DISNEY WORLD AND BEYOND
THE ULTIMATE FAMILY GUIDEBOOK

DISNEY WORLD AND BEYOND

THE ULTIMATE FAMILY GUIDEBOOK

Stacy Ritz

RAY RIEGERT

Executive Editor

LESLIE HENRIQUES

Production Director

GLENN KIM

Illustrator

ULYSSES PRESS

Published by: Ulysses Press
P.O. Box 3440
Berkeley, CA 94703-3440

Library of Congress Catalog Card Number 91-65094

ISBN 0-915233-37-1

Printed in the U.S.A. by the George Banta Company

10 9 8 7 6 5 4 3 2 1

Managing Editor: Claire Chun
Editors: Bob Drews, Judith Kahn, Roger Rapoport
Designer: Bonnie Smetts
Maps: Phil Gardner
Index: Sayre Van Young
Proofreaders: Wendy Ann Logsdon, Khoa Nguyen
Cover Photography: Robert Holmes (front cover);
    Pat Canova (top back cover); Steve Krongard/
    The Image Bank (bottom back cover)

Distributed in the United States by Publishers Group West, in Canada by Raincoast Books, and in Great Britain and Europe by World Leisure Marketing

Printed on Recycled Paper

For David,
My Rock of Ages

Acknowledgments

My husband, David, deserves the most thanks. As ride-tester, Orlando aficionado and friend superior, he provided unfailing support. To Ray Riegert, I owe sincere thanks for his advice and enthusiasm, and for overseeing every aspect of the Space Mountain-size project. Leslie Henriques kept everything on track while lending her unique combination of wisdom, wit and diplomacy.

Judith Kahn not only performed brilliantly as editor but extended encouragement and friendship. Claire Chun proved it was possible to perform ten tasks at once and make it look easy. Roger Rapoport contributed editorial assistance, as well as a much needed sense of humor. Special recognition also goes to Bob Drews for an editorial job well done.

Close to home, I want to thank Linda for being a sounding board, and Steve, who showed me the nightspots. Lastly, I am indebted to my parents, Fred and Duane, who first took me on all the rides and showed me Florida's "beyond."

Contents

Maps

Stacy Ritz's Best of Disney World and Beyond

THEME PARK ATTRACTIONS
Pirates of the Caribbean *(Magic Kingdom, pages 44–45)*
Haunted Mansion *(Magic Kingdom, pages 49–50)*
Space Mountain *(Magic Kingdom, pages 58–59)*
Spaceship Earth *(Epcot Center, pages 81–82)*
Star Tours *(Disney–MGM, pages 105–106)*
Back to the Future *(Universal, pages 141–42)*
The FUNtastic World of Hanna-Barbera *(Universal, page 151)*
Scorpion and Python *(Busch Gardens, page 249)*

SIGHTSEEING ATTRACTIONS
Green Meadows Children's Farm *(Kissimmee, page 193)*
Hot Air Ballooning *(Orlando, page 210)*
Bok Tower Gardens *(Lake Wales, page 227)*
Spook Hill *(Lake Wales, pages 227–28)*
Kennedy Space Center *(Merritt Island, pages 234–35)*

HOTELS
Grand Floridian *(Disney World, page 168)*
Hyatt Regency Grand Cypress *(Lake Buena Vista, pages 171–72)*
Holiday Inn Lake Buena Vista *(Lake Buena Vista, page 172)*
Marriott's Orlando World Center *(Orlando, page 172)*
Don CeSar Beach Resort *(St. Petersburg Beach, page 256)*

CAMPGROUNDS
Fort Wilderness *(Disney World, pages 175–76)*
The Great Outdoors RV/Golf Resort *(Titusville, page 237)*
St. Petersburg Resort KOA *(St. Petersburg, page 257)*

RESTAURANTS
Land Grill Room *(Epcot Center, page 181)*
Portobello Yacht Club *(Disney's Pleasure Island, page 186)*
Pebbles *(Orlando, page 214)*
Chris's House of Beef *(Orlando, page 214)*
Chalet Suzanne *(Lake Wales, page 230)*
Bern's Steak House *(Tampa, page 252)*

SHOPPING

World Showcase *(Epcot Center, pages 194–95)*
Universal Studios *(Page 198)*
Church Street Exchange *(Orlando, page 215)*
Park Avenue *(Winter Park, page 216)*
Ron Jon Surf Shop *(Cocoa Beach, page 240)*

NIGHTSPOTS

Pleasure Island *(Disney World, page 199)*
Top of the World *(Disney's Contemporary Resort, page 201)*
Church Street Station *(Orlando, pages 216–17)*

BEACHES AND PARKS

Wekiwa Springs State Park *(Apopka, page 231)*
Withlacoochee State Forest *(Brooksville, page 233)*
Canaveral National Seashore *(Cape Canaveral, pages 239–40)*
Daytona Beach *(Daytona Beach, pages 245–46)*
Clearwater Beach *(Clearwater Beach, page 259)*

SMALL TOWNS

Winter Park *(Page 210)*
Mount Dora *(Page 226)*
Lake Wales *(Pages 227–28)*

Games to Play While Waiting in Line

The lines at Orlando's theme parks can try anyone's patience. Fortunately, if you know how to create your own entertainment, the wait can be painless (well, almost).

Kids and adults alike can while away the time, use their creativity and even get a few laughs by playing the games described below. Some of these games relate to specific theme parks, others are appropriate for particular age groups. I have also added trivia questions for extra fun.

If you really want to speed up those waiting lines, create some games of your own!

Games for all ages

❖ *RHYME TIME* ❖

Everybody loves to make up rhymes. It's even more fun when you do it together. Begin with a line of poetry. The next player adds a rhyming line, the next player contributes another and so on. The player who rhymes the fourth line gets to start a new rhyme. Example:

> I read about Disney World in a book,
> And decided I'd go take a look.
> I left the dog, but my family I took.
> All because of that silly book.

❖ *"SENSITIVE" POETRY* ❖

Compose a poem that you can see, smell, taste, feel and hear. Give it a try, using the following example as a guideline:

> I love the smell of old socks.
> I love the taste of ham hocks.
> I hate feeling blue,
> But I love hearing something new.
> As you can see I'm a very good poet, too.

❖ *A IS FOR...* ❖

Look around you and choose objects that begin with particular letters. Start with "A" and proceed alphabetically. For example: animal, bus, carousel, dirt, entrance, etc. Each player must come up with a nearby object that begins with the next letter in the alphabet.

❖ *HAVE YOU EVER, EVER, EVER?* ❖

Begin this game by reciting the first three lines of the following ditty and inserting an animal or object in the last word of the third line. The next player then provides a rhyming word for the last word in the fourth line:

Have you ever, ever, ever?
Have you ever, ever, ever?
Have you ever seen a MOUSE
Eat a HOUSE?
OH! NO! We never saw a MOUSE eat a HOUSE!

The last line of the verse is said in unison. The second word doesn't need to be a "real" one; in fact, the sillier it is, the more fun you'll have with the children! Some other examples are:

Have you ever seen MICKEY
Be real PICKY?
Have you ever see a MANGO
Do the TANGO?

❖ *STUPID QUESTIONS* ❖

Making a fool of yourself is easy. Just ask the stupidest question you can think of. Then have everyone decide whose question is the dumbest. The stupid one is the winner!

❖ *PINK FLAMINGOS* ❖

Everyone poses a question that has to be answered with the phrase "Pink flamingos." Such as "What did you wear to bed last night?" Pink flamingos. "What did you barbecue for dinner?" Pink flamingos. If you giggle when you ask the question, you're out. The last remaining person is the winner.

❖ SILENCE IS GOLDEN ❖

Here's a game guaranteed to leave your group speechless. (Parents will love this!) Everyone pledges not to talk for a certain time period, say ten minutes. Only sign language can be used. It's a fun way to be imaginative with body language and visual communication. The last person to speak wins.

❖ NUMBER STORIES ❖

Storytelling is even more fun when you use numbers. Begin by using the number "one." The next person adds the word "two," etc. Example: Once upon a time. . . Two bullfrogs went on a date . . . They swam across three lakes. . . Then they saw four speedboats headed straight for them. . . But they escaped with five seconds to spare. . . .

❖ PICK A NUMBER ❖

One player picks a number between 1 and 100, but doesn't reveal it to the other players. Each person takes turns trying to guess the number. When someone guesses incorrectly, the player will say "higher" or "lower" depending on whether the guess is above or below the secret number. The person who guesses right gets to pick the next secret number.

❖ BODY MOVES ❖

A leader starts the game with a body move, such as winking an eye. The next player performs that move and adds another, like nodding his or her head. For example, they might wink and nod their head. The game continues with each player performing the previous body moves— in the correct order—and adding a new one. Someone who forgets a move, is out of the game.

❖ RHYME, RHYME, RHYME ❖

One player begins the game by saying a simple word, such as "mouse." The next player must say another word that rhymes, like "house." Each person takes turns rhyming the original word. When no one can think of a new word that rhymes, the group goes on to a new word.

❖ *SEE AND TELL* ❖

A leader asks each person about what they see in line. Some sample questions: What is the smallest thing you see? What is the prettiest thing you see? What is the brightest thing you see? Other things to look for: tallest, shortest, fattest, skinniest, strangest, funniest, saddest, etc.

❖ *STORYTELLING* ❖

Children are born storytellers. Encourage kids in your group to create tales based on park characters, rides or situations. If you saw Cinderella yesterday, let your child tell you what Cinderella is doing today while you're visiting Sea World—or what a visit to Sea World would be like with Cinderella.

❖ *COMMON FEATURES* ❖

How many people can you find wearing Mickey Mouse ears? How many have braces? Count them. If you're in line at a ride, count the number of people with black hair, children with cameras, people with hats on. . .You get it? Add to the fun by guessing the number of people you'll find in each category in five minutes.

❖ *HANG LOOSE* ❖

Here's an easy way to loosen up while standing in line. Have every player rub their head and pat their leg at the same time. Then have them touch their nose and their back at the same time. Next, have them lift their right leg and grab it with their left hand. Improvise other variations on this theme. Another familiar version is "Simple Simon Says."

❖ *QUESTIONS, QUESTIONS* ❖

What better way to pass the time than by discussing the highlights of your trip? One player asks the others a variety of questions such as: What is the best beach you've seen? Where is the prettiest place you've been? What is the best ride in all the parks?

❖ *COLOR ME PURPLE* ❖

One player picks a color and other members of the group try to iden-tify it by asking questions. Each player is allowed to ask up to three questions before making their choice. Example: Do you see lots of people wearing this color? Are there fruits this color? Is it the color of a grape?

❖ *CHALLENGES* ❖

Create challenges for your children. Here are four examples: Take ten hops with the left foot then another ten with the right. Count back-ward from 20. Take as many steps as possible to get from one place to another. Hold your breath for the duration of the song "Zippity Doo Dah."

❖ *20 QUESTIONS* ❖

The first player chooses an object. The other players then have (sur-prise) 20 questions to figure out what the object is. Each question has to be answerable by "yes" or "no." And remember, guesses count toward the 20 questions! A good strategy is to ask general questions in the beginning, such as: Is it alive? Is it very big? Is it soft?

As a variation on this classic game, limit the object to things within the theme park.

Another alternative is to allow each person five questions. After five tries, the next player takes a turn. The game continues until one of the players comes up with the correct answer.

❖ *I SPY* ❖

This old favorite is a great guessing game. A player says "I spy some-thing purple," referring to an object clearly visible to the other players. Then the other players ask questions to try to determine what the object is. I Spy can also be played by initially describing the shape, dimensions, smell or sound of an object.

Games for kids 6 to 90

❖ *ODD MAN OUT* ❖

The object of this counting game is to avoid saying a particular number. To begin, pick a two-digit, odd number like 25. Go around the circle. The first player can count "1" or "1, 2"; then the next player picks up the count, adding one or two numbers to the progression. For example, the first participant says "1." The next says "2, 3." The third person can say either "4" or "4, 5." Continue until someone (the loser) ends up saying "25."

❖ *SWITCH HITS* ❖

Pick a simple word. The first player must either change a letter in the original word to make another word or create an anagram. For example, start with "BAT." The next player says "BAR" or "TAB." No repeating words!

Extra challenge: After completing a round, try reciting the sequence of words from last to first.

❖ *ALPHABET SOUP* ❖

When hunger pangs begin to strike, try moving down the food chain alphabetically. Each player repeats the choices of the previous person. Begin at "A" and continue until you get all the way down to "Z." Here's how: First player: "I'm fond of asparagus." Second player: "I'm dying for asparagus and beets." Third player: "I want asparagus, beets and chicken soup."

❖ *HINKY PINKY* ❖

This word game begins with a player selecting a secret rhyming phrase like "fat cat." The player then defines the phrase—with a clue like "obese feline" or "tubby tabby"—and tells how many syllables are in the rhyming words by saying "Hink Pink" for one syllable, "Hinky Pinky" for two syllables or "Hinkety Pinkety" for three syllables. The other participants try guessing the rhyming couplet.

How about these? What Santa would say during Christmas: "Remember December." An insane flower: "Crazy daisy."

❖ *PATTERN WORK* ❖

Players use clues to discover a pattern. For example, you choose "double letters" as the pattern. Some clues you could give are: "Look at the crook" or "Poodles love noodles." Another example, a little easier for the young ones, could be the letter "C": "He likes cats and canaries, cars and cartoons."

❖ *LINKING UP* ❖

Here's a way to bring everyone together. The first player mentions a film, book, celebrity or city. Successive players offer a concept linked to the previous one. Example: First player: Teenage Mutant Ninja Turtles.   Second player: Pizza.   Third player: Cheesy.   Fourth player: Smelly.   First player: Socks.

❖ *BUZZ* ❖

Here's a chance to review your multiplication tables. Pick a number between one and nine. That's the buzz-number. Start counting in sequence around the circle of players. When the multiple of the buzz-number comes up in sequence, the number must be replaced by the word "buzz." Players are out if they forget to say "buzz" or if they say it at the wrong time. Example: Pick multiples of 5. When 10, 15, 20, 25, etc. come up they should be replaced by "buzz."

❖ *THE POWER OF NEGATIVE THINKING* ❖

One person thinks of a funny activity like trying to catch a greased pig. Only negative hints can be used to describe the activity: "It really smells." "You slip and slide around a lot." "There's a lot of squealing." The player who comes up with the right answer suggests the next mystery activity.

❖ *ALPHABET MEMORY* ❖

Another fun game involves picking words alphabetically. For example, the first player chooses an "A" word, the second player selects a "B" word and the third player picks a "C" word. Each player must name all the words chosen previously. The game continues through the alphabet, with players being eliminated when they forget the sequence of words.

❖ *INTERNATIONAL GEOGRAPHIC* ❖

See how well you know your way around. The first player names a country. The second player must come up with a city that begins with the last letter of the previously named country. For example, Greenland might be followed by Denver and China could be followed by Athens. Continue in sequence through your group.

❖ *SPELL CHECKER* ❖

Here's an easy game that's a great way to build vocabulary. Pick a word like "Lazy." Then have the players run through the alphabet. When you hit a letter that is in the designated word, say "check." For example: Instead of saying "A" the player will say "check." If you forget to say "Check" for the appropriate word you are out of the game.

❖ *COCONUTTING AROUND* ❖

Coconut is a noun, not a verb. But you can have a lot of fun with this word when you substitute it for a secret verb. Here's how: The contestant goes out of hearing range or covers his or her ears. Other members of the group pick a verb such as "swim." The contestant returns, and can ask up to 12 questions aimed at discovering the verb but must always use "coconut" in the question. For example: "Can you coconut at the beach?" or "Do kids like to coconut in the bath?" After the first contestant finishes, give everyone else a chance to guess other mystery verbs.

❖ *NAME THOSE RIDES* ❖

The first player starts by naming a theme park ride, such as Space Mountain, It's A Small World, etc. The next player must name a different ride, and the game continues with each person naming a new ride. Players have ten seconds to answer. A stumped player is excused from the game. The last person left wins!

You could also try naming Disney characters (Mickey Mouse, Pluto), Florida cities (Orlando, Daytona Beach) or movies (*E. T, Back to the Future*).

❖ *FANTASYLAND SEE AND TELL QUESTIONS* ❖

So you're waiting in line in the Magic Kingdom's Fantasyland. Ask your kids the following questions as you wait with anticipation for the line to move forward:

At Cinderella's Golden Carrousel

How many horses have swords?

How many horses have reins made of braided flowers?

Look at the murals above the Golden Carrousel and see who can answer these questions first:

What color is the staircase where Cinderella leaves her slipper?

What time is on the clock tower?

Who is sitting with Cinderella in the forest?

When Cinderella puts on the glass slipper, what color is her other shoe?

At Peter Pan's Flight

In the scenes outside the ride, what color are the clouds?

In the same scene, how many teepees are on the island?

How many totem poles?

At It's A Small World

How many of the following things can you find in the colorful panels outside this ride? Windmill. Flower. Castle tower. Archways. Nutcracker's face. Tree.

At Dumbo, the Flying Elephant

Each Dumbo is wearing a different color hat. How many colors can you spot?

Can you find the little animal that befriends Dumbo?

What do you see that made Dumbo think he could fly?

At Snow White's Adventures

In Snow White's forest scenes, what plant is sprinkled around the base of the big tree?

What shape are the trees near the castle steps?

Who is obviously missing from the forest?

At Mr. Toad's Wild Ride

In the countryside mural, how many policemen and wolves can you spot standing on the bridge?

❖ *Disney Trivia Contest* ❖

1. Who follows the White Rabbit down the hole?
2. What makes Alice shrink and grow?
3. The butterflies Alice meets are shaped like what food?
4. Who was Dumbo's mother?
5. What's the merry tune you hear on the Dumbo ride?
6. Who was Captain Hook's bumbling sidekick?
7. Who are the children Peter Pan takes to Never-Never Land?
8. What did the crocodile swallow in *Peter Pan*?
9. Who was Mr. Toad's horse?
10. What did Mr. Toad trade his family mansion for?
11. What was the name of Mr. Toad's mansion?
12. Why was Mr. Toad arrested?
13. Who sang "When You Wish Upon a Star" in Disney's *Pinocchio*?
14. Princess Aurora is better known by what name?
15. Who led the crew of Jules Verne's *Nautilus*?
16. What did Tommy Kirk turn into in a 1959 Disney movie?
17. What was the password for the D-Day invasion?
18. Who was the first voice of Mickey Mouse?
19. What kind of television characters were Doreen Tracy, Cheryl Holdridge and Cubby O'Brien?
20. Name Snow White's seven dwarfs.

Answers:

1. Alice.   2. Eating or drinking.   3. Bread. They are called Bread and Butterflies.   4. Mrs. Jumbo.   5. "You Can Fly, You Can Fly, You Can Fly."   6. Mr. Smee.   7. Wendy, Michael and John.   8. A clock.   9. Cyril Proudbottom.   10. A stolen car.   11. Toad Hall.   12. For driving that stolen car!   13. Jiminy Cricket.   14. Sleeping Beauty.   15. Captain Nemo.   16. The Shaggy Dog.   17. Mickey Mouse.   18. Walt Disney. 19. Mouseketeers.   20. Sneezy, Sleepy, Dopey, Doc, Grumpy, Happy and Bashful.

ONE

Disney Dreaming

It is the ultimate escape, a real-life passage to Never-Never Land. Walt
Disney World, purveyor of storybook illusions and cotton candy
moods, is the most popular travel destination in the world. Every year,
millions pass through the Disney door to indulge in its fountain of
fantasy, to drink its dreams.

That Disney is a world unto itself is undisputed: At any waking
moment, its 43 square miles contain more people, traffic, hotels and
restaurants than most cities. But more than this, Disney World is also a
state of mind. In a single generation, Disney World placed its stamp on
the American psyche, sharing the dreams of one man with an entire
nation. For here, in 1971, Walt Disney offered the world its biggest
playground. And the world accepted.

But by no means does the Orlando dream vacation end at Walt
Disney World. For the traveler in search of the true Central Florida
experience, there is much, much more. There are two other big theme
parks, Universal Studios and Sea World. The mammoth Universal Studios offers a surrealistic patchwork of theme park fantasy and Holly-
wood-style illusions, while the smaller Sea World combines relaxed
touring with a view to the sea. Along the fringes of these meccas are
miles of kitschy Americana, where you can lose yourself in places such
as Alligatorland and Shell World, the Tupperware and Elvis Presley
museums.

Then there is Orlando, which may well be the area's best-kept
secret. The city boasts a sleek new downtown, turn-of-the-century
architecture, fine museums and renovated shops, tony restaurants and
avant garde nightlife. Just outside the burgeoning downtown lies more
scenic reality. Citrus groves that stretch to the horizon, see-through
lakes cupped in cypress trees, endless pastures where only the cattle
roam—they too comprise the "world" beyond Disney World.

1

This book, *Disney World and Beyond: The Ultimate Family Guidebook*, takes you through Walt Disney's fantasy world, then shows you the beauty outside it. The focus throughout is on quality and value, the exemplary and the unique, while always keeping families in mind. Why families? Because every day, more and more travelers are choosing the family experience as parents and kids look to share what is offered here: the ultimate vacation.

Throughout this guide you'll discover the best of the Central Florida's "family friendly" establishments and attractions. You'll also find plenty of tips on saving time and money, as well as handling special family needs such as babysitters, breast-feeding and stroller rentals. And the book's short feature articles and one-liner teasers give you insider information, providing local trivia and history and little known hints at a glance.

Each of Disney's major theme parks is featured in a separate chapter. There's the *Magic Kingdom*, the genesis of Disney World and the supreme fantasy factory. The place that children love best, the kingdom features fanciful rides and scenes and happy vibes. More high tech and cultural, *Epcot Center* combines a permanent world's fair with futuristic attractions that fuel the imagination. At *Disney–MGM Studios*, Hollywood works its movie magic through starstruck shows and mind-blowing rides.

Disney's six minor parks are highlighted in the *Rest of the World* chapter. Often considered the jewels in Disney's crown, "the rest" includes Fort Wilderness, a vast wooded campground and family retreat; River Country, a backwoods, downhome swimming hole with water slides; and Discovery Island, a secluded nature preserve teeming with colorful, kooky birds. There's also Typhoon Lagoon, an oasis of raft rides and water slides and tropical lushness; Pleasure Island, a glitzy collection of nightclubs, restaurants and shops; and Disney Village Marketplace, a place for laid-back shopping and dining.

But the unfolding chapters of this tourist extravaganza don't stop here. There's *Universal Studios*, the biggest film and television studio outside Hollywood. Opened in 1989, the park is fashioned with thrilling movie scenes and rides and fabulous special effects. Nearby *Sea World* delves deep into the mysteries of the ocean. The world's most popular oceanarium, it puts humans in touch with 8000 creatures big and small.

When you're waiting to try all those theme-park rides, you'll undoubtedly want to use *Games to Play While Waiting in Line*. This special fun section, which you'll find near the front of the book, features an assortment of games, poems and theme park trivia to help pass the time in line.

The *Staying, Eating and Playing* chapter offers recommendations on hotels, campgrounds, restaurants, shopping and nightlife in and around the theme parks.

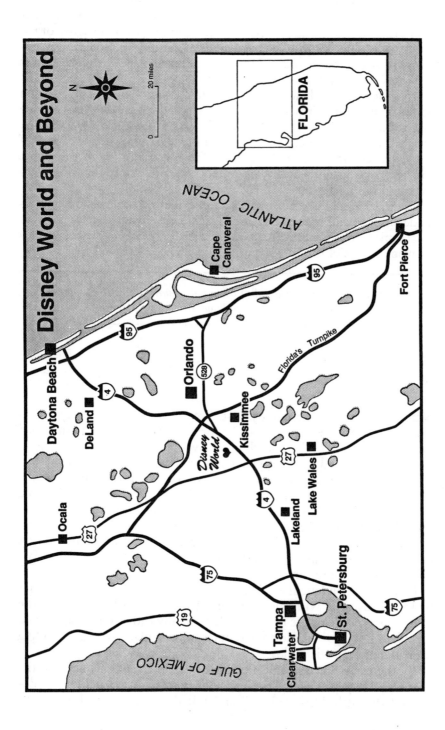

Disney World and Beyond

Away from the parks, the *Orlando* chapter portrays picture-perfect neighborhoods, tropical gardens and parks, and shimmering lakes that reflect a mix of historic and modern architecture. The chapter *Side Trips from Orlando* spans two coasts, taking in the lovely beaches of the Space Coast and the historic bay scenes of Tampa. It also combs Central Florida's outback, the cowtowns and fishing camps, orange groves and thick woods just outside Orlando.

Together with Orlando and all the theme parks, they form a region poised on the cusp of reality. A place where, on the same day, you can dine in a castle with Cinderella and canoe down a pristine river. Where you can fly through Bedrock with Fred and Barney, then stroll a real city of brick streets and grand old homes. Where you can cruise through a concrete lagoon with brightly painted fish, and catch a real one in a backwoods pond.

Central Florida, the ultimate paradox, is the keeper of both man-made empires and natural treasure. The treasure was there long before the empire. With a little luck and a lot of work, it just may stay a permanent part of the landscape.

Until 1845, Orange County was called Mosquito County for the insects that protected their territory more fiercely than the Indians.

History

Naturally, it began as a fantasy. Just three decades ago, Disney World existed only in the mind of a California dreamer. Walt Disney had built his California Disneyland, but he wanted more. So much more, in fact, he searched to the opposite end of the country to get it.

But long before Disney ever set eyes on Florida, the palm-studded peninsula had been indulging dreamers. In 1513, Ponce de Leon came looking for a magical "fountain of youth" and great caches of gold thought to be waiting for ambitious treasure-seekers. He found neither youth nor gold, but instead uncovered a place of balmy breezes and palmy shores and year-round blossoms. He called it "Florida," Spanish for "feast of flowers."

Ponce de Leon left, after exploring the eastern coast, to return again in 1521, this time with the hope of setting up a little colony on the southwestern side of the peninsula. Unfriendly Indians soon squelched this plan, but by then Florida's reputation as a place worth struggling for had begun to take hold.

By the early 1700s, English colonists began causing trouble for the Spanish. They laid waste the missions across northern Florida, destroyed the little "first colony" and killed many of the Indians. As

Spain's hold grew weaker, England's desire for the territory strengthened. Finally, in 1763, following the devastating Seven Years' War, Spain traded Florida for Cuba, abandoning the glorious dreams of eternal youth and gleaming treasure.

The English had great plans for Florida but were able to fulfill few of their dreams as their attention soon turned from palm trees and sunny shores to the dark battlefields of the American Revolution. Even the Spanish, who took the colony back from the preoccupied Redcoats, found it impossible to maintain and sold it to the United States in 1821.

By 1845, Florida had become a state, and the golden age of steamboats had begun fueling both tourism and agricultural enterprise. Rumors that a fountain of youth lay at DeLeon Springs near DeLand, and word of incredibly warm and colorful waters at Silver Springs, kept river traffic at a full head of steam. Glamorous steamers, toting produce and freight below, carried the wealthy and powerful on sightseeing tours of Florida's interior.

By the late 1880s, two millionaires with dreams as grand as Ponce de Leon's made accessible the sea-surrounded paradise and set in motion a land development that has steamrolled through the 20th century. It all began when Henry B. Plant and Henry Flagler built railroads down each coast, establishing lavish resorts that summoned the rest of the nation to paradise. In subsequent decades, the nation did indeed come, thousands of people fueled by fantasy. Some sought better jobs or the perennial chance to "start a new life." Others simply wanted to soak up rays and bask in the warm seas.

Meanwhile, the Orlando area was hosting its own brand of dreamer: the Florida cowboy. These earthy, hard-working settlers made a living off the ocali, or scrubland, that proved perfect for raising cattle. When they drove the cows they'd crack their whips, earning themselves the nickname *crackers*. The crackers also planted vast groves of oranges and grapefruit, giving birth to Florida's citrus empire.

But not all citrus farmers fared well. In the late 1800s, a Canadian named Elias Disney lost his 80-acre orange grove to a devastating

---

BEST SEAT IN THE HOUSE

Few people know that you can ride in the front of the Disney World monorails. It's by far the best spot, because you get wonderful views out the curved glass windows as you're cruising through the air. Just as fun, you can sit with the driver and watch him work the control panels. The drivers are extra friendly, offering Disney anecdotes and information on their favorite rides. To ride up front, just ask any attendant. He will escort you to your very own special waiting area. Happy monorailing!

freeze. Elias had moved from Kansas to Central Florida, hoping to share in this land of promise. Initially he ran a Daytona Beach hotel— one of the first in the area—then bought the grove in nearby Paisley. The hotel failed to draw enough tourists, and the farm went bust. In 1889, Elias moved to Chicago and became a construction worker. He died in the 1930s, never to return to Florida.

How ironic that 30 years later, Elias' son Walt Disney would open his own hotels not far from Daytona Beach. And while his father's hotel had failed, Walt's resorts would become a legacy.

When Walt Disney came to Orlando in the early 1960s, the area was still a babe to tourism and development, "virgin territory" as the crackers called it. In the city's small downtown, low-slung buildings gathered along several blocks. From here suburbs unfolded for a few miles but soon gave in to wide open space where sky met scrubland. Though nearly 90,000 people called it home, Orlando only had two "big" attractions, Gatorland and the Tupperware Museum.

Before Walt Disney ever laid the cornerstone of his fantasy world, the area was already a purist's dreamland: deep pine forests, clear, bottomless lakes and miles of silent frontier. This was important to Disney. What he needed most was untouched land, and lots of it. Lack of land had shut him out of California, where his 100-acre Disneyland was hemmed in by outside development.

In 1964, Disney bought 27,500 acres about 20 miles southwest of Orlando. Then he set about building his kingdom. Disney died in 1966, but his Magic Kingdom became a reality five years later, opening on October 1, 1971. Within a year it drew 10.7 million visitors—more people than lived in the entire state of Florida at the time. The dawning of Disney World sent Orlando for a spin and launched a cultural and physical metamorphosis across Central Florida. All at once, the cowtown became a boomtown. The opening of the Magic Kingdom also decided how millions of Americans would vacation the rest of this century.

But the Magic Kingdom was just the beginning, a mere pinpoint on Disney's Florida drawing board. His real dream was a city where people worked and lived, an air-conditioned, computer-controlled community with apartments, stores, golf courses, churches and a hospital. It would be crowned with a glass dome, Disney said, to shut out the heat and humidity. Its name would be Epcot, Experimental Prototype Community of Tomorrow.

Epcot did open in 1982, but not as Walt had planned. Instead, the billion-dollar "community" took root as a theme park housing a permanent world's fair and an array of scientific attractions. In the process, it fueled the fire of growth already blazing across Central Florida. In the ten years since the Magic Kingdom had opened, the Greater Orlando population had almost doubled. Sea World had opened an oceanarium that competed for Disney World's millions. And dozens of chain

Worldwide, 600,000 people ride monorails each day. Of those, 150,000 are Disney World passengers; most of the rest are in Japan.

motels, fast-food joints and slap-em-up tourist attractions had latched on to Disney World's perimeter, ready to feast on the Disney pie. Across Florida, Orlando was being called a Mickey Mouse Town, while greater America was pumping millions of dollars into this vacation promised land.

The wildfire development continues today. Just as it lured Elias and Walt Disney, Central Florida remains a magnet to countless visionaries with dreams, schemes and plenty of room to grow. Today's Walt Disney World boasts two water-theme parks, a mammoth campground, nature preserve, ten resort hotels, more than 150 restaurants, and shopping and nightclub complexes. The Magic Kingdom parking lot alone could hold all of California's Disneyland, the seed of Walt Disney World.

The supply simply can't meet the demand. *Each week*, the Orlando area hosts over 240,000 visitors—a quarter of its total population. More than 18 million people fly into Orlando's airport every year—three times the number arriving ten years ago. The metropolitan area is adding 50,000 residents annually.

Lately, the most exciting player on the Orlando dream scene is Hollywood. Both Disney World and Universal Studios have opened film and TV production centers that double as theme parks. "Hollywood East" is what people are calling Orlando this decade.

But Hollywood is only part of the frenzy gripping this fountain of fun. Declaring the 1990s "The Disney Decade," Disney World is adding 29 new attractions, half a dozen major resorts, a fourth big theme park, and an 8400-acre community that will include homes, condominiums, schools, churches and a million-square-foot shopping mall.

Outside Disney World, other worlds are evolving. A 450-acre theme park called Veda Land promises visitors mental and spiritual enlightenment through such attractions as a courtyard of illusions and a chariot ride inside a rose. Scheduled to open in 1994, Veda Land is the idea of magician Doug Henning and transcendental meditation guru Maharishi Mahesh Yogi. Meanwhile, a group of Soviet and Alaskan investors are planning a Russian-style theme park. Called Perestroyka Palace, it will feature an $18 million imitation of St. Basil's Cathedral in Red Square.

If it all goes according to plan, visitors can soon experience Mickey Mouse, spirituality and Moscow during their Orlando vacation.

And as the fantasy makers continue to build their worlds, Greater Orlando continues to define its identity. Some say the area grew too fast too soon and tried to please too many. Plagued by traffic, littered with billboards and tinged with tacky tourism, it walks a tenuous line between welcoming growth and resenting it. But that's only half of Orlando's story. The other half is of a place holding fast to its home-spun ideals, intrinsic beauty and peace of mind. It is a place with one foot in fantasy, and one planted firmly in reality.

Tourist Seasons

Timing is the key to a successful Disney World visit. If you go during the busy season, you'll spend much of your vacation standing in lines and sitting in traffic. Plus, you'll pay top dollar for everything. One family who went to the Magic Kingdom on Easter Sunday (a peak day) calculated they spent 6 hours in line and only 35 minutes riding. By contrast, if you go when it's slow your experience will be the oppo-site—a *real* vacation.

Unfortunately for families, summer—when the kids are out of school—is high season. Holidays are also a bad time to visit. Disney World has its worst crowd crunch from Christmas Day through New Year's Day. Thanksgiving weekend takes a close second, followed by the weeks surrounding Easter. During these frenzied days, Disney World and Universal Studios often reach capacity—over 80,000 people *per theme park*—and close their gates by mid-morning. Pity those who make it inside.

The very best time to visit Disney World is after Thanksgiving weekend up to the week before Christmas. Other slow times: Septem-ber and October, and the second week of January through May (ex-cluding holidays).

If you must visit during the busy season, plan to be at the theme parks on Friday or Sunday. Incredibly, because many people travel to and from Disney World on weekends, these are the slowest days. Natu-rally the reverse is also true: Mondays, Tuesdays and Wednesdays are the craziest. The only exceptions are Typhoon Lagoon and River Country, which are popular with locals on weekends.

For 50 cents, you can get an up-to-the-minute Orlando weather report by calling 407-976-1611.

Climate

Summertime means more than crowds: It also brings sizzling hot days with afternoon showers that arrive like clockwork. The rain takes the edge off the heat, delivering breezy nights with silent lightning that leaps across the black sky. Fall and spring bring chamber-of-commerce weather, those crisp, blue, cloudless days that make your energy level soar. Winter can be warm or freezing—in a matter of hours—though most days are refreshingly cool. Central Floridians, you may as well know, rarely wear coats. To help plan your trip, the following chart lists average highs and lows, as well as rainfall, by month.

	Avg. High Temp. (F)	Avg. Low Temp. (F)	Avg. Rainfall (in inches)
January	72	49	2.1
February	73	50	2.8
March	78	55	3.2
April	84	60	2.2
May	88	66	4.0
June	91	71	7.4
July	92	73	7.8
August	92	73	6.3
September	90	73	5.6
October	84	65	2.8
November	78	57	1.8
December	73	51	1.8

Calendar

JANUARY

Orlando   The **Citrus Bowl Parade** kicks off the **Florida Citrus Bowl** game on New Year's Day.

Tampa   Fabled buccaneer José Gaspar leads a "takeover" of Tampa, complete with dancing, feasting and a lavish parade during **Gasparilla Day**.

FEBRUARY

Walt Disney World   The **Disney Village Marketplace Wine Festival** showcases dozens of winemakers from around the world.

Orlando   Highland games, shortbread contests and bagpipe music highlight the **Scottish Highland Festival**.

Daytona Beach   The **Daytona 500** marks the culmination of Speed Week with a 200-lap stock car race at the Daytona International Speedway.

MARCH

Orlando   It's Shakespeare by the water at the **Shakespeare Festival**, which runs through mid-April. Performances are at the Walt Disney Amphitheater on Lake Eola.

Kissimmee   Top name performers appear at the **Kissimmee Bluegrass Festival**.

Around Central Florida   Baseball professionals arrive for **Spring Training**. Watch the Houston Astros in Kissimmee, the Kansas City Royals in Baseball City, and the Boston Red Sox in Winter Haven.

APRIL

Walt Disney World   Mickey Mouse and the Easter Bunny go all out for the **Easter Parade** down Main Street in the Magic Kingdom (sometimes held in March).

Sea World   The **Easter Sunrise Service** features nationally known speakers and singers (sometimes held in March).

Orlando   Fingerpainting, puppet shows, pony rides and other kidstuff highlight the **4C Children's Festival** at Lake Eola Park.

Winter Park   Artisans across North America convene for the **Winter Park Sidewalk Art Festival**, one of the South's most prominent art events.

Mount Dora   Over 100 colorful schooners set sail across Lake Dora for the annual **Sailboat Regatta**.

MAY

DeLand   Hot air enthusiasts take to the skies during the **Central Florida Balloon Classic**.

JUNE

Kissimmee   For ropin', ridin' and square dancin' on horseback, head over to Kissimmee's **Silver Spurs Rodeo**, the oldest in Florida.

JULY

Walt Disney World   **Independence Day** ends with a big bang (fireworks, that is) above the Magic Kingdom and Seven Seas Lagoon.

AUGUST

Bartow   The **Annual Bartow Youth Villa Classic** benefits youth projects with an open golf tournament, dance, fashion show and more.

Busch Gardens   Rubber duckies cruise neck and neck at Adventure Island for the zany **Great Florida Duck Race**.

SEPTEMBER

Orlando   The city celebrates October early with the **Octoberfest Street Festival** at Church Street Station.

Kissimmee   Arts, crafts, food and games highlight the **Osceola Art Festival** along Lake Tohopekaliga.

OCTOBER

Walt Disney World PGA pros tee off at the **Oldsmobile/Walt Disney World Golf Classic**, held in the Walt Disney World Village.

Orlando Outrageous costumes and lively entertainment headline the **Halloween Street Party** at Church Street Station.

Winter Park The **Winter Park Autumn Art Festival** features local and national exhibitors.

NOVEMBER

Walt Disney World One of the state's best art shows, the **Festival of Masters at Disney Village Marketplace** showcases stellar artwork from across the country.

Lake Buena Vista Join the masters for the **World Cup of Golf** at the elegant Grand Cypress Resort.

Orlando Santa Claus arrives early to lead the gala **Christmas Parade** through downtown.

DECEMBER

Walt Disney World Disney's favorite mouse throws **Mickey's Very Merry Christmas Party** on Main Street U.S.A. **New Year's Eve** celebrations feature big parties with fantastic fireworks and bands in every theme park and in many Disney resorts. The bash at the Contemporary Resort's Top of the World lounge is considered the ultimate.

Around Central Florida Several cities usher in the season with **Christmas Parades**, tree trimmings and other yuletide festivities.

To kill traveling time, take along audiotapes of classic Disney stories.

Before You Leave Home

Nothing makes a trip more enjoyable than a little prep work. This goes for every family member. Parents can learn the layout of the theme parks and what each has to offer, thus avoiding confusion and hurried decision-making after they arrive. Preteens and teens who plan to sightsee on their own should definitely know how to get around. And young children can prepare (and get wildly excited) by reading Disney stories and watching the classic animated films. This helps acquaint them with characters and rides they'll see after they arrive. Some families rent Disney videos before their trip and hold movie nights. A few entertaining classics to rent: *Cinderella, Peter Pan, Alice in Wonderland, Dumbo* and *The Wind in the Willows*. And don't forget to bring along your *Disney World and Beyond Family Fun Cards* (see last page of this book), arranging them in the order you plan to see the various theme park rides. Each card highlights a different attraction.

Children should also be told about height restrictions. Certain rides require minimum heights, including the Magic Kingdom's Space Mountain (44 inches), Big Thunder Mountain (40 inches) and Universal Studios' Back to the Future (46 inches). The theme parks strictly adhere to these rules. If your kids are too short to ride, it's best they know *before* you leave.

Packing

There are two important rules to remember when packing for a "Disney World and Beyond" vacation: Pack light and pack casual. Unless you plan to spend your trip dining in ultra-deluxe restaurants, all you'll need in the way of clothing are some shorts, lightweight shirts or tops, cool slacks, a bathing suit and coverup, and something relatively casual for any special event that might call for dressing up.

The rest of your luggage space can be devoted to a few essentials. These include a good hat, high-quality sunglasses and some insect repellant. You should also take along plenty of strong sunscreen (preferably not oils). Even the cloudiest winter days bring out that classic tourist look: scorched skin. A light jacket and rain poncho are also musts. The best ponchos are the hooded kind that come folded in a package the size of your hand. Pharmacies sell them for about a dollar while Disney and other theme parks sell them for several times that amount.

Good soft, comfortable, lightweight shoes are critical for foot survival. A theme park visitor walks an average of four miles a day (often on blazing hot concrete, no less), so you're going to need sole support.

CAR TROUBLE?

If your car breaks down at Disney World, Universal Studios or Sea World, a security officer will come to the rescue. Security vehicles patrol the parking lots, making rounds every five to ten minutes. Simply hail one of the vehicles, which resemble police cruisers. The officers will either start your car or call someone who can.

In addition, Disney World has a **Car Care Center** *(407-824-4813) right outside the Magic Kingdom. Universal Studios has a vintage 1940s* **Texaco Station** *(407-345-4860) adjacent to its parking lot.*

Tennis shoes are ideal for sightseeing; save the sandals and flip flops for poolside.

If you're driving and have extra room, bring plenty of baby formula and disposable diapers. You can buy them inside the various theme parks, but you'll pay dearly. For those afternoon munchies, pack some snacks in ziplocked bags. Crackers, the kids' favorite cereal and popcorn are a few that will hold up well. Juiceboxes are also great substitutes for carbonated soft drinks sold in the theme parks.

The closer you are to Disney World, the more expensive the gas. Fill up before you get there.

Getting There

BY CAR

Several major highways lead to the Orlando area. From the northeast United States, take **Route 95** south to Daytona Beach, then pick up **Route 4** west. Route 4 makes a beeline for Orlando.

From the midwestern United States, pick up **Route 75** south to **Florida's Turnpike**. Head south on the turnpike to **Route 528** (Beeline Expressway), then west on Route 528 to Route 4.

Route 4, which runs from Daytona Beach to Tampa, is the major artery through Orlando. Walt Disney World, Universal Studios and Sea World all have exits along Route 4.

BY AIR

Orlando International Airport is the air gateway to the Walt Disney World area. A state-of-the-art facility, it lies 27 miles northeast of Disney World and 15 miles southeast of downtown Orlando. It is served by over 20 domestic and foreign airlines including Air Canada, American Airlines, British Airways, Continental Airlines, Delta Air Lines, Icelandair, KLM Royal Dutch Airlines, Midway Airlines, Northwest Airlines, Trans World Airlines, United Airlines and USAir.

Once you arrive, the Walt Disney World information desk (main building) can help you get organized. Inexpensive shuttle service to the Disney World area is provided by **Mears Transportation** (407-423-5566) and **Transtar Transportation** (407-856-7777). Both companies also provide ground transportation around the Orlando area.

BY TRAIN

In Central Florida, **Amtrak** (800-872-7245) makes stops at Orlando (1400 Sligh Boulevard), Kissimmee (416 Pleasant Street), DeLand (2491 Old New York Avenue) and Palatka (11th and Reid streets). If you're traveling to the Orlando area from the vicinity of New York City, consider Amtrak's **Auto Train**. You can board your car at Lorton, Virginia, four hours from New York, and depart at Sanford (400 Persimmon Avenue), about 25 miles northeast of Orlando.

BY BUS

Traveling by bus is not the quickest way to arrive, but it's usually the least expensive. **Greyhound-Trailways Lines** has a station in Orlando (555 Magruder Boulevard; 407-843-7720) and near Walt Disney World in Kissimmee (16 North Orlando Avenue; 407-847-3911). The Kissimmee station offers van service to the Magic Kingdom and Epcot Center.

CAR RENTALS

Companies at the Orlando airport include **Avis Rent A Car** (407-851-7600), **Budget Rent A Car** (407-850-6700), **Dollar Rent A Car** (407-851-3232), **Hertz Rent A Car** (407-859-8400) and **National Car Rental** (407-855-4170). Current companies that provide free airport pickup service include **Alamo Rent A Car** (407-855-0210), **Enterprise Rent A Car** (407-859-2296) and **Thrifty Car Rental** (407-380-1002).

For car rentals close to Walt Disney World, call **Alamo Rent A Car** (407-396-0991), **Avis Rent A Car** (407-827-2847), **Budget Rent A Car** (407-827-6088), **Dolphin Car Rental** (407-396-6050), **General Rent A Car** (407-396-7772), **Hertz Rent A Car** (407-239-6565) or **Superior Rent A Car** (407-396-4446). **Ugly Duckling Rent A Car** (407-847-5599) supplies used rental cars.

Getting Around Walt Disney World

Walt Disney World is so built up and spread out that it may seem intimidating at first. Not to worry. The Disney folks are quite practiced at getting visitors where they want to go. Theme park exits are well-marked on all the major roadways. And once you're inside Disney World, all you have to do is follow the signs.

Disney's own transportation network parallels the public transportation systems of many big cities. Yet despite its size and state-of-the-

Flash photography is not allowed in most theme park theaters and in many indoor rides.

art design, it doesn't always move you quickly or easily. Generally, monorails are the fastest way to travel, and buses are the slowest. But the monorail links only a few places, stopping at the Magic Kingdom, Epcot Center, the Grand Floridian Resort, Polynesian Resort, Contemporary Resort and the Ticket and Transportation Center, while buses can take you anywhere.

The Ticket and Transportation Center is Disney's Grand Central Station.

If you're staying at a Disney resort, you'll receive maps and detailed instructions on how to get around. For the general public, transportation maps are available at the Ticket and Transportation Center and at the theme park ticket counters. No matter where you're going, a Disney attendant can tell you the quickest route.

Technically, you must have a special transportation ID to ride the Disney monorails, buses and boats. The ID card is issued to guests of Disney resorts and to those with four- or five-day theme park passes. In reality, this is not the case. Transportation attendants and bus drivers rarely require ID for passengers. Perhaps this will change in the future, but for now, you can ride almost anytime without a card.

Visitor Information

WALT DISNEY WORLD
General Information: P.O. Box 10040, Lake Buena Vista, FL
   32830-0040; 407-824-4321

Lodging Reservations: P.O. Box 10100, Lake Buena Vista, FL
   32830-0100; 407-934-7639

Restaurant Reservations (Disney resort guests only): 407-828-4000

Lost & Found
   Magic Kingdom: 407-824-4245
   Epcot Center: 407-560-6105
   Disney–MGM Studios: 407-560-4668

UNIVERSAL STUDIOS
General Information: 1000 Universal Studios Plaza, Orlando, FL
   32819-7610; 407-363-8000

SEA WORLD
General Information: 7007 Sea World Drive, Orlando, FL 32821;
   407-351-3600

OPERATING HOURS

Theme-park operating hours seem to change more often than the Florida tides, but this is to your advantage. Walt Disney World, Universal Studios and Sea World all base their opening and closing times on crowds. If heavy crowds are expected, the parks open early and close late and vice versa. However, there are a few rules of thumb:

❖ During the summer and holidays, the theme parks stay open late, usually closing at 10 p.m., 11 p.m. or midnight.

❖ In the winter, the parks close around 6 or 7 p.m.

❖ Last but most important: At Disney World, advertised opening times are not always the real opening times. If the Disney folks expect crowds, they may open the parks 30 to 60 minutes before the scheduled time. There's no way to anticipate this, but you can take advantage of it by being there early. I recommend arriving at least an hour early at the Magic Kingdom and Epcot, and 30 minutes early at Disney–MGM Studios.

TICKET OPTIONS AND PRICES

WALT DISNEY WORLD   Disney World offers four ticket options: (1) one-day ticket good for one of the three big theme parks (the Magic Kingdom *or* Epcot *or* Disney–MGM Studios); (2) four-day ticket good for all three big theme parks; (3) five-day PLUS Super ticket, good for the three big parks PLUS Typhoon Lagoon, River Country and Discovery and Pleasure islands; and (4) annual passport good for the Magic Kingdom, Epcot and Disney–MGM Studios, including parking at each park.

MICKEY MOUSE MONEY

Leave it to Disney to come up with Mickey Mouse money. As if your own greenbacks aren't good enough, Disney World offers visitors "Disney dollars." Here's how they work: When visitors enter the theme parks, they can exchange their own U.S. currency for Disney bills, dollar for dollar. Disney dollars are good at restaurants and stores throughout Disney World. Unused Disney money can be traded in for regular cash at the end of the day.

Of course, there's no logical reason to buy Disney dollars. They're not more convenient than real money, and they don't provide any discounts. They can, however, tempt you to spend more. Says one mother: "Disney dollars seemed like play money. I could spend them with wild abandon—something I'd never think of doing with my own money."

The four- and five-day passes let you come and go in the theme parks, entering more than one park on the same day. In addition, the passes *do not* have to be used on consecutive days but are good indefinitely. For instance, you may buy a four-day pass and go to the Magic Kingdom on August 5, 1992, then use the second day of the pass to go to Epcot on November 10, 1993—or whenever. With the five-day pass, this applies only to the big theme parks. Admission to the smaller theme parks—Typhoon Lagoon, River Country, Discovery Island and Pleasure Island—is good only for *seven days* after the ticket is stamped.

Now for the bad news: prices. Considering Disney World has raised its admission over a dozen times since 1984, it's likely the following prices will increase as soon as this book goes to press. However, to give you an idea of what you'll spend (and it's a pretty penny), here are the prices, including tax, as of summer 1991:

	Adults	Children 3–9
One-day/One-park Ticket	$34.85	$27.45
Four-day passport	$117.20	$92.90
Five-day PLUS super pass	$153.15	$122.50
Children under 3 are free		

UNIVERSAL STUDIOS   There are three ticket options here: a one-day ticket, two-day ticket or an annual pass. Again, all prices are subject to increase.

	Adults	Children 3–9
One-day Ticket	$32.86	$26.50
Two-day Ticket	$51.94	$41.34
Annual Pass	$90.10	$71.55
Children under 3 are free		

SEA WORLD   Admission options include a one-day ticket, a week-long pass and an annual pass. If you plan to visit for two or more days, definitely go for the week-long pass (good for seven days).

	Adults	Children 3–9
One-day Ticket	$28.55	$24.30
Week-long Pass	$33.55	$29.30
Annual Pass	$49.95	$39.95
Children under 3 are free		

No matter which theme park you're visiting, the single most important ticket tip is to *buy ahead of time!* If you arrive with ticket in hand, you can avoid standing in long lines. Really, who wants to start their day with a 20-minute wait?

Most area hotels sell tickets to all the theme parks and will even help plan your itinerary. You can order tickets by mail before you leave home or by telephone: Disney World (407-821-4321); Universal Studios (407-363-8000); Sea World (407-351-3600).

When you're sightseeing, carry money and other small items in a waist pouch instead of a purse.

DISCOUNTS

Everyone who goes to Disney World can get bargains. If you know where to look and whom to ask, you'll find discounts galore for restaurants, hotels, nightclubs, shops and even the theme parks. Disney World itself offers only minimal discounts for:

❖ Members of the Magic Kingdom Club. Many employers, including federal, state and local governments, subscribe to the club. If your employer is a member, it will issue you a Magic Kingdom Club card. As a member, you receive small discounts on Disney admission ($2 off one-day passes and $5 off four-day passes, for instance) and on Disney store purchases. The best discount is 40 percent off some Disney resorts during certain days in August, September, January and February. (Resorts and days vary each year). Club membership also entitles you to discounts with National Car Rental and Delta Air Lines fares to Orlando. However, the discounts aren't always off the lowest rates, so check with each company. Discounts change frequently; call the club headquarters at 714-490-3200.

❖ Florida residents. During certain months—usually May and September—residents receive up to 30 percent off Disney theme park admission. A Florida driver's license is required for proof of residency.

❖ Those 55 or older. Seniors also receive up to 30 percent off during Young at Heart Days, usually from October through early December. A driver's license or passport is required for proof of age.

Universal Studios and Sea World have similar discounts for Florida residents and senior citizens. Check with each park for specifics.

The best discounts are outside the theme parks. The **Florida Traveler Discount Guide** offers numerous bargains at family-style lodging across Central Florida. To order a copy, send $2 to Exit Information Guide, 3014 Northeast 21st Way, Gainesville, FL 32609; 904-371-3948.

The **Kissimmee-St. Cloud Convention and Visitors Bureau** (1925 Route 192, Kissimmee; 407-847-5000) has stacks of free booklets offering discounts at restaurants, shops, nightclubs and attractions outside the big theme parks.

You'll also find motel and hotel bargains advertised in the Sunday travel sections of major newspapers. Many are good deals, but some are not. Beware of cheap accommodations that say "close to Disney" but are really out in the boondocks. If the place is more than five miles away, forget it. You'll waste half your day getting to and from the theme parks. You're better off paying a few extra dollars for convenience and peace of mind.

VACATION PACKAGES

There is a dizzying number of packages available for the Disney World traveler. Whether to buy one depends on your individual needs. If you're flying to Orlando and staying at a Disney resort, a package can probably save you money. Check for packages that combine airfare, accommodations, car rental and theme-park tickets; they often save up to 20 percent. Packages also clue you in on what your vacation is going to cost since you pay for much of it up front. And they can eliminate a lot of "what are we going to do?" decisions.

On the down side, many packages come with extras you'll never use. Golf green fees, boat rentals, even meals represent lost dollars if you don't use them. Disney's ultra-deluxe Gold Key Plan packages, for instance, include everything from a deluxe room and three meals a day to unlimited tennis, boating and golf. For some families, these are useless plus they take away the flexibility of being able to enjoy non-Disney restaurants and sights.

Above all, shop around. Travel agents can help compare package prices and options. Considering the intense competition among area hotels and attractions, you can't help but find a bargain.

LOCKERS AND KENNELS

A locker can be a lifesaver. Great for stowing extra items such as jackets, packages and diaper bags, they're available for a small fee at all the big theme parks.

Disney World kennels offer convenient, inexpensive lodging for pets. Besides Fido and Fluffy, the kennels also accept many unusual boarders such as snakes, birds, hamsters, rabbits, goldfish and even monkeys. (One chimpanzee is a regular boarder.) If your pet falls into

---

SAY "CHEESE!"

There's hardly a bad place to take pictures inside the area's theme parks, but there are some extra choice spots. Here are ideas for great shots of the kids:

❖ *With Cinderella, in front of Cinderella Castle (Magic Kingdom)*
❖ *On Dumbo, before takeoff (Magic Kingdom)*
❖ *Next to the dancing fountains at Journey Into Imagination (Epcot)*
❖ *With "actors" and "actresses," in front of The Great Movie Ride (Disney–MGM Studios)*
❖ *With Jaws, in the Amity town square; or in front of Brown Derby Hat Shop in Hollywood (Universal Studios)*
❖ *Feeding the dolphins, at the Dolphin Community Pool (Sea World)*

the "unusual" category, bring its cage. Kennels are located at the Ticket and Transportation Center, Epcot Center, Disney–MGM Studios and at Fort Wilderness.

Universal Studios provides inexpensive lodging for dogs and cats, while Sea World will keep your pets for free.

CREDIT CARDS

Don't leave home without your plastic; at Disney World, you're gonna need it. The major cards—Visa, MasterCard and American Express—are accepted throughout Disney World and surrounding attractions. However, theme-park vendors and fast food restaurants *do not* take credit cards. Sun Bank, located inside the Magic Kingdom and Epcot Center, gives credit card cash advances.

CAMERAS AND CAMCORDERS

What would a trip to the Disney World area be without photographs? Whether you take your camera or camcorder (or both), you'll have plenty of opportunities to get those classic Disney shots. If you forget your equipment, you can rent 35mm cameras or camcorders at the Kodak Camera Centers inside the Disney theme parks. There's a nominal fee, plus a small deposit. Both Universal Studios and Sea World will lend you a 35mm camera, free of charge, with a refundable deposit.

Bring your own film and video tapes; you can buy them inside the theme parks but at premium prices. Two-hour film developing is available at all the Disney parks; one-hour developing is provided by Universal Studios.

Star System

One of the primary goals of this book is to help you sort through the overwhelming number of theme-park attractions, and I've judged them by originality, imagination, design and *overall* family appeal. Obviously, family members aren't always going to agree on the "best" rides, so I've geared my ratings toward the people in charge: the parents. For instance, some rides extremely popular with young children received low ratings because they don't appeal to adults or even older children.

One Star signifies "one to be missed," a dullsville attraction that's a waste of time. *Two Stars* means below average, but with some redeeming entertainment value. *Three Stars* indicates an average attraction, one that shows at least a little imagination but may not appeal to the majority of visitors. *Four Stars* signifies above average, offering ingenuity, fantasy and top-notch design. *Five Stars* is "not to be missed," a very popular, state-of-the-art attraction that makes you want to ride over and over and over.

Lodging

With more hotel rooms (over 75,000) than any other city in the country, Greater Orlando offers a smorgasbord of lodging. From mom-and-pop motels and family-style apartments to lavish resorts that resemble mini-cities, you can choose many ways to sleep in the Orlando area. No matter where you stay, you should book well in advance. During high season, I recommend reserving Disney resorts a year ahead of time. Disney World is, after all, the world's most popular travel destination.

In *Disney World and Beyond: The Ultimate Family Guidebook*, I have chosen the best family- oriented accommodations the area has to offer. Included are all the Disney World resorts, as well as nearby lodging with specialties such as children's check-in and kids-only restaurants. To help suit your budget, I've organized the accommodations according to price. Rates referred to are high-season rates, so if you are looking for low-season bargains, it's good to inquire.

Budget hotels are generally less than $50 per night for two adults and two children; the rooms are clean and comfortable but lack luxury. The *moderate* hotels run $50 to $90 and provide larger rooms, plusher furniture and more attractive surroundings. At a *deluxe* hotel you can expect to spend between $90 and $130 for two adults with children. You'll check into a spacious, well-appointed room with all modern facilities; downstairs, the lobby will be a fashionable affair, and you'll usually see a restaurant, lounge and a cluster of shops. If you want to spend your time in the finest hotels, try an *ultra-deluxe* facility, which will include all the amenities and cost over $130.

Camping

For families, camping is a great way to stay in the Orlando area. First and foremost, it saves money. Not only is camping much less expensive than staying in a hotel, but it also saves on food bills. By cooking some of your own meals, you avoid falling into the trap of eating overpriced theme-park food three times a day. Camping also provides a physical and mental break from the rigors of theme-park touring. Best of all, most campgrounds are family-oriented, providing myriads of outdoor activities for all ages.

Campers will need basic cooking equipment and, except in winter, can make out fine with only a lightweight sleeping bag and a tent with good screens and a ground cloth. A canteen, first aid kit, flashlight, mosquito repellent and other routine camping gear should be brought along.

Walt Disney World has its own campground, Fort Wilderness, and there are several private campgrounds just minutes from Disney's door. For campground listings, see Chapter Eight.

On a diet? All the major theme parks offer light, low-calorie fare. Check with guest relations at each park.

Restaurants

It seems as if Central Florida has more restaurants than people. To help you decide on this army of eateries, I've organized them according to family appeal and cost with price ratings of budget, moderate, deluxe or ultra-deluxe.

Dinner entrées at *budget* restaurants usually cost $8 or less. The ambience is informal, service usually speedy and the crowd often a local one. *Moderate*-priced restaurants range between $8 and $16 at dinner; surroundings are casual but pleasant, the menu offers more variety and the pace is usually slower. *Deluxe* establishments tab their entrées from $16 to $24; cuisines may be simple or sophisticated, depending on the location, but the decor is plusher and the service more personable. *Ultra-deluxe* dining rooms, where entrées begin at $24, are often the gourmet places; here cooking has become a fine art and the service should be impeccable.

Some restaurants change hands often and are occasionally closed in low seasons. In every instance, I've endeavored to include places with established reputations for good eating. Breakfast and lunch menus vary less in price from restaurant to restaurant than evening meals.

Family Necessities

STROLLERS AND CAR SEATS   A stroller can be a lifesaver inside a theme park. If you don't bring your own, you can rent one at any Disney World park, Universal Studios or Sea World. I recommend using a stroller for children younger than three. Those three to five years will definitely need one in Epcot Center and Universal Studios, but probably not at Disney–MGM Studios (it's much smaller). At the

Take your children to the restroom before getting in a long line, especially at Dumbo!

Magic Kingdom, it's nice to start the day without one, then pick one up later if little legs start to give out. Keep your stroller receipt; stolen strollers are replaced free of charge with a receipt.

If you're flying to Orlando and renting a car, **Kids in Safety Seats** (407-857-0353) will provide car rental seats and strollers. For a small fee, they will deliver in the Disney World area. Remember, Florida law requires car seats for young children.

BABYSITTERS   Guests of Walt Disney World resorts can use the **KinderCare** babysitting center, available for infants through 12-year-olds. Reservations should be made at least eight hours in advance by calling 407-827-5444. Disney resorts and most area hotels also offer in-room babysitting, though it's considerably more expensive. Several private services provide bonded babysitters that will accompany you to the theme parks and watch the kids while you're sightseeing. Call **Mothers Babysitting Service** (407-857-7447) or **Super Sitters** (407-740-5516). Both companies also provide in-room babysitting.

BABY SERVICES   Available at the Magic Kingdom, Epcot, Disney–MGM Studios and Universal Studios, Baby Services offers quiet, dimly lit rooms with changing tables and comfortable rockers for nursing. High chairs, bibs, pacifiers, formula, cereal and jars of food are also on hand for a fee. Disposable diapers are available here and at many Disney stores. The stores usually keep them under the counter, so you'll have to ask.

NURSING NOOKS

Disney World's relaxed family atmosphere and abundance of cool, dark attractions make it a good place to discreetly nurse an infant. In the Magic Kingdom, try the quiet theaters at The Walt Disney Story, The Hall of Presidents, Magic Journeys and Carousel of Progress.

At Epcot, there are theaters at Future World's Universe of Energy, Wonders of Life (Cranium Command and The Making of Me) and The Land (Symbiosis). In World Showcase, France, Norway and The American Adventure all have dark cinemas. Over in Disney–MGM Studios, you'll find comfortable seats with some privacy at SuperStar Television, Here Come the Muppets and the Disney Classics Theater.

For those apprehensive about these locations, there are comfortable rocking chairs at the Baby Services area of each park.

---

*Brought your plants? Disney World's plant sitters will watch them for free. Call
407-824-4321 for information.*

Disabled Travelers

For the most part, Walt Disney World and surrounding theme parks are
easily accessible to the disabled. Attractions feature wide, gently sloped
ramps, and restrooms and restaurants are designed with the disabled in
mind. Wheelchairs and motorized three-wheel vehicles are available
for rent at the entrance to every theme park. For hearing-impaired
guests, Disney World offers written descriptions of most attractions as
well as a Telecommunications Device for the Deaf inside each park.
For a small deposit, sight-impaired guests can borrow portable tape
recorders and cassette tapes with narrative on each attraction. Check at
the Guest Relations desk.

For information on Central Florida facilities, contact the **Center
for Independent Living** (720 North Denning Drive, Winter Park;
407-623-1070).

For advice on travel contact **Travelin' Talk** (P.O. Box 3534, Clarks-
ville, TN 37043; 615-552-6670), a networking organization. Also
providing helpful information for disabled travelers are the **Society
for the Advancement of Travel for the Handicapped** (347 5th
Avenue, Suite 610, New York, NY 10016; 212-447-7284), **Travel Information Center** (Moss Rehabilitation Hospital, 12th Street and
Tabor Road, Philadelphia, PA 19141; 215-329-5715), **Mobility International USA** (P.O. Box 3551, Eugene, OR 97403; 503-343-1284)
and **Flying Wheels Travel** (P.O. Box 382, Owatonna, MN 55060;
800-533-0363).

Be sure to check in advance when making room reservations. Many
hotels and motels feature facilities for those in wheelchairs.

Senior Travelers

As millions have discovered, Central Florida is an ideal place for older
vacationers, many of whom turn into part-time or full-time residents.
The climate is mild, the terrain level, and many destinations offer sig-
nificant discounts. Off-season rates make the area exceedingly attractive for travelers on limited incomes. During slow season, visitors 55
and older enjoy discounts at Walt Disney World, Universal Studios,
Sea World and other local attractions. Florida residents over 65 can
benefit from reduced rates at most state parks, and the Golden Age

Passport, which must be applied for in person, allows free admission to national parks and monuments for anyone 62 and older.

The **American Association of Retired Persons (AARP)** (3200 East Carson Street, Lakewood, CA 90712; 213-496-2277) offers membership to anyone over 50. AARP's benefits include travel discounts with a number of firms; escorted tours and cruises are available through **AARP Travel Service** (P.O. Box 5850, Norcross, GA 30091; 800-927-0111).

Elderhostel (75 Federal Street, Boston, MA 02110; 617-426-7788) offers reasonably priced, all-inclusive educational programs in a variety of Central Florida locations throughout the year.

Be extra careful about health matters. In addition to the medications you ordinarily use, it's a good idea to bring along the prescriptions for obtaining more. Consider carrying a medical record with you—including your medical history and current medical status as well as your doctor's name, phone number and address. Make sure that your insurance covers you while away from home.

Foreign Travelers

PASSPORTS AND VISAS   Most foreign visitors are required to obtain a passport and tourist visa to enter the United States. Contact your nearest United States Embassy or Consulate well in advance to obtain a visa and to check on any other entry requirements.

CUSTOMS REQUIREMENTS   Foreign travelers are allowed to carry in the following: 200 cigarettes (or 100 cigars), $400 worth of duty-free gifts, including one liter of alcohol (you must be 21 years of age to bring in the alcohol). You may bring in any amount of currency, but you must fill out a form if you bring in over $10,000 (U.S.). Carry any prescription drugs in clearly marked containers. (You may have to produce a written prescription or doctor's statement for the custom's officer.) Meat or meat products, seeds, plants, fruit and narcotics are not permitted to be brought into the United States. Contact the **United States Customs Service** (1301 Constitution Avenue Northwest, Washington, DC 20229; 202-566-8195) for further information.

DRIVING   If you plan to rent a car, an international driver's license should be obtained *before* arriving in Florida. Some rental companies require both a foreign license and an international driver's license. Many car rental agencies require a lessee to be 25 years of age; all require a major credit card.

CURRENCY   United States money is based on the dollar. Bills come in six denominations: $1, $5, $10, $20, $50 and $100. Every dollar is divided into 100 cents. Coins are the penny (1 cent), nickel (5 cents), dime (10 cents) and quarter (25 cents). Half-dollar and dollar coins are rarely used. You may not use foreign currency to purchase goods and services in the United States. You may, however, exchange your currency at the Sun Banks located inside Disney World's Magic Kingdom, Epcot Center and Disney–MGM Studios. Inside Universal Studios, change your money at Southeast Bank; at Sea World, the Special Services desk provides a foreign currency exchange. Disney World resorts, except for the Disney Inn, and many area hotels will also exchange your money.

LANGUAGE ASSISTANCE   Disney's Magic Kingdom, Epcot Center and Disney–MGM Studios provide translated recordings for many attractions. Check with Guest Services inside each park. Universal Studios' Guest Relations has foreign language maps.

ELECTRICITY   Electric outlets use currents of 117 volts, 60 cycles. For appliances made for other electrical systems you need a transformer or other adapter.

Spend a day in a theme park and you've walked three to four miles. If you're not in good walking shape, better get moving!

Planning Your Visit

The phenomenal scope of Walt Disney World and surrounding sights makes a short visit stressful, if not maniacal. I recommend staying at least three days, especially if you're coming from outside Florida. To me the ideal Disney vacation is seven days, with two to three days spent outside the big theme parks. Even the most energetic visitors get tired of pounding pavement ten hours a day, and Central Florida has much to offer in the way of side trips.

However long you stay, rarely do two visitors agree on how to see the Disney World area. Still, there are good ways and bad ways to spend your days, and following a few touring guidelines can help make your vacation less of a hassle. First and foremost: *Arrive Early!*, at least a half hour before the official opening time. Second, eat a big breakfast *before* you get to the parks. For the rest of the day, eat during "off" hours, which is before or after the dining rush hour. Third, have a good idea of the order you'd like to see the various attractions. This guide's five-star rating system can help you decide what goes at the top (and bottom) of your list. You should also remember that kids (as well as adults!) like to ride their favorite attractions over and over. Allow extra time for riding again.

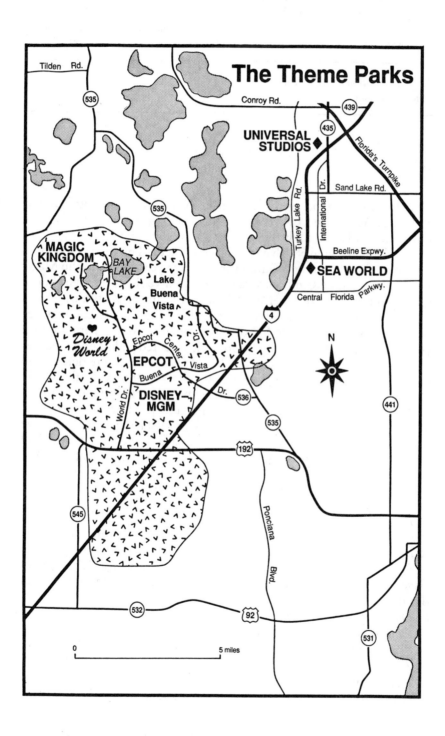

Last, don't try to cram too much in. Decide what you'd really like to see—then cut that in half. One mother, writing for *Parents* magazine, says she made a "tough decision that enhanced our quality of life in Disney World: We wouldn't try to see everything on this trip."

Fancy an old-time shave? Visit the Harmony Barber Shop on Main Street in the Magic Kingdom.

Sample Itineraries

To help you along, below are itineraries for a family spending four days at Disney World and other theme parks, along with suggestions for fifth, sixth and seventh days if you have time for them.

For the first two days, I've given two choices: The Magic Kingdom for families with young children three to five years old, and the Magic Kingdom for families without young children. I've also given two choices for the fourth day: Disney–MGM Studios or Universal Studios.

These itineraries are guidelines, not marching orders. You may decide, for instance, to visit Epcot instead of the Magic Kingdom on your second day. Because Epcot is an adult-oriented park, I don't recommend it for families with young children. However, if you're determined to take them, consider going to Epcot the first day. If they see the Magic Kingdom first, Epcot will most certainly be a disappointment to them.

All itineraries assume you're staying at a hotel either inside Disney World or just a few miles outside. If you're staying more than five miles away, you can take the midday breaks at a Disney restaurant. And however you plan your days, remember this is a vacation, not a chore.

DAY ONE: MAGIC KINGDOM (WITH TODDLERS)

Early morning   Be on Main Street early—it opens a half hour before the rest of the Magic Kingdom—to pick up maps, strollers and other touring essentials. As soon as the rest of the Magic Kingdom opens, go to Cinderella Castle and make 6 p.m. reservations for *King Stefan's Banquet Hall.* Then proceed to the heart of Fantasyland and ride, in this order:

Dumbo, the Flying Elephant
Cinderella's Golden Carrousel
Snow White's Adventures (may be scary for some youngsters)
20,000 Leagues Under the Sea
Magic Journeys
Peter Pan's Flight (may be scary for some youngsters)
It's a Small World

Lunchtime   Head back to the hotel for lunch and a nap.

Afternoon   Stroll to Mickey's Starland and see *Mickey's House and Musical Show*. If there's a wait for the show, the kids can roam *Grandma Duck's Farm*.

Late afternoon to early evening   After the show, board the *Walt Disney World Railroad* at Mickey's Starland. Ride it to Main Street, then disembark and take a jitney or horse drawn carriage to *Cinderella Castle* for your 6 p.m. dinner.

If you have time after dinner (and aren't too exhausted), take the kids for a twinkling night ride on *Cinderella's Golden Carrousel*.

DAY TWO: MAGIC KINGDOM (WITH TODDLERS)

Early morning   Be on Main Street early again. When the Magic Kingdom opens, go to Adventureland and ride the *Jungle Cruise*, then see the *Enchanted Tiki Birds*. Walk across to Tomorrowland and ride *WEDway PeopleMover*, *Star Jets* and *Grand Prix Raceway*. Then take the *Skyway to Fantasyland*.

In Fantasyland, ride the *Mad Tea Party* (no spinning the teacups). Then repeat other Fantasyland rides the kids like.

Lunchtime   Around lunch time, go to Frontierland and take a raft over to *Tom Sawyer Island*. Relax while the kids burn off some energy. Have a sandwich at Aunt Polly's Landing, which is rarely crowded. Ride the raft back to the mainland and see the *Country Bear Jamboree*.

Afternoon   After the jamboree, exit the Magic Kingdom and take an afternoon break.

Evening   Here are some suggestions for the evening: (1) see the *Polynesian Revue* (for adults) and *Mickey's Revue* (for kids), staged simultaneously at the Polynesian Village in Disney World (2) have dinner at *Trails End* in Disney's Fort Wilderness, then catch the fort's 8 p.m. campfire party (3) visit Disney's *River Country*, if it's open at night.

DAY ONE: MAGIC KINGDOM (WITHOUT TODDLERS)

Early morning   Be on Main Street early—it opens a half hour before the rest of the Magic Kingdom—to pick up maps and other touring essentials. On Main Street, make a 12:15 p.m. reservation for the Diamond Horseshoe Jamboree. As soon as the Magic Kingdom opens, make a mad dash to ride *Space Mountain*. Next head to Adventureland for:

   Pirates of the Caribbean
   The Jungle Cruise
   Swiss Family Treehouse

Lunchtime   Then go next door to Frontierland and see the *Diamond Horseshoe Revue* at 12:15 p.m. After the revue, exit the Magic Kingdom, have lunch and spend the afternoon relaxing.

Early evening   Around 5 p.m., have dinner outside the Magic Kingdom, then return.

Evening   Walk over to Fantasyland and go on *Mr. Toad's Wild Ride, Mad Tea Party, It's a Small World* and any other Fantasyland rides you'd like. Walk next door to Liberty Square and see *The Haunted Mansion* and *The Hall of Presidents*. Next go to Adventureland and ride *Big Thunder Mountain*—a great finale to any evening!

If it's summertime or the holiday season, stay for the *Fantasy in the Sky Fireworks*.

DAY TWO: MAGIC KINGDOM (WITHOUT TODDLERS)

Early morning   Be on Main Street early. When the Magic Kingdom opens, go to Tomorrowland and ride *Space Mountain* again. Then ride, in this order:

WEDway People Mover
Carousel of Progress
American Journeys

Mid-morning   Walk across to Adventureland, stopping to repeat *Pirates of the Caribbean* or any other rides you'd like. Then stroll next door to Frontierland and see the *Country Bear Jamboree*. Afterwards, hop aboard the nearby *Liberty Square Riverboat* for a relaxing cruise.

Lunchtime   Grab a bite to eat at the nearby Turkey Leg Wagon.

Afternoon   After lunch, visit *Mickey's House* in Mickey's Starland, or re-ride favorite Fantasyland attractions. At 3 p.m., head over to Main Street for the *Disney Character Hit Parade*. After the parade, exit the Magic Kingdom.

Evening   Some options are: (1) visit *Pleasure Island* (2) visit *Typhoon Lagoon*, if it's open late (3) have dinner at one of Epcot's *World Showcase restaurants* (assuming you've made a previous reservation), then catch the *IllumiNations* laser show.

Walt Disney once said, "I love Mickey Mouse more than any woman I've every known."

DAY THREE: EPCOT

(Note to Parents: While *you* visit Epcot, you might want to consider letting the kids take a half- or full-day Disney guided tour. The tours are for ages 8 through 15. For more specific information, see Chapter Five.)

Early morning   Arrive early—Spaceship Earth and the surrounding area open a half hour before the rest of Epcot. At Earth Station, you should make a 5:30 p.m. dinner reservation for one of the World Showcase restaurants. Then ride *Spaceship Earth.*

Mid-morning   As soon as the rest of Epcot opens, walk directly to World Showcase. Rejoice! because it will be empty. Stroll counter-clockwise around World Showcase, starting at *Mexico*, then *Norway*, and so on.

Lunchtime   Plan to have a fast-food lunch at the American Adventure.

Afternoon   Around 2 p.m., leave Epcot and take an afternoon break. If you're still hungry, stop by *The Land Farmer's Market* on your way out of the park.

Evening   Return to Epcot at 5 p.m., allowing yourself plenty of time to get to World Showcase. Have dinner at 5:30, then walk across to Future World. Visit these pavilions in the following order:

> *Journey Into Imagination*
> *The Land*
> *Wonders of Life*

If you have time, visit the *Universe of Energy*. As the park is closing, find a spot around World Showcase Lagoon to watch the spectacular *Illumi-Nations* laser show.

DAY FOUR: DISNEY–MGM *or* UNIVERSAL STUDIOS

DISNEY–MGM

Early morning   Arrive on Hollywood Boulevard early—it opens a half-hour before the rest of the park. When all of Disney–MGM opens, make a beeline for Backlot Annex and ride *Star Tours* (Note: Children under three are not allowed to ride, and some older than three are frightened). Then walk back to the end of Hollywood Boulevard and go on *The Great Movie Ride.*

Mid-morning   Next, walk over to Lakeside Circle and make a 1:30 p.m. lunch reservation for the '50s Prime Time Café. Then see *Super-Star Television* show and *The Monster Sound Show.* Walk across the street and catch the 12:15 p.m. *Indiana Jones Epic Stunt Spectacular* show.

Lunchtime   Have lunch at the *'50s Prime Time Café.*

Afternoon   After lunch, there are two options:

   (1) If you have young children, see *Here Come the Muppets*, then *Honey, I Shrunk the Kids* and then *Teenage Mutant Ninja Turtles.*

   (2) Without small children, take the *Backstage Studio Tour.* This takes two to two-and-a-half hours (including time in line). If you're not completely exhausted, go for the *Animation Tour.*

UNIVERSAL STUDIOS

Early morning   Arrive 30 minutes before the park opens. At the Front Lot, pick up maps, strollers and other touring essentials. Warm up those legs and, when the park opens, dash to Expo Center and ride

Back to the Future (Note: Children shorter than 46 inches are not allowed to ride.) Walk around the corner and ride *E. T. Adventure.*

Morning   Keeping up the brisk pace, head to Production Central and ride *The FUNtastic World of Hanna-Barbera.* Relax. If you have small kids, stroll down the street to *Nickelodeon Studios.* If not, take the *Production Tour*, then see *Alfred Hitchcock: The Art of Making Movies.*

Lunchtime   Have a late lunch at *Mel's Drive-In* in Hollywood.

Afternoon   After lunch, peruse Hollywood's street sets. Walk around the lagoon to San Francisco-Amity and ride *Earthquake, The Big One.* Then go next door to New York and ride *Kongfrontation.* Then watch *Ghostbusters.*

Evening   By now, if you're not totally zapped of energy, you should find a spot around the lagoon and watch the 7 p.m. *Dynamite Nights Stunt Spectacular* boat race.

OPTIONS FOR DAYS FIVE, SIX AND SEVEN

❖ *Disney–MGM* or *Universal Studio*s. If you're a real movie buff, see the park you skipped on Day Four.

❖ *Sea World.* Kids love the animals, and adults enjoy the break from crowded high-tech attractions.

❖ *Orlando Area.* Explore downtown Orlando (including Church Street Station) or lovely Winter Park.

❖ *Space Coast.* Only 50 minutes away are pretty, white sand beaches and the Kennedy Space Center.

❖ *Tampa's Busch Gardens.* Spend a day at Busch Gardens. If you can, spend the night (it's 90 minutes one-way from Orlando). The next day you can explore Tampa's historic districts or visit Clearwater beach.

AFTERNOON DELIGHTS

On those sweltering summer afternoons, the last place you want to be is rubbing sweaty elbows in a crowded theme park. Instead, leave the parks and head for:

❖ *Your air-conditioned hotel room (the kids can nap while you catch an in-room movie).*

❖ *A Disney resort swimming pool, where you can lay prone in the shade and slurp an icy drink (the Polynesian Village pools are convenient).*

❖ *A Disney hotel restaurant. They're cool and uncrowded in the afternoon.*

❖ *Pleasure Island's ten-screen movie complex.*

You can also spend these days at the minor Disney theme parks, including *Typhoon Lagoon*, *River Country* and *Discovery Island*. And definitely use one of the mornings to take the kids to a Disney character breakfast—they'll love you for it.

TWO

The Magic Kingdom

To many people, the Magic Kingdom *is* Disney World. For here is **35** where Walt Disney first worked his fantasy formula on Florida, recasting a swath of swampland into fairy-tale architecture, whimsical artistry, flourishing gardens and state-of-the-art attractions. Here the brilliant cartoonist pushed make-believe to its extreme limit, devising a fictional kingdom woven with cartoon characters, simulated towns and jungles, lighthearted music, squeaky clean streets, shimmering lakes and thrilling rides all spun into one colorful, jubilant experience.

The Magic Kingdom takes up only 100 of Disney World's 28,000 acres—little more than a drop in a pond—yet it is the heart of that world. A virtual clone of California's Disneyland, the kingdom is fashioned with 45 attractions, 37 eateries and 54 shops spread across six imaginative—and vastly different—"lands." The most popular is Fantasyland, a dreamy web of storybook architecture, boat rides, carousels and merry music. Adventureland, with its thatched buildings, squawking parrots and jungle journey, offers a tame trek through the wilds of Africa and South America.

Frontierland presents a stony profile of rust-colored knolls and cowboy-and-Indian scenes, while adjacent Liberty Square emulates early America with colonial storefronts and patriotic attractions. Like a page out of the Sunday comics come to life, Mickey's Starland features roaming cartoon characters, kid-size houses and stores painted in a riot of colors. In contrast, Tomorrowland's whitewashed buildings and endless pavement paint a stark picture. This land portrays the future as Disney saw it in the 1960s and is home to the park's most popular ride, Space Mountain.

Then there's Main Street, U.S.A., the key to the Magic Kingdom and the first sight that greets visitors. Here brick streets, old-fashioned lampposts and intricate building facades create a splendid facsimile of an idealized American town. There's also the colorful depot for the

Walt Disney World Railroad, a steam train that chugs around the perimeter of the Magic Kingdom. Just beyond Main Street is a lush park known as Central Plaza that is ringed with indigo water and dotted with grand oak trees and lacquered park benches. The magnificent Cinderella Castle looms ahead, and all day long visitors gather to stare and marvel at its many spires and to dream fairy-tale dreams.

Each area's remarkable attention to detail—from the decorated trash cans to employee costumes and clever restaurant menus—never ceases to awe even frequent visitors. There is true joy in immersing yourself in the mood of one land and then being transformed by the aura of a thoroughly different realm. Even on the worst days, when the park is crushed with people and the sun threatens to suffocate, it is impossible not to be caught up in the spirit of the Magic Kingdom.

Nighttime brings more illusions to the kingdom, as beads of light trace intricate rooflines and the castle spires glow high in the inky sky. This is the most festive time, when triumphant music pulsates from parades, costumed singers pour through the streets and fireworks blast against the eastern stars.

Since the Magic Kingdom's opening in 1971, Disney World has spawned its other theme parks, including the 260-acre Epcot (more than twice the size of the Magic Kingdom). But despite the competition, the Magic Kingdom remains the ultimate escape valve, the spot farthest from reality. It is a place for children, and a place where adults can think like children. It is a place that tugs on the hearts of dreamers and even those skeptics who chide its corny humor, conservative overtones and idealistic approach.

Anyone who has experienced the fascination of Cinderella Castle, the adrenaline rush of Space Mountain or the happy vibes of *It's a Small World* knows the Magic Kingdom has no parallel. In fact, more people visit the Magic Kingdom than any other theme park *in the world*.

ARRIVAL

Getting to the Magic Kingdom can be quite a chore, complex and time-consuming. Because of this—and because early arrivers can avoid long lines—it is imperative to get there *one to two hours* before the advertised opening time. Trams and monorails are usually operating two hours prior to opening, and Main Street typically opens 30 minutes to an hour before the rest of the park.

From the Contemporary, Polynesian Village and Grand Floridian Resorts: Take the hotel monorail directly to the Magic Kingdom.

From Epcot Center: Take the Epcot monorail to the Ticket and Transportation Center, then transfer to the Magic Kingdom monorail or ride the ferry.

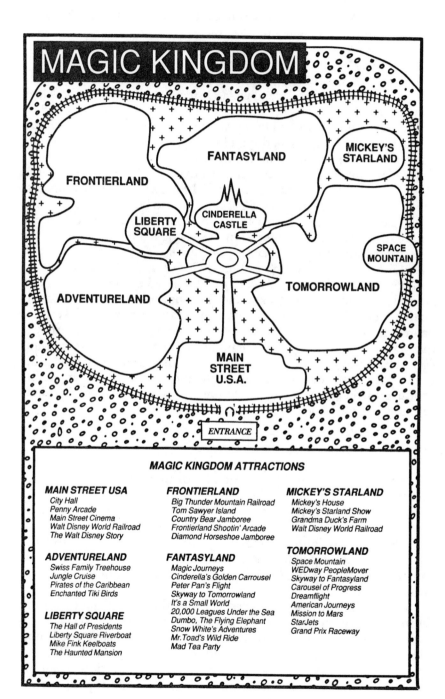

MAGIC KINGDOM

FANTASYLAND

MICKEY'S STARLAND

FRONTIERLAND

LIBERTY SQUARE

CINDERELLA CASTLE

SPACE MOUNTAIN

ADVENTURELAND

TOMORROWLAND

MAIN STREET U.S.A.

ENTRANCE

MAGIC KINGDOM ATTRACTIONS

MAIN STREET USA
City Hall
Penny Arcade
Main Street Cinema
Walt Disney World Railroad
The Walt Disney Story

ADVENTURELAND
Swiss Family Treehouse
Jungle Cruise
Pirates of the Caribbean
Enchanted Tiki Birds

LIBERTY SQUARE
The Hall of Presidents
Liberty Square Riverboat
Mike Fink Keelboats
The Haunted Mansion

FRONTIERLAND
Big Thunder Mountain Railroad
Tom Sawyer Island
Country Bear Jamboree
Frontierland Shootin' Arcade
Diamond Horseshoe Jamboree

FANTASYLAND
Magic Journeys
Cinderella's Golden Carrousel
Peter Pan's Flight
Skyway to Tomorrowland
It's a Small World
20,000 Leagues Under the Sea
Dumbo, The Flying Elephant
Snow White's Adventures
Mr. Toad's Wild Ride
Mad Tea Party

MICKEY'S STARLAND
Mickey's House
Mickey's Starland Show
Grandma Duck's Farm
Walt Disney World Railroad

TOMORROWLAND
Space Mountain
WEDway PeopleMover
Skyway to Fantasyland
Carousel of Progress
Dreamflight
American Journeys
Mission to Mars
StarJets
Grand Prix Raceway

From Disney–MGM Studios: Take a Disney bus directly to the Magic Kingdom.

From the Yacht Club or Beach Club Resorts: Take a Disney bus directly to the Magic Kingdom.

From the Swan or Dolphin hotels or the Caribbean Beach Resort: Take a Disney bus directly to the Magic Kingdom.

From Fort Wilderness, Typhoon Lagoon, Pleasure Island or the Disney Village Marketplace: Take a Disney bus directly to the Magic Kingdom.

From area hotels not in Disney World: Most hotels provide shuttles to and from the Magic Kingdom. However, they often run only on the hour or every two or three hours. In this case, it's better to drive.

By Car: On Route 4, look for signs that say "Walt Disney World" exits. Take the Magic Kingdom exit and follow it about two miles to the toll plaza. Here you'll pay a parking fee and be directed to a mammoth parking lot that seems to fall off the horizon. At this point, you're still at least 20 minutes from the Magic Kingdom.

It's imperative to *make a note of your parking row* (sections are named after Disney characters such as Pluto, Goofy, and Chip and Dale) or you might not be able to find your car at the end of the day. From here you take a tram to the Ticket and Transportation Center, a sort of Grand Central Station where you purchase admission tickets and board a monorail or ferryboat for the one-and-a-half-mile journey to the Magic Kingdom. The monorails make the faster trip (two minutes compared to the ferry's five minutes), but lines are usually longer because visitors avoid the extra walk to the ferry launch. If the monorails appear crowded, opt for the ferry: the trip will be quicker *and* more relaxing.

SIGHTSEEING STRATEGIES

Remember once again that it's a good idea to get to the Magic Kingdom an hour or two before the announced opening time. Then it will be easy to plan your morning. For instance, if the Disney people say the park opens at 9 a.m., you can park your car at 7:30 a.m. and be on Main Street between 8 and 8:30 a.m. Here you can rent a stroller or locker, get maps and information, secure reservations for live shows, eat breakfast and stroll Main Street's shops and sights—before the crowds arrive.

Most important, you may even get into the rest of the park early. During the summer, holidays and other busy times, the Magic Kingdom sometimes opens as early as an hour before the advertised time. This helps prevent traffic gridlock and record-breaking ticket lines on days when the place fills up—and visitors are turned away—well before noon. There's no way to surmise when this will happen, but one thing is certain: Arriving early can save you *up to several hours* of wait-

A spacious apartment near the top of Cinderella Castle was designed for the Disney family, but no one ever moved in.

ing in line for attractions. Best of all, it removes the aggravation from an experience that should be pure entertainment and fantasy.

This flexible opening axiom doesn't apply to quitting time, however. Attractions and rides usually close pronto, although Main Street stays open a half hour to an hour later and buses and monorails operate about two hours after closing. This, of course, is a prime time to see Main Street. While the rest of the park is funneling out, you can experience the sights and shops at leisure. And buying souvenirs just before closing means you won't have to rent a storage locker or lug the bags around all day.

OTHER STRATEGIES

❖ Try to see all of one theme area, or "land," before moving on to the next. The Magic Kingdom is so complex it's disastrous to sightsee checkerboard style.

❖ Take your time. Trying to see all of the Magic Kingdom in one day is like trying to watch ten movies in one night. It's impossible!

❖ Eat an early or late lunch—before 11:30 a.m. or after 2 p.m. Ditto for dinner, which should be before 4:30 p.m. or after 8 p.m. You'll avoid the meal crowd crush and have more time to do what you really came here for.

NUTS & BOLTS

Stroller and Wheelchair Rentals: Both are available at the Stroller Shop, on the east side of the main entrance.

Baby Services: Located next to the Crystal Palace restaurant on Main Street U.S.A. Services include changing tables and comfortable rockers for nursing. Diapers, formula and other baby needs are also available here, as well as in some stores throughout the Magic Kingdom.

Lockers: Available under the Walt Disney World Railroad Station at the foot of Main Street, and at the Ticket and Transportation Center. Be forewarned: Lockers cost 50 cents each time you open them.

Pets: Pets are not allowed in The Magic Kingdom. You can, however, board them for the day at the kennel near the parking toll plaza.

Lost Children: Report lost children to City Hall or Baby Services on Main Street.

Package Pickup: Serious shoppers should consider this free service, which lets you forward all your Magic Kingdom purchases to

Guest Relations (on the east side of the main entrance). You can pick up your packages on your way out and avoid lugging them around all day. One note: Package pickup sometimes has human traffic jams between 5 p.m. and 6 p.m., and during the half-hour before park closing.

Lost & Found: Report lost or found articles to City Hall.

Banking: Traveler's check services, cash advances and automatic teller machines are available at Sun Bank, located on the west side of Main Street next to City Hall. Open from 9 a.m. to 4 p.m. every day.

GETTING AROUND

To get a feel for the place, think of the Magic Kingdom as a giant wheel whose spokes lead to each of the six lands. At the base of the wheel is Main Street U.S.A., which serves as the park's entrance and the place to get oriented. The Walt Disney World Railroad travels the rim of the wheel, while overhead Skyway buckets trickle across the northeast sky.

At the wheel's hub sits Central Plaza, a verdant park in front of Cinderella Castle. The plaza is a good meeting place if your party decides to split up during the day—or if someone gets lost. There are also plenty of broad grassy areas where parents can rest while children release some energy. Families sometimes picnic here, spreading out blankets under shade trees and sorting out which rides to go on next.

From the hub, bridges and walkways lead to each land. Traveling counterclockwise, you'll encounter Adventureland, then Frontierland, Liberty Square, Fantasyland, Mickey's Starland and Tomorrowland. On a map the transitions between lands look fairly easy, though in reality there's plenty to foul you up. The entire kingdom is riddled with sinuous waterways and curving lanes that don't always take you from here to there. Anyone who's just ridden Space Mountain and attempts a dash to Big Thunder Mountain with kids in tow will find he's undertaken a trying trek.

Translation: Use a map to plot your course, taking it slow until you get your bearings. If you get lost, a Disney employee can always help.

JITNEYS, CARRIAGES AND OTHER WACKY WHEELS

To see Main Street on four (or more) wheels, board one of the zany vehicles that tools around this brick-lined thoroughfare. There are bright red jitneys and fire engines, carts pulled by muscled horses, double-decker buses and horseless carriages whose drivers wear handlebar mustaches. Most make one-way trips from the foot of Main Street to Cinderella Castle.

The Main Street trolleys are drawn by husky Belgian and Percheron horses, breeds that were once used to pull plows in Europe.

Main Street U.S.A.

What finer introduction to an enchanted kingdom than a postcard-perfect street? This replica of a beautiful American town affords a visually exciting collage of wrought-iron balconies, ornate balustrades, gingerbread designs, old-fashioned lampposts, painted benches, shade-giving trees, merry music, espresso and pastry carts, and hanging pots brimming with flowers. Bright red fire engines clang, jitneys whiz around and muscled horses haul trolleys packed with visitors.

Much of Main Street is lined with clever shops and businesses whose task seems to entertain as well as sell. The House of Magic, for instance, has giant monster masks and costumes, while Uptown Jewelers displays gorgeous ceramic eggs. One great spot is the Harmony Barber Shop, where people (particularly children) press their faces against the front window to watch mustached barbers give old-time shaves and haircuts (see Chapter Nine for information on shopping in Disney World).

Interspersed among the shops are nifty sights and eateries that funnel heady aromas out their propped-open doors. There's a pastry shop, an ice cream parlor with red-and-white awnings, and a confectionery where candy makers swirl huge vats of peanut brittle. Each place has its own ambience, some busy and bright, others formal and Victorian, and still others rustic and woody.

There is so much to keep the eye (and mind) busy here that it takes a lot longer than 40 minutes—the average time a visitor spends on Main Street—to absorb everything. Best of all, this area is rarely clogged with people and can be visited anytime. Plan to come between midmorning and midafternoon, when more popular attractions are crowded and the sun is most intense. Main Street is also a good place for one parent to take the kids while the other goes solo on Space Mountain or any other ride closed to small children.

To explore Main Street, begin by stopping at **City Hall** for maps, entertainment and dining schedules, lost and found, and general information. Across the street from City Hall is a booth where you sign up for the **Diamond Horseshoe Jamboree**, a popular saloon-style revue in Frontierland. The five daily shows usually sell out within an hour of the park's opening. If you can't get a reservation, show up 30 minutes before any jamboree and get in the standby line. Chances are excellent that you'll get a seat.

One of Main Street's best spots is the **Penny Arcade**, where a cent will buy you time on an old-fashioned reel machine. There are also nickel and dime machines and a few modern video games that, of course, accept quarters.

Vintage Disney flicks, including some great silent cartoons, run continuously at the **Main Street Cinema**. Though it's standing only, the octagonal room with six screens is cool, dark and a welcome respite from lines and summer heat. Kids are often fascinated by these unfamiliar black-and-white cartoons, but it's the adults who can while away a half-hour or more watching such classics as *Steamboat Willie*. The first cartoon with sound, *Steamboat* has a particularly nostalgic story line: a clever mouse named Mickey falls in love with a rosy-cheeked beauty named Minnie.

Main Street is also home to two larger attractions:

Walt Disney World Railroad ★★★ With their striped awnings, brightly painted bench seats and thunderous choo choo, these old-fashioned steam trains offers loads of fun. You can hop on one of four turn-of-the-century trains that circle the Magic Kingdom, stopping at Frontierland and Mickey's Starland and traversing what a narrator terms "original Florida frontier"—fern hammocks and scrub palmetto—as well as some hokey Disney character cutouts. Kids love the open-air experience and the chance to ride on what they often call "a real live train." For adults, it's a great way to rest tired bones while getting a splendid introduction to each land. In fact, the train is the only ride that offers close-up views of the Magic Kingdom.

TIPS: Lines frequently form at the Main Street and Frontierland depots but rarely at Mickey's Starland. Trains are five to seven minutes apart.

STREET SHOWS

You're strolling along Main Street, enjoying the handsome architecture, when suddenly a barbershop quartet breaks into harmony. Dressed in bright-colored pin-striped suits, the men belt out a comical song and lift their hats to a cheering crowd. You round the corner into jungly Adventureland, and there's a Caribbean band tapping away on steel drums. Nearby at Cinderella Castle, a piano player sends ragtime tunes across the balloon-filled courtyard.

Live street shows, lending whimsy and festivity to the Magic Kingdom, are staged daily at various locations across the park. Times change frequently, so stop by City Hall on Main Street for a show schedule.

The Walt Disney Story ★★ Possibly the least popular Magic Kingdom attraction, this place provides some interesting insights into the man who made it all happen. A minimuseum features Disney nostalgia such as Walt's awards and letters from U.S. presidents and the original cels, or frames, from the movie *Snow White*. A movie traces Walt's life, including the train ride from New York to California where he hatched the idea for a witty, intelligent mouse named Mickey. The whole thing pushes the Disney line, of course, but it's informative nonetheless.

TIPS: Most appealing to seniors; children may find it boring. There's rarely a line, so plan to visit during midday when popular rides are crowded.

The Walt Disney World Railroad's Lilly Belle *train is named for Walt's wife.*

Adventureland

The crude wooden bridge from Central Plaza to Adventureland is like a tunnel of metamorphosis: on one side are brick lanes, cropped lawns and the bright orderliness of the plaza; on the other are dim, watery passages, tangles of vines and croaks of toads. Here in Adventureland, Disney's interpretation of exotica thrives with totem poles and carved spears, waterfalls that gush down algae-covered rock and bright blooms that poke across footpaths. The jungly scheme is peppered with the flavors of Africa, Polynesia and the Caribbean: parrots squawk, drums pound and mechanical elephants trumpet. Even the air is heavy with the musty scent of the tropics.

The "faraway place" theme is emphasized by the architecture, a fusion of thatched huts, tin-roofed buildings washed in sherbet hues, and carved wood and adobe facades crowned with clay tile.

One of the best buildings is the Caribbean Plaza, a breezy network of shops where goods are stacked under stucco arches. Pirate hats, bangle jewelry, treasure chests and other "loot" are sold by women in batik prints and harem garb, giving the place a festive, freewheeling feel.

Perhaps of all the lands, Adventureland most appeals to all ages. Families, singles, couples, seniors—they all savor Adventureland. No rides here can be classified as "just for kids," and none prohibits young children. From the mammoth treehouse and adventure-packed jungle cruise to the boat that braves pirate attacks, all the rides feature something for every person.

Swiss Family Treehouse ★★★ Some visitors pooh-pooh this attraction as dull and even hard work but most love the challenge of scaling

The Swiss Family Robinson tree is manmade, but the Spanish moss on its branches is real.

such a magnificent tree. Spanning 90 feet in diameter and boasting some 600 branches, this multilevel banyan treehouse is fashioned after the island home in the classic tale *Swiss Family Robinson.* A marvel of design and ingenuity, the tree boasts some 800,000 perfectly applied vinyl leaves (costing a dollar a leaf in the early 1970s) and a trunk that's stupendous. Narrow wooden steps twist around the trunk and through limbs, providing views of rooms furnished so warmly it seems as if the shipwrecked family indeed lives there. Patchwork quilts are tossed across poster beds, and wood pipes deliver fresh water to each room. Notice the spacious kitchen, located at the tree's base, with its stone floors, brick oven and array of pots and pans.

TIPS: The tree requires a somewhat arduous climb that may be too strenuous for small children and seniors.

Jungle Cruise ★★★★ One of Disney's most famous and best loved rides is this fun-filled, crazy cruise through a skillfully simulated jungle. Visitors sit elbow-to-elbow on bench seats in canopied riverboats with names such as *Nile Nellie* and *Amazon Annie.* A captain, outfitted in safari hat and belted jacket, guides the group on what he warns is a "perilous" subtropical trek. It's one of the few rides narrated by "real" people—a refreshing feature—and these narrators are amusing, with their corny jokes and zany antics. During the ten-minute, action-packed voyage, explorers elude elephants, hippos, zebras, wildebeests, giraffes and pythons. They also dodge waterfalls, escape from pygmies and sneak through a Cambodian temple beaded with humidity. In one shore scene, savages have plundered a camp, leaving a jeep on its back with its wheels still turning and radio blasting.

None of the stuff is real, of course, though some scenes are authentic enough to frighten some preschool children. Most kids are easily calmed, though, and by the end of the ride don't want to get off—despite admonition by the guide to "leave all your jewelry and other valuables but make sure you take your children."

TIPS: This ride ranks with Space Mountain when it comes to perpetual lines. Most aggravating, though, is that lines are deceiving. Every time you round a corner, you realize (miserably) that there are still more lines. Plan to visit first thing in the morning, or try during the 3 p.m. Main Street Parade.

Pirates of the Caribbean ★★★★★ Arguably one of Disney's greatest feats, this attraction combines the best of the best rides: realistic scenery, spirited music, nonstop action and a short but stomach-loosening drop. Unlike the bright outdoor scenery of Jungle Cruise, this boat trip takes you through the dark and clammy hollows of pirates' dens. In early scenes, crooked-toothed, peg-legged men are chained to stone floors and buzzards pick at skeletons strewn on a deserted beach. For most of the ride, the swashbucklers are plundering, frolicking and raising hell on an island. During a chaotic fortress raid, they carelessly fire pistols, chase women and set the town ablaze. Chickens cluck, dogs bark and drunken pigs twitch their legs in strangely realistic ways. Several sights border on the raucous—including the auctioning of women—though Disney manages to make it all seem good fun. The attention to detail is masterful, down to the wiry hair on one pirate's leg.

Tips: Small children may be frightened by some of the scenes. Though a very popular ride, lines move quickly and there is rarely more than a 30-minute wait. Not to be missed.

The Enchanted Tiki Birds ★   An air-conditioned bamboo villa is the venue for this tropical serenade by dozens of Audio-Animatronics, or robotlike, parrots and flowers. It was Disney's first Audio-Animatronics attraction, and maybe that's why the 15-minute show seems low-budget. The music is repetitive and eventually becomes obnoxious, as evidenced by the dozen or so visitors (including children) who inevitably slip out midshow. The totem poles that blink and sing are proof that Disney can be overly fatuous.

Tips: If the idea of listening to faux birds and flowers sing for 15 minutes sounds dull, skip this one. One to be missed.

To keep the Jungle Cruise jungly, 100 gas heaters and electric fans (concealed in rocks) send warm air to the plants and trees.

Frontierland

Cross into Frontierland, and the caws of Adventureland parrots transform into the whines of a locomotive (a.k.a. Big Thunder Mountain, one of the fastest and most exciting rides at Disney). Reminiscent of an 1800s mining town, Frontierland poses a rugged skein of cactus, rust-colored rock, adobe buildings, trading posts and a town hall coated in brick. There's Pecos Bill Café, bordered by wood sidewalks; Westward Ho; Mile Long Bar; and a Turkey Leg Wagon that serves oversized vittles. Employees are wrapped in leather duds and occasionally talk with a twang, and kids dart around with new coonskin caps.

Big Thunder Mountain, with its ruddy, jagged, vertical profile, is *the* reason many folks wander into Frontierland, though they usually stay a while once they discover the multitude of activities. Indeed, the place is a utopia for families: There's an big woodsy island where kids can

Big Thunder Mountain Railroad took 15 years to plan and two years to build.

run free for hours, a carnival arcade that's mobbed by teenagers, and two family-style revues that combine good entertainment with relaxation. Plan to spend some time here; even with minimal lines, it take several hours to see the best this "land" has to offer.

Big Thunder Mountain Railroad ★★★★★ Wild and rambunctious, this roller coaster easily competes with the big boys. The plummets aren't steep but they are sudden, and there are enough curves and speed to get the adrenaline flowing. Set in the Gold Rush Days, the coaster is a runaway mine train that whirls across two acres of Disney's most creative scenery.

Keep your eyes open, or you'll miss the mining town caught in a flash flood, the Audio-Animatronics animals (including chickens, opossums and donkeys), the falling rocks and the goofy guy in long johns laid out in an old-fashioned bathtub. There are also dozens of nifty mining antiques sprinkled across the nubby terrain, and bats that loom overhead. Then there is the mountain: rising some 197 feet, it took two years and 650 tons of steel to build. About 16,000 gallons of paint and 4,675 tons of cement were slapped on, along with plenty of good old dirt and rocks.

Once you've ridden during the day, return for a night trip. With the mountain and rocks aglow, surroundings are supreme. Arrive about 30 minutes before the park closes, and lines should be short (or even nonexistent).

TIPS: Children must be 40 inches or taller to ride; not recommended for seniors or the weak at heart. Not to be missed.

Tom Sawyer Island ★★★ One of the few nature-oriented Disney attractions, this cleverly designed island is a must for families. Like a reverse doughnut, it rests in the center of the Rivers of America. Steamboats, rafts and keelboats ply the water, tossing blue-green ripples against the island shore. Visitors crowd onto timber rafts (it's standing only) for fun, motorized transportation to the island.

Cool and woodsy, Tom Sawyer Island offers a retreat from lines and plenty of places where children can romp: winding footpaths, hills, bubbling streams, a barrel bridge and old-fashioned swing bridge, a windmill and grist mill, and a "magnetic mystery mine" whose moist walls seem dusted with gold. The best spot, though, is Fort Sam Clemens, a log fortress where you can fire air guns (with great sound effects) at startled passengers on the Liberty Square Riverboat. The guns blast incessantly all day and can be heard across Frontierland.

While children spend some energy, parents can stroll leisurely or rest on one of the many benches sprinkled across the island. Families particularly like Aunt Polly's Landing, which serves just-squeezed lemonade and peanut butter and jelly sandwiches. You can linger on the wood loggia and watch the riverboats go by or mingle with other families.

The island's shady, relaxed environs and lack of crowds make it an ideal spot to spend steamy afternoons when most other attractions feel the crush of people. A good strategy is to arrive just before noon and enjoy a picnic lunch.

TIPS: Not recommended for seniors; adults without children may want to see the island on their second day at the Magic Kingdom. There's rarely a line, so visit when other attractions are packed. Island closes at dusk.

Country Bear Jamboree ★★★★ A long-standing Disney favorite, this show is an amusing rendition of the world from a bear's point of view. A crew of wacky Audio-Animatronics bears (with remarkably lifelike features and mannerisms) crack jokes, sing songs and tell tall tales to a usually packed Grizzly Hall. Two of the most memorable performances are a trio of beach bums singing "Wish They All Could Be California Bears" and a slick bruin doing Elvis imitations. The venerable Big Al, who plays emcee, has become so popular that his mug shows up on Disney hats, T-shirts and postcards.

TIPS: An attraction for all ages, the jamboree draws big crowds for its relatively small auditorium. Plan to visit before 11 a.m. or during the 3 p.m. Main Street Parade.

Frontierland Shootin' Arcade ★ Kids are the main fans of this arcade, which is typical of carnival shooting galleries. For a quarter you can fire at "wilderness" targets such as cardboard tombstones and vultures. The place is nothing special and should be visited on your second day at the Magic Kingdom.

TIPS: The arcade costs a quarter for five shots. The arcade won't appeal to many adults and seniors. Rarely a line, so visit anytime.

The Diamond Horseshoe Jamboree ★★★★ Possibly the best of Disney's live performances, this 30-minute hand-clappin', foot-stompin' show is definitely a good time. Presented in a horseshoe-shaped Dixieland hall with wood floors and brass railings, it headlines a cast of husky young cowboys, flashy cancan girls and Lilly, a bosomy songbird who's been poured into a red satin dress. The singing and dancing are better than average, and the jokes, which often focus on embarrassed spectators, are corny but entertaining.

TIPS: A few drawbacks: Reservations should be made *at the beginning* of the day at the Main Street booth in front of Disneyana Collect-

---

The Frontierland Shootin' Arcade's guns are authentic Hawkins 54-caliber buffalo rifles.

ibles. If you miss reservations (which fill up fast), show up a half-hour before one of the five daily shows and get in the standby line (shows are at 10:40 a.m., 12:15 p.m., 1:45 p.m., 3:30 p.m. and 4:45 p.m.). Chances are, you'll get in, despite Disney assurances that you won't be admitted without an advance booking. The best show to try is the last one of the day.

Although sandwiches were once sold before the show, only potato chips and brownies (the vending machine kind) are now offered. Families who plan to have lunch at the jamboree have been aggravated to find out (as they stood in line) that their hungry children would have to wait another hour for a meal. Worst yet, it takes attendants 30 minutes to serve the crowd before the show—time better spent on other attractions.

Liberty Square

At first it's difficult to know where Frontierland ends and Liberty Square begins. Both places share the same ambience of American nostalgia, and both are accented with riverboat landings and shady waterfront sidewalks.

But the heart of Liberty Square is quintessential colonialism: saltbox homes tinted in vanilla, storefronts of cranberry-colored brick, gabled roofs, weather vanes, and no lack of American flags. As with most other "lands," Disney's replicas here are ingenious. Tidy shops stock antiques, jams and jellies, and crocheted blankets, and a homey tavern beckons with rough-hewn wood floors and a big stone hearth. With so much coziness everywhere, the humid Florida air almost feels a little brisk.

The flora, too, is nothing short of stunning. Brilliant azaleas and Japanese yews form colorful palettes around trees, along the river and in window flower boxes. Center stage is a vast live oak, appropriately named the "Liberty Tree," that's more than 130 years old. From its branches dangle 13 lanterns recalling the original 13 states.

Frontierland's homey aura and all-American overtones appeal to families, who often kill an hour strolling the riverfront and shops. Parents will find secluded relaxation behind the Silversmith Shop, where a handful of benches, umbrella-topped tables and big shade trees pose a sort of secret resting place.

The Hall of Presidents ★★★ When this attraction opened in 1971, it was hailed as a hallmark of Disney achievement. The fantasy makers had duplicated human likeness in robots so well that it was almost eerie. Still today, visitors are awed by the realistic expressions, features, motions and voices of America's 41 presidents. The wrinkles, the eyebrows, the freckles, down to the brace on Franklin Delano Roosevelt's

To keep the Haunted Mansion good and dusty, crews shoot five-pound bags of dust from a gadget that looks like a fertilizer spreader.

leg, are remarkable. Notice that while Abe Lincoln is calling roll, a few fellow presidents become restless and start fidgeting.

Set in a comfortable theater that seats more than 700, the production highlights U.S. achievement with the expected patriotic overtones. A preshow film, which is average at best, portrays a textbook story of American history.

TIPS: A favorite of seniors, though small children may find it difficult to pay attention.

Liberty Square Riverboat ★★★ It's impossible to miss this triple-decker paddlewheeler as it chugs along the manmade "Rivers of America" through Liberty Square and Frontierland. Steam pours from its stacks, and passengers crowd against white gingerbread railings for nice views of the mainland and Tom Sawyer Island. There's no captain (the boat travels via underwater rail), and the 15-minute ride is super slow and relaxing. It's a great break for parents, who can sit down while their children roam around. Kids love exploring the boat, and getting shot at (with air guns) by other kids camped out at the fort on Tom Sawyer Island. There are usually plenty of seats, but to ensure you get one, be one of the first aboard the boat.

TIPS: Covers the same territory as the Mike Fink Keel Boats, and is by far a better ride. If you don't fancy a boat trip, you can explore Tom Sawyer Island on foot. The riverboat draws moderate crowds, with an average wait of 15 to 20 minutes.

Mike Fink Keel Boats ★ These two low-slung craft are named for a Mississippi riverboat captain and renowned marksman who lived from 1770 to 1823. The keel boats explore the same scenery as the Liberty Square Riverboat, so there's no need to ride both—particularly since the keel boats are much less exciting. Passengers are crowded into a small space, and the narrator uses an annoyingly loud microphone to deliver a dull spiel and lackluster jokes. On the positive side, there's rarely a long wait for this attraction.

TIPS: Save this attraction for your second day at the Magic Kingdom—or don't ride at all.

The Haunted Mansion ★★★★★ "Here lies old Fred. A great big rock fell on his head." So reads one of the wacky graveyard epitaphs outside The Haunted Mansion, a vast, ominous house at the crest of a hill. It's a fitting introduction to one of Disney's best-ever attractions, an ingenious design with so many special effects and illusions that you find yourself saying, "I know this isn't real, but. . . ."

Despite its granite-like appearance, Cinderella Castle is made of fiberglass and steel beams and sports a 500-gallon coat of paint.

A gloomy butler greets visitors at the front doors and ushers them into an eight-sided gallery with cobwebbed chandeliers and a ceiling that rises—or is the floor sinking? After much doomsaying, he leads everyone to their coffins (called "doom buggies") for a spirited ride through rooms with phantoms, ghoulies and various eebie geebies. There's a piano player who's nothing more than a shadow, a spooked cemetery and its petrified watchman, a teapot pouring tea and a screeching raven that won't go away. Voices howl, figures skate across ceilings and ghosts become more vivid as the darkness gets thicker.

All the special effects are great, but the show stoppers are the holograms. Using advanced technology and imagination, Disney pushed 3-D projection to its limits. Life-size human images, dressed in everyday attire, float around and mimic the mannerisms of their living counterparts. In one dance hall scene, holograms whirl around the floor in sync to the music. Perhaps the most fascinating (and talked-about) hologram is the woman's head in the crystal ball: her lifelike image chatters nonstop.

The kicker, though, is at the ride's end, when you gaze into a mirror and see a spook (read hologram) nestled beside you.

Despite the attraction's expert effects, it's not really scary for most people. Small children, however, will likely be frightened by what to them is most certainly "real."

TIPS: Though a popular ride, the mansion is tucked away in a corner of Frontierland and so has sporadic lines. In fact, lines here are usually dictated by when crowds leave the nearby Hall of Presidents and Liberty Square Riverboat. Every 20 to 30 minutes, both attractions release several hundred people who then wander over to the Haunted Mansion. Translation: Wait till those attractions are *almost* ready to release visitors, and make a beeline for the Haunted Mansion. Not to be missed.

Fantasyland

Truly a colorful, whimsical place, Fantasyland is a combination of circus-style canopies, gleaming turrets and gingerbread houses, with the whole land crisscrossed by streams filled with shiny pennies. Dominated by the grandiose Cinderella Castle, Fantasyland is fashioned as a palace courtyard. Indeed, strolling these fanciful lanes is like roaming the chapters of a fairy tale.

The best way to arrive is via the Skyway to Fantasyland, which begins in Tomorrowland. These brightly colored sky buggies whisk you above the Magic Kingdom, providing a splendid prelude to Fantasyland's quixotic architecture and ambience.

Fantasyland has more attractions than any other land (11, more than twice that of most lands). Obviously, children are the biggest fans of these rides, which feature the happy lyrics and themes from many of Disney's best-loved films and characters. There are flying Dumbos, whirling Mad Hatter teacups, Cinderella's white carousel horses and Snow White's forest. Most adults enjoy the rides, and those who don't still delight in the imaginative setting and remarkable attention to detail (in true Disney style, even the garbage cans are splashed with glowing color).

Not surprisingly, Fantasyland is usually the most popular and crowded area of Disney World. Perhaps that's because this make-believe land epitomizes what Disney does best: bring out the kid in everyone.

Cinderella Castle ★★★★★ Technically, this tremendous structure is part of Fantasyland, though realistically it's *the* frame of reference for all of Disney World. Towering 180 feet above Main Street and encircled by a rock-rimmed moat, the castle is a masterful facsimile of the medieval palace in the classic French fairy tale. Its royal blue turrets and gold spires glisten in the sun, and its myriad towers, parapets and balconies provide visual inspiration.

The castle is beautiful even from miles away. Indeed, each year dozens of couples marry at Disney resorts, using the castle silhouette as a romantic backdrop. And some hotels advertise rooms "with a castle view."

TIPS: Musical shows are offered throughout the day in front of the castle. Check the schedule in the castle forecourt, and plan *not* to peruse the castle during those times. Another time to avoid the castle:

REFLECTIONS OF A PRINCESS

Lining the archway of Cinderella Castle are spectacular mosaics that qualify as one of Disney's premier creations. Five panels—each spanning 15 feet high and 10 feet wide—tell the moving tale of a little cinder girl, her hateful stepmother, fairy godmother, a pumpkin and a prince.

Designed by Disney artist Dorothea Redmond and crafted by mosaicist Hanns-Joachim Scharff, the palettes contain a million pieces of Italian glass in some 500 colors—as well as real silver and gold. Even a brief look at the walls reveals many treasures: a glimmering gold jewel in the stepmother's tiara, the striking royal blue of Cinderella's eyes, and columns carved with birds and mice that are making her gown.

Cinderella's Golden Carrousel is a 1917 gem built by Italian woodcarvers working for the Philadelphia Toboggan Company.

during the 3 p.m. Main Street parade when crowds gather all along the route. Not to be missed.

Magic Journeys **★★★** Epcot fans will remember this 3-D fantasy film as the one that played at "Journey into Imagination" before the arrival of *Captain EO.* Despite the movie's lack of plot, there are enough clever special effects to keep almost everyone intrigued. The 25-minute flick follows the mind travels of five children, playing to the familiar Disney theme of "you can imagine anything." Viewers journey through outer space, circus shows and some spectacular outdoor settings. If you're wearing the goofy purple 3-D glasses, you'll likely reach out for the bats and other creatures that appear to hover about the theater.

TIPS: Some small children may be frightened by the special effects, while some seniors may find the theme frivolous. Don't miss the preshow, *Working for Peanuts,* a splendid 1953 classic and the first 3-D cartoon ever made.

Cinderella's Golden Carrousel **★★★** As carrousels go, this one's a showpiece. From the hand-painted scenes across the canopy to the fiberglass steeds that heave up and down, everything is beautifully detailed and animated.

The 18 scenes, taken from Disney's 1950 movie *Cinderella,* depict the cinder girl in vivid, cinematic colors. Below, horses are embellished with gleaming swords, chains and even yellow roses. Notice that although most horses are white, no two are identical. Also, instead of traditional merry-go-round music, this carrousel organ renders such Disney song classics as "Chim-Chim-Cheree" and "When You Wish Upon a Star." Together with the melodies, the glittering lights, mirrors and almost constant motion make this a singular experience for all ages.

TIPS: As with most carrousels, lines don't move fast. Arrive before noon or after dusk, when a profusion of lights makes this one of the prettiest rides at Disney.

Peter Pan's Flight **★★★** Small children love this air cruise in colorful pirate ships. The setting is Never-Never Land, from Sir James Matthew Barrie's 1904 fairy tale about a half-elfin boy who "couldn't grow up." Passengers glide around brightly lit indoor scenes for rendezvous with Tinkerbell, Captain Hook, Mr. Smee and other favorite *Peter Pan* characters.

Because of its popularity with families, the short (two-and-a-half-minute) ride typically has long lines. My advice: If the wait is more than 20 minutes, skip it. No matter how good it is, a two-and-a-half-minute ride is not worth a long wait.

TIPS: Not popular with seniors and adults without children.

Skyway to Tomorrowland ★★★ This five-minute ride in aerial cable cars offers superb views of the Magic Kingdom and a chance for a quick rest. (For a detailed description, see "Skyway to Fantasyland," in this chapter.)

It's A Small World ★★★★ This leisurely cruise in sherbet-colored boats takes you through glittery scenes of hundreds of singing and dancing dolls. There are red toy soldiers, hip-swaying hula girls, leprechauns, kings and queens and nursery rhyme stars such as Little Bo Peep and Jack and Jill. The theme of world unity shines through in the detailed costumes and settings from countries around the globe. A favorite (if not *the* favorite) Disney ride of small children, it is a feel-good experience with lighthearted lyrics you can't get out of your head.

TIPS: Though a very popular ride, it has fast-moving lines and rarely more than a 15-minute wait.

20,000 Leagues Under the Sea ★★ Jules Verne's epic ocean-exploration fantasy novel sets the theme for this submarine outing in a blue-green lagoon. Fashioned like the vessel in Disney's 1954 movie of the same name, the sub somewhat resembles a slender reptile with barbs and beady eyes. The inside is dim, humid and narrow, with just enough room for passengers to sit single file and peer out small port-

---

THE KEY TO THE CASTLE

Many visitors are disappointed to learn that there's no tour of Cinderella Castle. There is, however, a way to get "into" this enchanting building: dine at **King Stefan's Banquet Hall.**

Named for Sleeping Beauty's father (hey, whose castle is this anyway?), this second-floor dining hall is at the peak of a broad staircase that spirals through silvery castle walls. Elaborately designed, it features a soaring rotunda, Gothic arches and stained-glass windows that dispense fine views of the Magic Kingdom. Hostesses wear long medieval gowns and dramatic French headdresses, and medieval court melodies pour across the room.

Castle fare—a lunch and dinner lineup of prime rib, seafood and fruit salads, fish and chicken dishes—is overpriced and mediocre, but the novelty of being inside a palace keeps people begging for tables. And, to the delight of small children, Cinderella makes frequent appearances. Reservations are essential; call 407-824-4321, or visit a hostess as soon as the Magic Kingdom opens.

holes. The view is of sunken ships, lost cities, rippling sea grass, color-ful fish and coral, seahorses and icebergs.

Though the ride was refurbished in early 1991, its special effects are not on par with Pirates of the Caribbean or Epcot's Living Seas. Adults may find the scenery so fake it's comical, although small children do love the bright colors and underwater feeling. Despite its drawbacks, the ride remains one of Disney's most popular. Sadly, it also features some of the longest, slowest lines. If you arrive to find a long wait, trust me: it's not worth it.

TIPS: Not recommended for those who easily get claustropho-bic. Ride early in the morning or just before the park closes.

Dumbo, the Flying Elephant ★★ Disney's version of a carnival midway ride is based on the endearing elephant with oversized ears. Super tame but fun, it features several Dumbos that glide in a circle and lift up when riders press a button inside. Kids plead to go on this attraction—over and over again.

TIPS: Popular mainly with small children.

Snow White's Adventures ★★★ This Disney-style spookhouse ride features wooden cars that bump and twist their way around screaming witches, ghoulish trees and other creepies. The idea, of course, is that you accompany Snow White on her perilous journey through the for-est. Some of the cardboard cutouts and other set work seem hokey, but the rock that nearly lands on your head at the end is a hoot. Though it's not really scary, small children are often frightened.

TIPS: Not popular with seniors and adults without children. Long lines are a tradition here. Go before 11 a.m. or after 6 p.m., or plan to wait at least 40 minutes.

IT'S CHARACTER TIME

Kids love meeting characters from their favorite Disney films. Sometimes the characters just roam the park, but they do have their hangouts: Goofy, Minnie and Donald Duck like the spot in front of City Hall on Main Street, while Mickey is usually in his dressing room in Mickey's Starland. Cinderella, Snow White and other charac-ters frequent the Cinderella Castle courtyard, though it's often very crowded. If it's raining, check for characters outside Disneyana Collectibles on Main Street.

Characters are always eager to sign autographs and pose for family snapshots. Before you get there, it's good to remind children that characters don't talk but com-municate (quite effectively) through body language. Also, they appear much larger in person than in movies or on television, which can sometimes startle a small child.

Mr. Toad's Wild Ride ★★★ Like Snow White's Adventures, this spook house jaunt jostles you along a track through various calamities. Following the escapades of Mr. J. Thaddeus Toad from the classic fantasy *The Wind in the Willows*, you plow through cardboard barn doors and haystacks and meet up with an oncoming locomotive in a dark tunnel. A hit with older kids, the ride is often too wild for young children.

TIPS: Lines move fast so there's rarely more than a ten-minute wait; ride during midday when most other attractions are jammed.

Mad Tea Party ★★ The madness here is that you spin in one direction for two minutes at can't-see-a-thing velocity.

When it's over, you still can't see a thing—and feel like you've gone mad. Nonetheless, the midway-style ride can be a blast. Indeed, some teenagers head straight here after Space Mountain, waiting in line for consecutive rides in the giant pastel teacups. The attraction's fanciful theme is taken from an *Alice in Wonderland* scene where the Mad Hatter throws a tea party for his unbirthday.

TIPS: If you don't like getting the spins, skip this ride.

It's a Small World debuted at the 1964-65 World's Fair in New York.

Mickey's Starland

If you were to design a place from a child's point of view, it could easily be Mickey's Starland. Like a scene from Saturday morning cartoons, the street is lined with Lilliputian-sized houses splashed in pink, lime green, yellow and purple. Driveways are teeny, yards are trimmed in little picket fences, and signs seem scribbled with finger paint. Mickey, Minnie and other Disney celebrities skip along the sidewalks and pose for snapshots with giddy children.

Located in the imaginary town of Duckberg, the fanciful area opened in 1988 as Mickey's Birthdayland to celebrate the mouse's 60th birthday. The theme was later changed, but the comic strip ambience endures. Most of the action takes place at Mickey's House and his Starland Show, which has live character revues all day. There's also a barnyard with small animals and a playground that gives parents a much needed rest.

Though a colorful place, the three-acre niche hardly qualifies as a "land." There are no rides or major attractions, and the area is so small compared to other lands that it seems like an afterthought. Still, it's a must for visitors with small children.

Magic Journeys was directed by Murray Lerner, who won an Academy Award in 1981 for his documentary From Mao to Mozart: Isaac Stern in China.

Mickey's House ★★★ Before you enter this whimsical address, notice the imaginative touches on the outside. Fashioned with mustard-colored clapboard, it is crowned with sloping, rust-red shingles and a weathervane. Windows are framed with teal shutters shaped like tulips, and the porch sports fat columns like ones you might find in a coloring book.

The inside is a Mickey museum, and each room looks as if the mouse was just there. His red pants lie across a chair, and his furry slippers and golf clubs are nearby. A shopping list full of cheese is tacked on the refrigerator, and an old-fashioned TV plays cartoon reruns starring (who else?) Yours Truly. Check out the fireplace racks styled like mouse ears.

The rest of the cartoon gang lives right behind Mickey. Minnie's tidy house is there, as is Donald's Houseboat and Goofy's ramshackle dive.

TIPS: This attraction is almost never crowded, so visit between 11 a.m. and 4 p.m. when other attractions have long lines. Though primarily a children's attraction, adults will enjoy the architecture and Disney mementos.

Mickey's Starland Show ★★★ A Disney character stage show is the gala affair here, but the preshow is just as popular with kids. Held under a yellow-and-white big top ringed with televisions, the preview features a cartoon where pop star Cyndi Lauper sings "Hey Mickey, You're so fine. . .Hey Mickey!" It's tough to hear Lauper, considering about 100 children are usually chiming in and dancing frenetically on the carpet.

The live musical comedy follows the capers of the Gummi Bears, Chip and Dale, Scrooge McDuck and Lunchpad McQuack. Mickey, assisted by a peppy, shrill-voiced cheerleader, hosts the event.

After the show there's traditionally a mad dash to Mickey's dressing room, where kids get their picture taken with the mouse.

TIPS: This show is strictly for kids; most adults don't find this interesting.

Grandma Duck's Farm ★★ An enhanced version of a carnival petting zoo, the farm offers the requisite pens housing sheep, calves, rabbits, ducks, pigs, and other barnyard animals. A small garden of tomatoes, eggplant and sunflowers help amplify the "realness" of the place, as do the imitation windmill and water tower. Best, though, are the long-legged billy goats that scale the roof on their house.

TIPS: The farm is rarely crowded, so visit when other rides are packed.

Tomorrowland

With its saucer-style buildings, sharp planes and miles of pavement, Tomorrowland is stark and geometric. The forerunner of Epcot, this futuristic place uses rides, innovative films and imaginative surroundings to portray technological advancements. Like a scene from the cartoon "The Jetsons," a boxy train snakes silently through the air and a three-story spaceship aims for the stars. A monotone voice, expounding on one of the rides, echoes against concrete buildings. Shrubs are shaped like spheres and squares, and overhead train tracks form concrete spaghetti in the sky. Except for a few splashes of bright orange, coral and yellow, everything is crisp white.

Yet despite its initial starkness, many people find this land their favorite. The theme itself is exciting, immediately coaxing curiosity and intrigue. And the attractions actually aren't so futuristic but portray what *used to be* the vision of the future. Mission to Mars, for example, depicts the 1970s view of a trip to the red planet. Carousel of Progress, Dreamflight and American Journeys give flashbacks of technology, and the Grand Prix Raceway—amusement park race cars—is hardly futuristic.

Of course, *the* reason most people keep coming to Tomorrowland (sometimes several times a day) is Space Mountain. Set along Tomorrowland's eastern edge, it is the only attraction situated outside the Walt Disney World Railroad tracks—the unofficial boundary for the Magic Kingdom. Both in location and thrills, Space Mountain symbolizes the outer limits.

Because Space Mountain is perpetually crowded, other Tomorrowland attractions usually are not. By the time some Space Mountain riders have killed an hour-plus standing in line, they're ready for some new scenery (or a dash to the restroom). And most of Tomorrowland's less popular rides are designed to handle big crowds. Plan to visit every-

---

The word "Leagues," painted on the flags outside 20,000 Leagues Under the Sea, was originally spelled S-E-U-G-A-E-L when the ride opened. A Navy visitor discovered the mistake.

thing *but* Space Mountain during the middle of the day, when the rest of the park is predictably packed.

Space Mountain ★★★★★ Looming 180 feet above the area, this concrete and steel structure resembles a ribbed white cone spiked with icicles. Touted as "Florida's third highest mountain," it is Disney's zenith. It is arguably the fastest, scariest, most imaginative mind trip in the theme park lineup. Its futuristic silhouette is permanently etched in the minds of thousands who worship this attraction as the best in the universe.

This ultimate in state-of-the-art thrills is a roller coaster ride in the dark that feels like a trip through outer space in warp drive. Passengers board fluorescent-striped capsules for what's supposed to be a journey through the depths of the galaxy. During the 2-minute-and-38-second ride, strobe lights flash, tunnels flicker and saucers spin as you probe deeper and deeper into inky blackness. Top speed is only about 28 mph, but there are enough twists and turns and sudden drops to plunge you into euphoria (or nausea, in some cases).

Besides its technology, what sets Space Mountain apart from most rides is its universal appeal. Grandparents queue up as readily as ten-year-olds, and pregnant women will plead with attendants to go on (despite posted warnings against expectant mothers riding). But popularity has its pitfalls, and in the case of Space Mountain, these are long, unrelenting lines. Riding during the morning or late afternoon may reduce your wait from one-and-a-half hours to 30 or 45 minutes. However, Space Mountain groupies know the best strategy is to join the Space Mountain Dash. Here's how it works:

BENEATH THE MAGIC

Below the Magic Kingdom's fanciful landscape lies a stark, otherworldly cosmos. This is the "guts" of the kingdom, a vast labyrinth of concrete tunnels connecting computer centers, dressing rooms and prop warehouses. The computers are the kingdom's lifeline, controlling everything from restaurant menus to the timing of the bears' jokes at the Country Bear Jamboree.

Another series of rooms contains thousands of Magic Kingdom employee costumes—the world's largest working wardrobe.

*A tour of this fascinating "underground" is offered to groups of 15 adults (ages 17 and older) or more who are staying at a Disney resort. Called **Innovations in Action**, the three-and-a-half-hour tour costs $50 per person and must be booked at least 30 days in advance by calling 407-363-6666.*

The floor under the Space Mountain track is the cemetery for some visitors' eyeglasses, cameras, wallets—and even false teeth.

Arrive 45 to 60 minutes before the park opens, when Main Street will be open. Walk down Main Street toward Cinderella Castle and hang a right at the Sealtest Ice Cream Parlor. Proceed past the Plaza Restaurant and stop at the sign that says "The Plaza Pavilion Terrace Dining." Here there's a rope (and probably already a small gathering) guarded by a Disney employee. The second the park opens, the employee releases the rope while dozens of people skip, briskly walk and/or run the 100 or so yards to Space Mountain. Employees dread working the rope because of the danger of being trampled by hyped-up visitors, who, incidentally, range from seniors to college students to parents with a slew of children.

The advantage of this spot is that it's about 120 yards closer to Space Mountain than the official starting point, located on the east side of the Magic Kingdom's central hub. Here hundreds of unenlightened people gather for their own dash to "the mountain." Even those who walk from the closer location will easily beat out those who sprint from the hub area.

Visitors who feel apprehensive about racing to a ride may (a) reconsider once they see how long the lines can be, or (b) find it's kind of fun after all. Despite initial repulsion to the idea, this writer found the experience quite comical and wacky, and not a bad way to make quick friends. The only unforeseen drawback was a stomach not fully prepared for a 9 a.m. sprint and roller coaster ride.

If you miss the Space Mountain Dash, try to ride about an hour before the park closes. This is when attendants sometimes "stack" the ride, which means queuing visitors *outside* to clear up long lines *inside.* Stacking makes it seem as if lines are never-ending (counting the supposed lines inside), when in fact what you see is what you get. An honest attendant will tell you if there's stacking. If that fails, try peeking in the ride's front door.

TIPS: Children shorter than 44 inches are not allowed to ride. Not recommended for pregnant women and people with weak stomachs or bad backs. If you're indecisive about riding, take the WEDway PeopleMover that tours portions of Space Mountain. The dark surroundings and squeals of Space Mountain riders will either scare you good or make you long to go on. Not to be missed.

WEDway PeopleMover ★★★ Make this your first ride in Tomorrowland (or second, after Space Mountain). Disney's prototype of fu-

---

The Skyway was the nation's first aerial cable car to manage a 90-degree turn.

---

ture mass transit, these open-air boxcars provide a great introduction to Tomorrowland as they scoot in and out of buildings on overhead tracks. The five-car trains plunge into the pitch-black belly of Space Mountain (listen for the screams of Space Mountain riders); coil through the Mission to Mars theater; circle StarJets, an outdoor rocket ride; and explore Dreamflight, a repertoire of aviation exhibits. A recording gives narration, including intriguing facts and figures, on each attraction. Notice that the trains, which move about ten mph, make a smooth, noiseless journey. That's because they're propelled by electromagnets and have no moving parts. And, for all the zipping around they do, they produce no pollution.

TIPS: Despite its appearance everywhere, the PeopleMover is not one of the park's more popular attractions. All for the better: Those who do ride know it as a relaxing, informative experience with rarely a long line. Most appealing to adults, though all ages find the ride entertaining.

Skyway to Fantasyland ★★★ These colorful, open-air cable cars pass over the northeast elbow of the Magic Kingdom, starting near Space Mountain in Tomorrowland and ending in the western corner of Fantasyland. The five-minute ride is leisurely and cool and yields sweeping views across the 100-acre park. Pastel awnings and kid-size houses merge with jungles and wild west towns to form a patchwork of storybook vistas. Best of all, the skyway affords an opportunity not just to be outdoors but to be *away from the crowds.*

TIPS: The skyway sometimes opens later and closes earlier (30 to 45 minutes in both cases) than the rest of the park. Lines average a 10- to 20-minute wait; for little or no wait, ride before 10 a.m. or during the afternoon or evening parades.

Carousel of Progress ★★★★ A revolving theater that circles six stationary stages, the carousel offers a nostalgic voyage through the history of technology. Having premiered at the 1964 World's Fair in New York, the show is slightly dated but still entertains through a charming cast of Audio-Animatronics characters and a sentimental tune the audience can't help but sing. The characters are a "typical" American family—father, mother, son, daughter and their trusty dog—who experience 20th-century advances. Each stage is detailed and different, from the late-1800s kitchen with gas lamps to the 21st-century living room of blinking video screens. The show is one of Disney's longest—22 minutes—and allows a comfortable, air-conditioned reprieve.

TIPS: Seniors and adults without children love this show, which does a big repeat business. Children and teenagers sometimes find it boring and long. Though fairly popular, it can accommodate several hundred people and so rarely has a long wait.

Dreamflight ★★ Magic Kingdom junkies will remember the early days when this ride was called "If You Had Wings." Other than the name, little has changed in this mildly entertaining aviation attraction by Delta Airlines. Visitors glide in continuously moving carts through scenes of flight history. Given Disney's special effects ability (Space Mountain, Pirates of the Caribbean), the ride seems passe. Much of the set work features corny cardboard cutouts, including big pop-up storybooks and less-than-convincing scenes of Tokyo and Paris. The five-minute ride does have some nice digital graphics, as well as a quick pass through a tunnel where film projections give you the feeling of flying. If nothing else, go on Dreamflight when everything else is crowded. For here, there's almost never a wait.

TIPS: Equally appealing to all ages, though not a popular attraction. Ride anytime of the day.

American Journeys ★★★★★ One of Disney's premier cinematic productions, this film is a vivid and spectacular portrayal of America's diverse scenery. Shown on a 360-degree "circle-vision" screen, it uses nine projectors and 16 speakers to take visitors across tableaux such as the rambling Midwest, the dramatic Pacific Coast and the idyllic Hawaiian islands. During the 21-minute presentation, viewers stand in a voluminous theater (capacity 3100) for visual trips down the mouth of Mount St. Helens, to a Tennessee bluegrass festival, and to a space shuttle launch in Cape Canaveral. Much more than a travelogue, *American Journeys* uses dynamic sound, tremendous images and high-tech camerawork to create the sensation of actually being there. And although aggressively patriotic, it's a show even extreme cynics will find compelling.

TIPS: Don't be fooled by the crowds at this one. The huge theater rarely fills up, so the maximum wait is seldom more than 21 minutes (the length of the show). On the downside, the theater has no chairs. This means small children must be held so they can see the screen, and infants have to be held since strollers are not permitted. As an option, one parent could take the kids on StarJets, while the other watches this superb film.

Mission to Mars ★ Nobody does everything perfectly, not even Disney. A case in point is Mission to Mars, definitely a dud. Set in a round theater, the show is supposed to simulate exciting space travel to the red planet. Instead, the mission fails when it becomes little more than a junior high school astronomy lesson. Viewers get jostled in their seats while listening to a dull narrative on Mars, including such tidbits of knowledge as that the planet is not inhabited and has a thin atmosphere (who would have guessed?).

What happened here is that Disney created the ride back in the '70s (then called "Spaceflight to the Moon") and gave it only minor updating through the years. Hence, the masterful technology of Epcot and rides such as Space Mountain make "Mission to Mars" seem little more than an aborted flight.

Tips: Preschoolers may be frightened by the seat shimmying and loud narrative, while anyone over age eight will likely be bored. Count on no (or very little) line here, so if you must see it, visit during midday.

StarJets ★★★ Kids adore this carnival-style ride, which puts them airborne for 90 seconds in futuristic jets. The open-cockpit aircraft are poised on the arms of a big rocket and look like flailing limbs every time they lunge through the sky. The trip can be tame or mildly exciting, depending on how often you raise and lower your jet. It also offers nice views into surrounding "lands," a reason why all ages enjoy the flight.

Tips: Children younger than seven must be accompanied by an adult. StarJets is a good place for one parent to take young children while the other rides nearby Space Mountain with the older children (children shorter than 44 inches aren't allowed on Space Mountain). This works timewise, too, because both rides usually have considerable waits. StarJets can only accommodate about 22 passengers per ride, and it takes some time to ferry people up and down a two-flight elevator.

Grand Prix Raceway ★★★ This is a typical amusement race with miniature gas-powered cars that thread along a steel track. Though not futuristic, the area is cleverly designed with Grand Prix billboards, twisting roadways and a small bleacher that's frequently packed with race car fanatics. Naturally, kids love the excitement of piloting a set of (seemingly) souped-up wheels, and parents hate the pervasive smell of fuel and the noise of the cars, which sound like a horde of angry bees invading Tomorrowland. Unfortunately, the four feet, four inches height restriction for drivers eliminates many children who would be big fans (though they can still ride with an adult). Worse yet, the entire ride involves much waiting: waiting to get on the raceway (30 to 60 minutes), waiting for your car to pull up (one to two minutes), then waiting to bring your car back (two to three minutes). For this writer, that's too much waiting for a three-minute ride where top speed is only seven miles per hour and you're not even allowed to bump the car in front of you.

TIPS: A very popular ride where the wait averages an hour during the park's busy season. Unless the kids are relentless about riding, don't waste your time on this one.

THREE

Epcot Center

Epcot was Walt Disney's lifelong dream. Everything else—Mickey
Mouse, the stunning animated films, Disneyland—were just stopovers
on the way to his futuristic world of peace and happiness. At Epcot
Center, nations exist in harmony and the future appears a not-so-distant
place of prosperity. Half the park is like a permanent world's fair, a
skein of striking architecture depicting various countries. The other
half features space-age buildings that explore the bounds of technology.

Epcot stands for Experimental Prototype Community of Tomorrow—words that sound too academic for a theme park. Yet Epcot
takes the academic subjects of laboratories and museums and serves
them up theme-park style. For lovers of knowledge and culture, Epcot
has all the right stuff: exhibits that inspire thought and a sense of adventure; rides and movies that inform and amuse; and buildings seasoned with history and design flair.

Theoretically, Epcot began in Disneyland. There, during the 1950s,
Walt Disney began to understand that his California theme park, land-
locked by development, could never expand. He vowed to start again,
this time creating a community with enough room to expand for centuries, an idealistic, futuristic place where people worked and lived.

Although his initial ideas have undergone a few changes (no one
actually lives at Epcot), most of Disney's dream has been played out.
Major industries sponsor many attractions and make them testing
grounds for cutting-edge ideas. Nations from around the globe con-
tribute money, materials and expertise to create attractions that exult
in each country's beauty. Environmentally ahead of its time, much of
the park is fueled by solar energy. Rainwater is collected from buildings and funneled into ponds and lagoons. And gardens grow without
the aid of pesticides or fertilizer.

Epcot is adult. Sophisticated. Even cerebral. A place that suggests
and explains, yet always entertains. Carved from 260 acres of central

The steel beams supporting Spaceship Earth extend some 185 feet underground.

Florida pine and palmetto, this billion-dollar "community" explores space and energy, transportation and biology, communication and agriculture—and people. The park is divided into two vastly different sections: World Showcase and Future World.

The heart of World Showcase is a sea-green lagoon speckled with ferry boats and verdant clumps of islands. Eleven "pavilions," each representing a different country, fan out around the lagoon in a repertoire of architectural styles spanning over a thousand years. From Tudor, Gothic and colonial styles to Aztec, Japanese and Moroccan, World Showcase is like a pie whose slices are all different flavors. Enjoyed individually, they are invigorating; when savored as a whole, they are intoxicating.

Walt Disney's city of countries is a world of peace and happiness. There is no talk of poverty at the Mexico pavilion, no hint of political unrest in China, no mention of recession in America. They are, as one Epcot guide put it, "countries as Americans perceive them."

Indeed, it is virtually impossible to explore a "country" without being overwhelmed by its beauty and intrigue. As visitors exit the pavilions, many ask the same question: "How can I go to this country?"

Details are duplicated with astounding accuracy in each pavilion, from the chimney pots on Parisian rooftops to the hieroglyphics of Mexico's Aztec Calendar. Restaurant menus offer ethnic flair, and shops employ native artists and craftspeople. And not only does each country's native foliage thrive across the pavilion, it changes with each season, just like back home.

Sprawled below the dynamic scenery of World Showcase, Future World looks like a galactic landscape. Silvery metal and glass buildings shaped like pieces of a jigsaw puzzle bear names such as Horizons, Universe of Energy and CommuniCore East and West. Near one cone-shaped building, a metal DNA molecule pirouettes; at another, water spouts do an aerial jig.

Eclipsing the entire area is Spaceship Earth. Coated in aluminum and propped up by steel beams, it resembles a huge silver golf ball. All day long, a conveyer belt delivers a stream of people inside for a journey through the center of the earth.

Future World's intellectual subjects and World Showcase's limited number of rides can make Epcot tiresome for small children. Over the years, the Disney company has introduced more attractions that appeal to kids, including character meals and shows. Still, in most children's minds, the Magic Kingdom is tops.

In fact, when Epcot opened in 1982, some adults received it curiously, if not cautiously. Not everyone was ready for such futuristic themes, at least not after the fantasy of the Magic Kingdom.

But over time skeptics have embraced Epcot, lured by its sophistication, its ability to inspire and its three-dimensional approach. Every year, more and more people tune into this place that combines fun with thought. A place that, in Walt Disney's words, "will never be

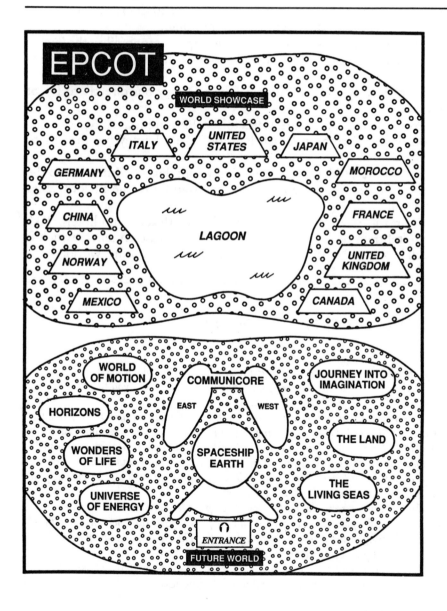

completed, but will always be introducing and testing and demonstrating. . ." A multicultural, cosmic experience poised on its prophetic launchpad.

ARRIVAL

From the Contemporary, Polynesian Village or Grand Floridian Resorts: Take the hotel monorail to the Ticket and Transportation Center, then transfer to the Epcot Center monorail.

From the Magic Kingdom: Take the express monorail to the Ticket and Transportation Center, then transfer to the Epcot Center monorail.

From Disney–MGM Studios: Take a Disney bus directly to Epcot Center.

From the Disney Village Marketplace, Pleasure Island, Typhoon Lagoon or the Caribbean Beach Resort: Take a Disney bus directly to Epcot Center.

From Fort Wilderness or the Disney Inn: Take a Disney bus to the Ticket and Transportation Center, then transfer to the Epcot Center monorail.

From the Swan, Dolphin, Yacht Club or Beach Club hotels: Take the hotel tram or ferry to Epcot's World Showcase entrance, which is much less crowded than Epcot's main entrance in Future World.

WORLDKEY UNLOCKS EPCOT'S DOORS

"Hi there! What restaurant would you like?" The perky voice belongs to a man pictured on the video screen before you. "Am I really talking to you live?" you ask, amazed. "Yes you are!" says the voice.

The man is wearing a plaid vest and sports perfectly combed hair and a name tag that reads "Doug." Doug is speaking to you via one of the video monitors, called WorldKey Service, that line an entire wall of Earth Station. WorldKey is activated by touching squares on the screen, allowing you to make lunch and dinner reservations at any Epcot Center restaurant. WorldKey attendants will also provide helpful Epcot information and help find lost children.

And the nifty screens do much more: They provide short, recorded vignettes on dozens of Epcot spots. You can preview the shops of the Mexico pavilion, the attractions of Norway or the inside of Spaceship Earth. The vignettes feature pictures, music, narrative and trivia on each subject.

One word of advice: Long lines usually form at WorldKey Service from 9 to 10:30 a.m. Arrive at 8:30 a.m., and it will be line less!

From area hotels not in Disney World: Most hotels provide shuttle buses to and from Epcot Center. However, shuttles often run only on the hour or every two or three hours. In this case, it's better to drive.

By Car: From Route 4, Epcot Center has its own exit, located about halfway between the exits for Route 192 and Route 535. Epcot is about one-and-a-half miles from Route 4.

After paying a $4 parking fee (free for guests of Disney World hotels), you'll park in one of 9000 spaces on what seems like a concrete wasteland. Trams will deliver you to Epcot's main entrance.

Like the Magic Kingdom, Epcot Center is frequently so crowded the parking lot closes well before noon. Because of this, and because early arrivers save hours of standing in line, it's critical to get there one to two hours before the advertised opening time. Trams and monorails usually operate two hours prior to opening.

SIGHTSEEING STRATEGIES

When plotting your Epcot strategy, it's vital to know that Spaceship Earth, Earth Station and the surrounding Future World hub area open 30 minutes to an hour before the rest of the park. Here you can get a head start on the competition by picking up maps and touring information; renting strollers, lockers or wheelchairs; and riding Spaceship Earth, one of the park's most popular attractions. At Earth Station, you can make lunch and dinner reservations for one of the World Showcase restaurants, avoiding that distressing phrase so often heard after 10 a.m.: "We're all booked."

During the summer, holidays and other busy times, Disney sometimes opens all of Epcot as early as an hour before the advertised opening time. There's no way to know when this will happen, though you can call 407-824-4321 the day before for the park's "official" hours.

Once you've ridden Spaceship Earth, your next move is crucial. No matter how great the urge, *do not* start exploring Future World. Instead, head for the World Showcase pavilions. Here you'll enjoy near-crowdless sightseeing until about 11:30 a.m., when the Future World sightseers head over for lunch. *This is when you head back to Future World.* This system always works because (a) it's a long hike to World Showcase, particularly first thing in the morning, and (b) humans can't resist the Future World attractions. One Epcot guide, who gives World Showcase tours in the morning, says she loves "having the place all to myself."

Most people travel clockwise around the World Showcase lagoon, so you should go counterclockwise. If you're sightseeing in the morning, the first few pavilions will be practically empty. The pavilions are so self-contained that it's best to see *all* of one country before moving on to the next. Once you've made the one-and-one-third-mile trek around the lagoon (and the sun is beating down), you won't want to backtrack. The only exception is when you dine at a pavilion. If you're coming from Future World, you can save steps by boarding a ferry across the lagoon to Germany (on the southeast corner) or Morocco (on the northwest corner). Doubledecker buses do transport visitors around the promenade, but bus lines are usually so long (and buses so crowded) that it's easier and quicker to walk.

All Epcot Center attractions do close promptly at the advertised time (8 or 9 p.m. most of the year), but most of its restaurants take reservations for times right up until closing. If you don't mind dining late—and missing the IllumiNations laser and fireworks show—take the late reservation. (Or, in most cases, you can show up without a reservation.) You can catch part of IllumiNations from a windowside table at the Chefs de France restaurant at the France pavilion.

NUTS & BOLTS

Stroller and Wheelchair Rentals: Available at the base of Spaceship Earth (on the east side) and at International Gateway in World Showcase. For replacement strollers and wheelchairs, take your receipt to the Germany pavilion or International Gateway.

Baby Services: Located at the Odyssey Complex in Future World, on the east side of the bridge to World Showcase. Services include changing tables and comfortable rockers for nursing. Diapers, formula and other baby needs are also available. Note: Baby Services opens an hour *after* and closes two hours *before* the rest of the park.

Lockers: Available on the west side of the Entrance Plaza near Spaceship Earth and at International Gateway. Additional lockers are located outside the main entrance at the bus station; however, these are inconvenient if you plan on retrieving items during the day. Most lockers cost 50 cents each time you open them.

Pets: Pets are not allowed in Epcot Center; however, you can board them for $4 per day at the kennels located on the east side of the Entrance Plaza. Pets cannot be left overnight.

Lost Children: Report lost children at Earth Station or Baby Services in Future World or call 407-560-7982.

Package Pickup: If you plan on doing some serious shopping, this free service comes in handy. Simply have the Epcot store clerks forward your purchases to Package Pickup, located just west of the Entrance Plaza. One drawback: If you're leaving during rush hour (5 to 6 p.m., or the few minutes before closing), you may face a lengthy line at the pickup counter.

Lost & Found: Located on the west side of the Entrance Plaza.

Banking: Credit card cash advances, currency exchange and traveler's check services are available at Sun Bank, on the west side of the Entrance Plaza. You can also cash personal checks up to $25 if you have proper identification. Bank hours are 9 a.m. to 4 p.m.

GETTING AROUND

Sprawled across 260 acres and the largest of Disney theme parks, Epcot is justifiably nicknamed "Every Person Comes Out Tired." If it's your first visit, know this fact: You can't see it all in one day. (Or three days, for that matter.) But that's really good news. After more than a dozen visits, this writer found Epcot so layered with information, entertainment and details that it was impossible to tire of the place.

Despite its exhausting size, Epcot is relatively easy to navigate. The park is split into two distinct "worlds": Future World and World Showcase. The main entrance is in front of Spaceship Earth in Future World. At the base of Spaceship Earth is Earth Station, where you'll find the Epcot Information desk and plenty of air-conditioned seating if you need to take a break. Earth Station is a good place to meet if someone in your party gets lost.

Future World forms an almost perfect circle that's ringed with seven sightseeing pavilions. Traveling counterclockwise, you'll encounter Universe of Energy, Wonders of Life, Horizons, World of Motion, Journey Into Imagination, The Land and The Living Seas. At the circle's north end is Spaceship Earth; at its center are two crescent-shaped buildings, CommuniCore East and CommuniCore West.

HIDDEN TREASURES

There are how many bricks in the American pavilion?

*If you want to get the real scoop on World Showcase, sign up for a behind-the-scenes tour. The four-hour excursions, called **Hidden Treasures of World Showcase**, are led by knowledgeable Disney employees who detail each pavilion's intricacies. From the architectural styles and singular design of each place to the country's music and history, the topics intrigue and inform. You'll also get inside the Epcot wardrobe—big as a city block—and learn all sorts of trivia (such as the number of bricks in the American pavilion—110,000!).*

The tour's highlight is a midmorning tea hosted by Morocco. While tour members sit cross-legged in a circle, a robed woman pours green tea into clear mugs. Later she sprinkles rosewater into everyone's hands, "so all day you will smell roses and remember the hospitality of Morocco."

Tours, which are for adults 16 and older, are held on Sunday, Wednesday and Friday from 9:30 a.m. to 1:30 p.m. The cost is $20 (plus Epcot admission), and reservations should be made at least three weeks in advance by calling 407-345-5860.

World Showcase rests south of Future World across a scenic bridge. Eleven "minitowns" border a promenade around the 40-acre World Showcase Lagoon. Traveling counterclockwise, you'll see Mexico, Norway, China, Germany, Italy, The American Adventure, Japan, Morocco, France, the United Kingdom and Canada. In between France and the United Kingdom is the International Gateway, which serves as Epcot's rear entrance. Here you can rent strollers and wheelchairs and have film developed in two hours.

World Showcase Lagoon could submerge 85 football fields.

World Showcase

The scenic bridge from Future World to World Showcase seems to create a time warp: On one side lies Future World's metal and mirror scenery, on the other, a skyline etched with ancient pyramids, painted pagodas and the Eiffel Tower. There is something comforting about these old buildings that at once captivate and stimulate. Time and space compress. A thousand years ago seems as today.

Flowers frame the paths that wend though World Showcase's 11 pavilions, each claimed by a different country. Like bustling town squares, the pavilions celebrate the architecture and customs born of different cultures throughout history.

Castles and temples, clock towers and stone churches reflect the beauty and lore of places such as Italy, Morocco, Norway, Germany, Japan and China. Gushing fountains, punctuated by sculpture, are sprinkled across plazas. Musicians and actors perform in the streets, providing a taste of their country's artistry. Quaint and exclusive shops peddle the specialties of each region, and some 21 eateries serve up native cuisine.

From the beginning, World Showcase was designed, as one Epcot guide noted, "so that no one country would stand above the others." In fact, the American pavilion, originally planned as a sleek highrise on stilts, was scaled down to a more modest colonial brick style so as not to outshine the others.

Now, this vast cultural apron, gathered around a 40-acre lagoon, is so collectively stunning that it's difficult to know where to start or how to see it all. Unlike any other Disney theme park, World Showcase is not a place to hop rides or play games or even participate in shows. Instead, it's a place for exploring and listening, or just sitting on a bench and absorbing the surroundings. In fact, to get the true World Showcase experience, all you have to do is *be there.*

The best way to see each "country" is to walk, and walk. Then walk some more. Start by strolling the streets, taking the time to notice each building's design details. Then peruse the shops. More than just stores, they reflect the history, architectural styles and craftsmanship of an entire nation.

Restaurants, too, provide cultural insight. If you don't plan to dine at a country's restaurants, ask to see them anyway. Several pavilions have fine minimuseums, and five show excellent movies. Two countries, Mexico and Norway, have tame but very enjoyable boat rides. And every pavilion has employees who are anxious to answer questions about their native lands.

Most important, you should see World Showcase *in the morning.* Even on Epcot's busiest days, more than three-fourths of the visitors remain in Future World until about 11:30 a.m. And if you travel counterclockwise, you can enjoy World Showcase's only two rides before midday lines form. Be there at 9 a.m., and you'll feel like you have the place to yourself.

Mexico ★★★★ A spectacular pre-Colombian pyramid, flanked by giant serpents' heads and somber sculptures of Toltec warriors, gives this pavilion a mystic aura. But the spectacle gives no clue to what's inside: a hillside town veiled in twilight. Fashioned after the Mexican village Taxco, the plaza is scattered with canopied carts where you can buy sombreros, flowers or sandals. Stores gather around the plaza, showing off their tile roofs, wrought-iron balconies and window boxes draped with flowers. A mariachi band strolls and strums, lending festivity. Down below, visitors dine by candlelight along a riverfront terrace.

The Mexico pavilion offers two formal attractions, an art exhibit and a boat ride. The exhibit, called **Reign of Glory**, possesses a splen-

---

MARIACHIS, BAGPIPES AND DARBUKAS

*One of the true joys of World Showcase is its **street performers**. Each country has its own brand of show, from Mexico's hunky mariachi men crowned with boleros to Canada's kilt-clad bagpipe players. Entertainers usually appear every 15 to 30 minutes, bursting out in song, dance or even quirky theater. The United Kingdom's Olde Globe Players, for instance, do a farce where audience members act amusing (and somewhat embarrassing) parts. Morocco has a procession where performers, clothed in caftans, play darbukas (drums), nfirs (trumpets) and 'uds (lutes). And China presents a miniature but elaborate version of a Chinese New Year celebration.*

To find out who's playing and when, pick up an entertainment schedule at Earth Station in Future World.

At China's Temple of Heaven, the circular beams represent heaven while the square patterns stand for earth.

did collection of pre-Colombian art, including clay vessels, masks and vases. You can peruse the display before or after the boat ride:

El Rio del Tiempo: The River of Time ★★★ This slow, peaceful journey is like a nighttime cruise that encounters ancient pyramids, rocky caverns and elaborate carvings. Flavored with Mayan, Toltec and Aztec scenes and artifacts, it spans thousands of years of Mexican history. Children love this colorful, leisurely trip and its beautifully costumed dancing dolls, reminiscent of those at the Magic Kingdom's It's a Small World. Video scenes of Mexican life (including cliff divers, flying dancers and speed boats) are interspersed everywhere, giving the ride an interesting travelogue edge. The finale—a dazzling fiber-optics fireworks show—is extra special.

TIPS: Arrive before 11 a.m. to avoid crowds. If you miss the morning, try again after 7 p.m.

Norway ★★★★ Perhaps one of the most extraordinary World Showcase pavilions, Norway is rugged, complex and stunning. Certainly, the singular beauty of the Land of the Midnight Sun shines through in these cobbled streets, rocky waterfalls, red-tiled cottages and a 14th-century stone castle. The focal point, though, is a wood stave church, modeled after one built in 1250 A.D., with thick shingles and stylized carvings. Notice the dragons that jut out from the eaves: They were added in case the villagers reverted back to paganism. Inside the church, an exhibit called **One Thousand Years of Discovery** recounts Norwegian exploration through art and artifacts. Besides this, Norway has a boat ride that's great fun:

Maelstrom ★★★★ Despite the ride's scary name and its encounters with grisly trolls, it's really very tame. A favorite of children and adults, it's an indoor glide in dragon-headed longboats just like the one Eric the Red sailed a thousand years ago. The vessels navigate around Viking villages, beautiful fjords and forests, and the slightly tumultuous North Sea. There's one steep but easy plunge, and a nearly backward tumble down a waterfall that's so gentle riders in the front sometimes miss it. After the ride, a five-minute film provides a quick but dramatic look at Norway's breathtaking landscape.

TIPS: A provocative pavilion, Norway usually gets very crowded after 11 a.m.

China ★★★★★ China's inspiring panorama seems architecturally spiritual. True to Chinese design and lore, the pavilion is a visual feast woven with symbols of life, death, virtue and the environment. As you pass through the Gate of the Golden Sun, you're greeted with an exquisite replica of Beijing's opulent Temple of Heaven, built in 1420 during the Ming dynasty. Coated in glimmering red (which stands for joy) and gold (imperialism), it is a three-tiered gem with delicate geometric patterns. The temple is edged by a meditation garden where soft tufts of grass and Chinese corkscrew willows invite contemplation. The Hall of Prayer, the temple's main wing, is where emperors prayed for good harvests. Outside, 12 columns represent the 12 months; inside, four columns symbolize four seasons.

The sights here are so detailed it would take several hours to see everything. It's best to try this on your second or third day at Epcot, and only after you've seen the pavilion's stellar movie:

Wonders of China ★★★★★ Rarely does a visitor witness this compelling film without yearning to visit China. For 19 minutes the movie soars across stone forests, rice terraces, cloud-tipped mountains and the Great Wall that's stamped across the forehead of this vast land. From the hustle of modern Shanghai to the awesome silence of the Gobi Desert, it's all dramatically portrayed on a 360-degree Circle-Vision screen.

TIPS: Despite the sensational subject and film work, the theater has one drawback: no chairs. Instead, lean rails are provided while viewers stand. For parents with small children, this may spell disaster. Toddlers can't see the screen unless they're held, and infants must also be held because strollers aren't allowed. Possible solutions: If there are several adults in your group, they can take turns holding young ones. Or one parent can take the kids on Norway's boat ride next door while the other parent enjoys *Wonders of China.* Unfortunately, the Canada pavilion also has a theater without seats.

Also, China may be World Showcase's most popular, and therefore most crowded, attraction. Try to see it before 11:30 a.m. or after 7 p.m. Not to be missed.

EPCOT'S PEOPLES

If the World Showcase employees seem like true representatives of their countries, that's because they are. Each pavilion employs people native to its hosts country, providing a cultural cornucopia of accents, costumes and traditions. The employees, who are mostly in their 20s, work in Epcot for one year as part of a World Fellowship exchange program. All the nationals live together in dormitories just outside the park.

Cultural exchange is integral to the World Showcase experience, and visitors are encouraged to ask questions at each pavilion. In fact, many employees are so enthusiastic that they're disappointed if you don't inquire about their homelands.

Take a good look at the American pavilion's clock tower: The Roman numeral four incorrectly reads IIII to distinguish it from the number V.

Germany ★★★★ This jovial alcove is a smorgasbord of gingerbread houses, turrets and wooden balconies, toy shops, beer gardens and blond men yodeling in the street. Modeled after no place in particular, the pavilion combines dashes of architecture, art and costumes from all across Germany. The result is like a fairy tale. In the middle of town square, called St. Georgsplatz, stands a sculpture of St. George slaying a dragon. The patron saint of soldiers, George was said to have slain the dragon during a trek to the Middle East. Nearby is Der Bucherwurm, a bookstore modeled after a *kaufhaus* (merchant hall) in Freiburg, Germany. Notice the facade bears statues of the emperors Ferdinand, Charles and Phillip. The original *kaufhaus* includes a fourth emperor, Maxillian, but there wasn't enough room for him on Disney's version of the building. Disney employees like to jest that "Max got the ax."

TIPS: Because Germany has no formal attractions, you can visit anytime.

Italy ★★★★ While the "historic" buildings of most other World Showcase countries seem fairly new, Italy's facades look marvelously cracked and weathered. It only adds to the authenticity of this place that emulates the Western world's longtime seat of art and thought. A 105-foot bell tower, or campanile, casts a slender silhouette across the broad piazza, a re-creation of St. Mark's Square in Venice. A nearby replica of the 1309 Doge's Palace is, like the real building, a study in architectural styles. As different doges came and went, they would leave their signatures: Romanesque columns here, Byzantine mosaics there, even a few Gothic arches. Also notice that the columns have no base. That's because the palace's Venice counterpart has none, a victim of flood erosion that has plagued the sinking islands for decades. Italy's genuineness spills across the World Showcase promenade to a tiny island where gondolas are hitched to moorings painted like barber poles. Olive and kumquat trees flutter in the wind, reminiscent of a Mediterranean vista.

TIPS: It takes at least an hour to truly absorb all the architectural and historic intricacies here. Best of all, you can visit any time; Italy is rarely overcrowded.

United States ★★★★★ Despite the heavy patriotic tones here, it's tough not to get caught up in this red, white and blue panorama. Graced by fragrant southern magnolias and palettes of blooming flowers, the pavilion features a replica of Philadelphia's Liberty Hall. All things considered, it's pretty incredible. The grand five-story building, crowned with a mansard roof and Liberty Bell, is coated in red mason bricks handmade from Georgia clay. The host pavilion of World Showcase, it sits smack in the middle of all the countries. From across the lagoon, it appears so familiar and inviting that it "acts as a carrot to draw people around the promenade," explains a Disney guide. Inside the building is a vast rotunda and a big, comfortable, air-conditioned theater where you'll see a film appropriately called:

The American Adventure ★★★★★ Truly a Disney great, this much-talked-about show combines superb set work and films with Audio-Animatronics characters so lifelike you feel you know them. Here the Disney imagineers took the technology of the Magic Kingdom's Hall of Presidents and went all out. Not only are characters' expressions, movements and voices realistic, but so are their personalities. Ben Franklin reveals characteristic insight and optimism, while cigar-puffing Mark Twain brandishes his wry humor. The pair narrate the 29-minute nostalgic adventure, which recounts major events such as the Boston Tea Party, the Civil War, the nuclear desolation of Hiroshima and man's first step on the moon. It also delves into the legacies of many notables, including a blond named Marilyn and a cowboy named John Wayne. In one folksy post-Depression scene, several men shoot the breeze on the porch of a country general store. One strums a banjo, another presses a bottle of Coke to his lips, and a third laments the price of gas (18 cents a gallon). Many of the show's sets are mounted on a carriage that moves about underneath the stage. Called the "war wagon," it weighs 175 tons, spans 65-by-35-by-14 feet and is supported by posts planted 300 feet into the ground. As John Wayne might have said, "That's some fancy rig ya got there!"

Tips: The bad news is this pavilion is usually thronged with people. Now for the good news: The American Adventure seats so many there's rarely more than a 20-minute wait, and that's in a beautiful air-conditioned rotunda. Preschoolers bored by the show often end up using the cool, dark theater for a quick doze. Not to be missed.

Japan ★★★★ First-time visitors to this attraction usually do the same thing: They stroll up to the pavilion and—stare. Little wonder, because the swell of winged pagoda roofs—painted so brilliantly blue they gleam like glass—is something to marvel at. Looming above the entrance is the mystic-looking *goju-no-to*, or five-story pagoda, inspired by the 8th-century Horyuji pagoda in Nara. Each of its five levels represents a different element—earth, water, fire, wind or sky—and at night they glow as one big beautiful Japanese lantern. The pagoda is set against a hill sketched with pebbled streams, arched bridges

---

"The American Adventure" has been revised over a thousand times.

and tightly cropped shrubs. Blue-tiled buildings gather around this serene knoll, and the sound of wind chimes drifts across the air.

TIPS: Toward the back, a superb replica of the 18th-century *Shirasagi-Jo* feudal castle houses the fine Bijutsu-Kan Gallery. Here changing exhibits display the delicate art of Japan and objects that have inspired its people.

Morocco ★★★★ Arguably Epcot's most exotic and romantic pavilion, Morocco is a cluster of fantastic fortresses, castles and prayer towers layered with stucco and carved wood and swirled by glimmering mosaics. Narrow, dusty streets wend through stuccoed archways and keyhole passages to a marketplace scattered with baskets, brass, horns and woven rugs. Moroccan men wear tasseled fezzes and women wear saris as they stroll the plaza. If it all seems strangely real, it should: Most of the pavilion was a gift from the Kingdom of Morocco, which sent nine tons of hand-cut tiles and 23 artisans to install them. All construction followed the rules of the Islamic religion. Notice that every tile has some small crack or other imperfection, and no tile depicts any living creature. That's because Muslims believe only Allah is allowed to create perfection and life. Much of Moroccan belief and custom is beautifully depicted in the Gallery of Arts and History, which has frequently changing exhibits. Take time, too, to step inside the exquisitely tiled Restaurant Marrakesh.

TIPS: Morrocco offers guided tours of the pavilion on request. Check with any pavilion employee.

France ★★★★★ Who, at least once in his life, has not longed to visit Paris? Keeping that in mind, you'll understand why this is one very popular (and very crowded) pavilion. The setting is turn-of-the-century France during *La Belle Epoque*, or beautiful time, when architecture took on a delicate, romantic flavor. Buildings boast mansard roofs, minarets, dormer windows and ribbonlike wrought-iron facades. A

EPCOT PROMISES YOU A ROSE GARDEN

A rose is a rose is a rose, right? Wrong, at least in World Showcase, where an astonishing 10,100 rosebushes in 40 varieties shape and color the scenery. That's just some of the "plantese" you'll learn on the **Gardens of the World** *tour. Led by a Disney horticulturist, it delves into the vast variety of flora across World Showcase. Tour members also learn some Disney growing secrets, such as that every plant and tree have several replacements in a mammoth nursery behind Epcot.*

Tours, open to those 16 and over, are offered every Monday, Tuesday and Wednesday from 9 a.m. to 1 p.m. There is an additional fee for this tour; reservations should be made at least three weeks in advance by calling 407-345-5860.

France's Eiffel Tower can be seen from anywhere in World Showcase except the France pavilion.

footbridge, modeled after the Pont des Arts, crosses an inlet of the World Showcase Lagoon meant to mimic the river Seine. Near the back of the pavilion lies an ornate facsimile of the barrel-roofed Les Halles Marketplace, built in Paris during the 1200s and later moved to the country. There's also a marvelous pastry shop and the requisite sidewalk café where the food smells so heavenly it commands perpetual lines. The Eiffel Tower, mounted atop the pavilion's theater, is built to one-tenth the scale of the real tower so visitors can see it from across World Showcase. After admiring it from afar, many people are disappointed to learn they can't get close to it. However, that underlying theater, the art nouveau Palais du Cinema, is where you can see an enlightening film called:

Impressions du France ★★★★★ This 18-minute flick takes a melodic, often whimsical journey across France. Shown on five screens spanning 200 degrees, it courses hills smothered in vineyards, sidewalks brimming with flower carts and castle estates so stunning you're ready to buy a plane ticket. There are dozens of other compelling scenes, including the serene French Alps, the sensual Mediterranean coast and gilded Versailles. And all seen in a cool theater with comfortable seats for resting tired bones. Not to be missed.

TIPS: Known for long lines. Arrive before 11 a.m. and you'll cut the wait to ten minutes or less.

United Kingdom ★★★ A waterfront pub, roving comedians and buildings representing over a thousand years of British history make this a jolly cultural experience. A brick street is lined with shops that range from neoclassical to Tudor to Georgian to Victorian—all in the course of 300 feet: A thatched cottage with plaster walls and stone floors leads to a wood house with plank floors and lead-glass windows. Next door, the polished Queen Anne room has tongue-and-groove floors and wainscotting. Outside lie a lush herb garden, rose garden and radiant flower beds skirted by wrought iron. It's so much fun to explore the detail-rich structures here that you don't even notice there's no main attraction.

TIPS: Watch for the Renaissance Street Players and their colorful antics.

Canada ★★★★ Flanked by a totem pole and profuse gardens and topped by stony mountains, Canada is romantic and rugged.

Copper-colored boulders reminiscent of the Canadian Rockies form a backdrop of gushing waterfalls, trickling streams and drop-off canyons. Willow, birch and plum trees are sprinkled across gentler

---

If it's raining, notice that no water falls from Spaceship Earth. Instead, it's collected within the globe and funneled into World Showcase Lagoon.

---

slopes that clone Victoria's Buchart Gardens. Here close-cropped hedges, blooming flowers and vines marble the landscape. Towering above the area is *Hotel du Canada*, a striking French Gothic brownstone with spires, turrets and a mansard roof.

A keen inspection, however, will reveal the hotel only *appears* to tower: It looks six stories tall but is actually only two-and-a-half. This is because of a technique, called "forced perspective," which involves making the bricks and windows smaller as they get higher. There's more visual trickery here, too: The trees that seem to "grow" out of the Canadian Rockies are really hidden in big pots. The trees are fed water and nutrients via a hidden tube. And the Rockies themselves are little more than painted concrete and chicken wire mounted on a platform similar to a parade float. One honest-to-goodness attraction here is a film called:

O Canada! ★★★★ The Royal Canadian Mounted Police seem to envelope you as they circle the screen at the start of this film. It's just a prelude to the smashing visual effects of this 360-degree film that rushes down waterfalls, across canyons and plains, and along straight and jagged shores. Canada's savoir-faire shines through in scenes from artsy Montreal and sophisticated Toronto, and its wildness is evident in clips of bobcats, bears, bison, reindeer and eagles. The superb filmmaking puts you mentally right in the scenes. Indeed, several scenes were shot by a camera dangling from a helicopter.

Tips: Like China's film presentation, *O Canada!* is a standing-only attraction. This is bad news for parents with small children, who have to be held for 18 minutes to see the show. Infants must also be held because strollers aren't allowed. As an option, one parent could take the kids for a snack at Canada's Le Cellier cafeteria while the other sees the film. The restaurant has plenty of moderately priced food kids like and is rarely crowded.

Future World

Epcot begins in the future. Here in Future World, plants are pod-shaped, walkways are angled and umbrellas resemble spaceships. Concrete extends for miles, and the slant-nose monorail coils overhead. Buildings of steel and glass reflect the sun's rays and aim for the heavens. Polishing this lunar look are twisted metal sculptures and fountains that mirror crisp white architecture. Spaceship Earth, a silvery sphere that towers overhead, is Future World's punctuation mark.

Future World's attractions delve into the subjects of travel, transportation, communication, biology, agriculture, sea life, energy and the human imagination. The challenge for Disney, of course, is to make these topics so interesting and entertaining that people keep coming back for more. For the most part, Future World more than succeeds.

Unlike the Magic Kingdom's Tomorrowland, which takes just a cursory (and not always accurate) look at what lies ahead, Future World offers forecasts that are comprehensive and believable. Indeed, many attractions combine the best of Disney's best: fantastic special effects, state-of-the-art motion pictures and set work, fascinating hands-on exhibits, and Audio-Animatronics figures so lifelike you're constantly doing a double take. And there are plenty of rides. Not fast rides, but clever ones that often last nearly 15 minutes. The Universe of Energy has a theater that travels from room to room, The Land offers a cruise through hydroponic gardens, and Spaceship Earth sends you forward *and* backward through the world's biggest manmade sphere.

Future World's complexity makes it impossible to see everything here in one day. Certain attractions should be on your must-see list, including Spaceship Earth, Wonders of Life and The Land, though you may choose to tour only one or two features *within* these attractions. Unless you're hooked on computers and sci-fi gadgetry, save CommuniCore East and West for your second Epcot visit. Both buildings offer technological displays and hands-on exhibits that require several hours of touring time.

Above all, don't rush through Future World. Much of the area's appeal lies in its fine tuning and details. The more you absorb and enjoy those details, the more you're likely to say: "Learning never felt so good."

Spaceship Earth ★★★★★ Rising some 18 stories and spanning 180 feet, this space-age spectacle seems dipped in aluminum and marbled with thousands of ridges. From far away—it is visible from an airplane

---

IT'S THE REAL THING!

Disney has really outdone itself with authentic details inside Spaceship Earth. Words dictated by the pharaoh are straight from the letter of an ancient Egyptian ruler. The scribble on the wall of Pompeii perfectly matches the wall's original graffiti. Gutenberg's press really is working, and the page it prints is identical to one from his original Bible. And that sleeping monk hunched over his desk appears to be breathing.

The Universe of Energy's traveling theater, powered by solar energy, is nicknamed "The Ride on Sunshine."

on either Florida coast—the million-pound globe appears otherworldly. Up close, as you stand in its vast shadow, it is overwhelming. Engineers call it "the world's largest geodesic sphere." Admirers call it "the big silver golf ball." Like Cinderella Castle in the Magic Kingdom, Spaceship Earth is Epcot's chief symbol, recognizable worldwide. By day it reflects the cerulean blue sky and chalky clouds; by night, it mirrors the very planets it emulates.

Inside Spaceship Earth is another world. Continuous moving trams, called "time machines," transport visitors through dim tunnels, fog and light and surrounds them with remarkable projected images and Audio-Animatronic figures. Sponsored by AT&T, the ride is an odyssey tracing the history of human communication. You slowly spiral higher and higher into Spaceship Earth, then at the globe's crown you pivot around for a backward descent. All the while, smells and sights and songs are fueling your senses.

During the 16-minute trip, Walter Cronkite talks in your ear (via a recording) and guides you through the days of cavemen, Egyptian hieroglyphics, Phoenician merchants, Roman theater, Gutenberg's printing press, Ed Sullivan and Beaver Cleaver, and finally to an executive at her computer. Along the way you smell the mustiness of ancient caves and the smoke from burning Rome, and hear a monk—quill pen in hand—snoring loudly in the abbey. In one impressive scene, Michelangelo puts the final touches on a Sistene Chapel fresco. Just as spectacular is the view at the top, where you plunge through a jet black sky peppered with millions of stars.

TIPS: Everyone seems to love Spaceship Earth. Parents enjoy the fabulous special effects, while children are mesmerized by all the colors, movement and music. Unfortunately, immense popularity means big-time lines. You can, however, avoid long waits by riding between 8:30 and 9 a.m. or after 7 p.m. *Not to be missed.*

Universe of Energy ★★★★ Shaped like a lopsided triangle, this mirrored building is sheathed in 80,000 tiny solar collectors that suck up sun rays and transform them into energy. Inside is a den of dinosaurs, forests, caves and mysterious movies. Split into four fast-paced parts, the Exxon-sponsored attraction begins with what seems like an ordinary film. Using stunning outdoor scenery, the movie explores heat, light, electrical and mechanical energy. And there's a fascinating twist: The 14-by-90-foot screen is made of 100 revolving triangles that change with every scene. Designed by noted Czech filmmaker Emile Radok, this "kinetic mosaic" screen amplifies every picture. Water seems to ripple across the wall, and fire appears to lick the theater.

Part two of the attraction, held in an adjacent theater, features a trio of 157-by-32-foot screens where Disney's largest animated film is shown. Only four minutes long, the flick is a brilliant reminder of Disney's phenomenal animation capabilities. Prehistoric animals, eerie insects and scary jungles set the scene for what will some day turn into oil, coal and gas. The depth and perspective of the scenery and the reality of the animals make this a film the whole family enjoys.

The movie's end brings a strange metamorphosis: Chunks of theater rows break away and head for the door. These clever, 97-passenger "traveling theaters" take a 300-million-year time trip through spooky forests scented with sulfur and veiled in fog. Here, lava sizzles, vines slither and dragonflies grow to be the size of cars. Monstrous millipedes edge toward the theater cars (causing some passengers to recoil), and two dinosaurs thrash on a plateau of crumbly rock. The scenes are spooky enough to scare small children—and delight teenagers.

The ride is followed by yet another film with a powerful message: We are running low on oil and need to develop other energy sources. Critics may label it hype, but the movie is delivered with such sincerity and stirring scenery that it comes across as a believable plea to help the earth.

TIPS: Some scenes may frighten small children. Don't be discouraged by long lines here: Every 15 minutes or so, about 600 new people are ushered in.

Wonders of Life—Sponsored by Metropolitan Life, this immensely popular place is a study in informative fun. Housed under a vast gold-crowned dome, it brims with dozens of games and gadgets that whiz, whirl, bleep and blink. Kids beg to spend hours here in this "Fitness Fairground," where they can test their tennis and golf prowess; zoom across the world on stationary bikes (while watching travel scenery);

IT'S MICKEY TIME

When Epcot opened in 1982, the only hint of Mickey Mouse was a clock mural on CommuniCore West's Age of Information exhibit. In recent years, however, Mickey has come to Epcot in a big way. Children can now meet their favorite mouse and other Disney characters at numerous Epcot pavilions throughout the day. The gang regularly shows up at the Odyssey Restaurant in Future World and Showcase Plaza in World Showcase. For specific times and places of appearances, pick up a schedule at Earth Station in Future World.

Before you go, it's good to remind children that Disney characters don't talk but communicate through body language. Also, the characters often seem larger in life than on television and can be overwhelming to a small child, so plan accordingly.

and fiddle around in the Sensory Funhouse, which has a "Room with a Skew." Every exhibit has health messages, but they're relayed so playfully it's tough to realize you're learning. In "Goofy About Health," a stressed-out Goofy gives up smoking and starts exercising, snoozing regularly and eating nutritious vittles. The eight-minute show, held in a small open theater, headlines great vintage Goofy cartoons and clever set work, with buildings such as Phast Pharmacy and Goofco store. In another open theater, the Anacomical Players deliver a corny, hilarious improv on human anatomy. Besides all this, Wonders of Life offers three splendid major attractions:

Body Wars ★★★★★ The swiftest, rowdiest ride at Epcot, Body Wars is a mind trip through the human body. Using the same technology that propelled Star Tours to Disney–MGM fame, Body Wars takes place in a simulator much like those used to train military pilots. The idea is that you've been miniaturized and "shot" into a patient's arm to rescue a scientist who's trying to pluck out a splinter. From here, the entire room starts rockin' and rollin' as the scientist gets sucked into the patient's circulation system. You plunge in after her, dodging blood cells, lungs and ribs and rebounding off artery walls. Together with terrific body images, the special effects and frenzied pace make this ride an ingenious psychological thriller.

TIPS: Expectant mothers and children under three are not allowed to ride. Some children old enough to ride will find it rough and frightening. Not recommended for people with bad backs or weak stomachs. Epcot's fastest ride is also its most popular. The only way to avoid a 45-minute-plus wait here is to arrive as soon as the park opens or during the hour before it closes. Lines sometimes dwindle between

---

DANCING WATERS

Water spouts rise and fall to the music, performing a liquid symphony. Tubes of water leap from one pond to another and children squeal, trying to snatch them from the air. Glistening water beads do the twist around a shrub sculpture of the baby dragon Figment.

*Welcome to **The Dancing Waters**, the main show outside Journey Into Imagination. Here frivolous fountains, each with its own routine, play to big crowds all day and much of the night. The Jellyfish Fountains shoot streams that flatten and jiggle at the top, while the Serpentine Fountains form temporary water bridges between gardens.*

A perfect prelude to Journey Into Imagination, The Dancing Waters rank as one of Disney's most inventive inventions. As Tigger might say, it's absolute imaginationimity!

That gem of a stagecoach in the World of Motion's wild west scene is a 150-year-old Wells Fargo rig imported from Phoenix.

---

6 and 7 p.m., the peak dinnertime for World Showcase restaurants. Not to be missed.

Cranium Command ★★★★ This delightful, highly entertaining attraction is Epcot's best-kept secret. Tucked in the back of Wonders of Life, the show is smashing, with newfangled effects and witty script delivered by some of America's best-loved comedians. Set in a 200-seat theater, it combines a fast-paced movie with elaborate set work. The show's star is the Audio-Animatronics robot Buzzy, a bumbling, bigger-than-life kid who pilots the brain of a 12-year-old boy for a day. Somehow, Buzzy puts the boy's biological clock off kilter: He dashes off to school without getting dressed, forgets to eat breakfast or lunch and wilts in the presence of a certain pretty female classmate. Along the way, Buzzy has quite a time figuring out which brain part controls what. Body parts are played hilariously by familiar television characters, including "Saturday Night Live's" (pump YOU up) Hans and Frans as the heart pumpers and Cheer's barfly Norm as the stomach.

TIPS: Don't miss the preshow cartoon, which sets the scene for the main presentation. This engaging show is still largely undiscovered, so lines are rarely longer than 20 minutes. See it during the middle of the day.

The Making of Me ★★★ This 14-minute film takes a tasteful and enlightening look at human conception and childbearing. Martin Short stars as a man who, wondering where he came from, journeys back in time to his parents' births and later their decision to have him. Directed by Glenn Gordon Caron (director of television's "Moonlighting"), the movie features compelling footage from an actual birth. The adult themes are handled delicately, though parents should know that some scenes and information are explicit. An unusual but welcome offering from a company as conservative as Disney.

TIPS: Sadly, this worthwhile and popular film is shown in a very small theater, making lines long all day. Forget the morning; see it after 6 p.m., when the wait should be 25 minutes or less.

Horizons ★★★ Future World's most amusing prophecies exist in this building styled like a flying saucer. A 15-minute tram ride that includes colorful settings, detailed architecture and lifelike robots, Horizons takes a look *back* at the future, with peaks at what folks back then thought life would be like someday. Some portrayals are irresistibly comical, like the 1800s perception of 1950s Paris, where fish-shaped dirigibles provide mass transit. There's also Jules Verne's notion that spaceships would look like bullets with tiny portholes. And the 1930s view of the 1990s home, where robots dressed as butlers vacuum the floor and remote controls provide instant suntans from Hawaii, Florida or the Bahamas (take your pick). Children naturally poke fun at this stuff that their "parents actually believed," while parents enjoy the kitchsy nostalgia of it all. Presented by General Electric, the ride offers a cool, leisurely respite from the crowds and heat.

TIPS: Horizons does draw big crowds, but lines are usually swift-moving. About the only time the wait exceeds 15 minutes is when nearby Universe of Energy releases its audience of about 600 people.

World of Motion ★★★ Automobile buffs adore this chrome-splashed, wheel-shaped pavilion that features two attractions: a relaxing car ride and an auto exposition. The former is a zany, whimsical tour of human transportation endeavors, from the days of foot travel to space shuttles. Through 24 elaborate sets and over 140 Audio-Animatronics characters, humorous scenes show how man has tried riding ostriches, soaring on magic carpets and rolling square wheels. Notice the dozens of antiques and precise reproductions (some purposely beaten up a bit), including chariots, balloons, riverboats, buckboards, airplanes, locomotives and, of course, cars. A longtime Epcot favorite sponsored by General Motors, this is a feel-good experience accompanied by an addictive tune appropriately named "It's Fun to be Free."

After the ride, guests can tour a 33,000-square-foot auto showroom called TransCenter. Not surprisingly, the place showcases GM's newest cars as well as some great experimental models. But you'll also find intriguing exhibits and short theater presentations on milestones of 20th-century transportation. One vaudeville minishow, "The Bird and The Robot," is narrated by a cigar-smoking toucan who drawls about the latest in car robotics. There's also a wind tunnel demonstration of aerodynamic drag, and Design 2000, where cars of the future look like spaceships. It's fun to watch the families split up as they enter

---

TOURING THE LAND

If you enjoyed the Listen to the Land boat ride, don't miss the attraction's free 45-minute **Harvest Tour**. *A guide provides details on The Land's experimental growing techniques, taking you through the hydroponic garden, tropical and desert farms, and the garden with simulated lunar soil. The tour explores what's covered during the boat trip, but in much greater depth. Best of all, it allows visitors the chance to ask questions.*

Harvest Tours are offered every 30 to 45 minutes from 9 a.m. to 1 p.m. daily. Reservations must be made the day you plan to tour; stop by the Guided Tour Waiting Area just outside Kitchen Kabaret on The Land's first floor.

Much of the produce and seafood at The Land Grille Room come from the restaurant's own hydroponic garden and fish farm.

the TransCenter. Inevitably, dads and sons head for the cars while moms and daughters peruse the exhibits.

TIPS: Happily, this ride accommodates big crowds and so almost never has a long line. There's a rear entrance for the TransCenter if you opt to skip the ride. A thorough tour of the TransCenter takes several hours and so is best saved for your second day at Epcot.

Journey Into Imagination—A dreamy ride, a Michael Jackson movie and oodles of nifty electronic games make this place the hands-down Epcot favorite of children. The building itself, composed of two slightly crooked glass pyramids, is wonderfully illusionary. All day long, the sun's rays wink across the glass and lure visitors to these geometric top hats. The formal welcoming committee, though, is an orange-bearded professor called Dreamfinder and his purple baby dragon, named Figment. The pair, who are *very* popular with kids, hang around outside the pavilion, signing autographs and posing for snapshots. Inside the Kodak-sponsored building, you'll find three attractions with imagination gone wild:

Journey Into Imagination Ride ★★★ This soothing glide through mind pictures takes you to lands of imaginometers, barrels of laughs, boxes of "childish delights," fairy-tale murals, storms and supernatural creatures. Dreamfinder and Figment (played by Audio-Animatronics characters) narrate the 14-minute odyssey and keep popping in and out of scenes. The colorful sets, fantasy themes and relaxing pace make this a warm, happy experience that leaves you feeling "you can dream anything."

TIPS: The "imagination" theme makes this ride a big hit with many people, particularly children, while others find it slow and insipid.

Captain EO ★★★★ The mere mention of this movie makes some kids go wild with delight. (Translation: If they aren't already hounding you, don't say anything until you arrive). This 3-D, sci-fi experience is a special-effects bonanza that pulses with rock music, lasers, fiber optics and space-age scenery. For most people, it's a rush. Directed by Francis Ford Coppola, the 12-minute flick stars Michael Jackson as a silver-suited spaceship captain who has to turn a planet from evil to good. Jackson's sidekicks are the loony but adorable characters Hooter, Fuzzball and Geex. During one scene, audience members claw at the air when Hooter (a little fuzzy owl) seems to hover across the theater.

TIPS: The rock 'n roll music is loud, but don't let that deter you: This movie is pure fun. Small children are often frightened.

Some 5000 sea creatures thrive in The Living Seas' jumbo aquarium.

The Image Works ★★★ When it comes to fantastically clever stuff, few attractions parallel The Image Works. Filled with electronic wizardry, this place has "the works": hundreds of devices for toying with light, sound, color, images and time. At the Magic Palette, you can paint a picture using an electronic paintbrush and video images and colors. At the Electronic Philharmonic, you can conduct an orchestra with the wave of a hand. And in the Time Machine, you're propelled to the days of cavemen, Shakespeare's England or even the wild west (take your pick). Everyone, regardless of age, seems to find a favorite activity. I played the Stepping Tones—where jumping up and down on the carpet creates light, music and psychedelic colors—so long one night I was politely kicked out at closing time. For children, the place inspires creative expression. For adults, it's a reminder that, in our fast-paced world, daydreaming really is a lot of fun. Perhaps the best part, though, is that there's never a line to get in. Midday crowds do create short waits at individual games, but there's always an activity without any line.

TIPS: There's a separate entrance for those who are just visiting The Image Works.

The Land—This tremendous building, shaped like a galactic greenhouse fused with sunlight, overflows with earthly delights. Colorful food counters line the first floor, dispensing homemade pastries, baked potatoes, barbecue, frosty ice cream, gourmet coffees, chocolatey desserts and bread so fresh it warms your hand. This initial scene is so heady and the aromas so overwhelming that it's impossible to take just a "quick peak" at The Land. And that's good, because the food-themed attraction takes an engrossing and often amusing look at our body's fuel. Three very good and very different attractions, presented by Kraft foods, are featured:

Listen to the Land ★★★★★ One of few Epcot attractions with a live narrator, this enlightening boat trip delves into the history and future of farming. The crew first winds through a simulated rain forest, desert, prairie and old-fashioned barnyard, then journeys through actual thriving farms. There's a miniature tropical farm with papayas so fleshy you long to reach out and pluck them. There's a fascinating hydroponic garden and a seafood farm brimming with colorful paddlefish and freshwater shrimp. At the prolific Desert Farm, a computer delivers water to the roots of cotton, sunflowers, buffalo gourds, sorghum and cucumbers. Fascinating trivia delivered by the boat captain and smooth sailing make this an informative and relaxing 14-minute cruise.

TIPS: Much of the information is too academic for preschoolers, though they usually love the scenery and the idea of being in a boat. Not to be missed.

Kitchen Kabaret ★★★ A delightful tribute to nutrition, the kabaret headlines a nutty cast of Audio-Animatronics foods who sing, dance and pun their way through the kitchen. The many memorable characters include the Boogie Woogie Bak'ry Boys who pop out of the fridge, Mr. Hamm and Mr. Eggz, and the Cereal Sisters (Mairzy Oats, Rennie Rice and Connie Corn). Mr. Mayonnaise's Groucho Marx-style eyebrows and Mr. Broccoli's punk hair and pink shades are a riot. If you enjoy the lighthearted humor of the Magic Kingdom's Country Bear Jamboree, you'll love this show.

TIPS: This is one Epcot attraction that's not popular but should be. All for the better: There's rarely more than a 15-minute wait, so go between 11 a.m and 3 p.m. No matter what time you go, the show offers a cool, dark reprieve from the sun and walking.

Symbiosis ★★★ This probing film examines the delicate thread between people and their environment. The film's mood swings from disgust at the vast polluting of world lakes and streams to jubilation at the deliverance of a few waterways and forests. The 70mm motion picture, shown on a 23-by-60-foot screen, features spectacular footage from over 30 countries.

TIPS: Despite its erudite name, Symbiosis will intrigue most any-one over 12. Smaller children tend to use the dark, quiet environment for a quick (20-minute) nap, while parents use it to rest tired feet.

The Living Seas ★★★ Water lashes at imitation boulders outside this wavy building trimmed in swimming-pool blue. Sponsored by United Technologies, The Living Seas is one of Epcot's most ambitious attractions—and sadly one of its most overrated. Even hard-core

THE TALK OF THE TOWN

"Hel-lo. My Name is Phra-ser." The voice is friendly but methodical, separating each syllable. "What is your name?" Curious, you type "Count Dracula" on the computer keyboard before you. "Count Drac-u-la?" the voice says, almost skeptically.

Meet **Phraser,** *a CommuniCore West computer who will enunciate virtually any word or phrase you type across his light blue screen. He'll recite poetry, read backward sentences, tackle foreign words—anything that's pronounceable. Phraser is the talk of CommuniCore, and he's fun to talk to. Mostly, he keeps people asking how he can be so smart.*

sea lovers find the attraction sorely lacking. The preshow movie on the origin of the seas is dramatic but bookish, and the **Caribbean Coral Reef Ride** ★ —the attraction's main event—seems over before it begins. Too bad, because the idea for the ride is marvelous: You literally cruise through the world's largest manmade saltwater aquarium. Moving trams take visitors through an acrylic-lined cylinder in the center of the aquarium. The 5.7-million-gallon tank, some 24 feet deep and 200 feet in diameter, is chock-full of fascinating sealife such as barracudas, dolphins, sea lions, stingrays, parrot fish and yes, sharks. Scuba divers roam the tank, testing new dive gear, training dolphins and talking to observers via wireless radios. Unfortunately, no sooner are you engrossed in all this than the three-minute ride is over.

The best part of The Living Seas comes after the ride, when visitors can peruse two floors of interesting marine exhibits. Kids go nuts over this area, called **Sea Base Alpha** ★★★ where they can play ocean-themed video games and slip into an atmospheric dive suit. Numerous aquariums feature some unusual life forms, including camouflage fish, kelp forests and minuscule zooplankton.

TIPS: The Living Seas draws big crowds from about 9:30 a.m. to 6 p.m. If there's more than a 20-minute wait, skip it. Orlando's Sea World, an entire theme park devoted to marine life, is more extensive and entertaining—and less crowded.

CommuniCore ★★★ A two-building maze of digital panels, computers and video screens, CommuniCore seems alive with electric energy. Here, in Epcot's most technical attractions, you can preview faraway lands in a "vacation station cubicle" or see the person you're

---

REACH OUT AT EPCOT

If Epcot is an information center, then **Epcot Outreach** *is the core of that center. Located in CommuniCore West, these vast archives stock enough reams of Epcot information to bridge Florida and California. Using a computer data service, a friendly librarian will investigate virtually any Disney-related question that pops into your mind: the number of Disney employees (35,000), the number of monorail passengers per day (150,000) and the largest single bed of annuals (25,000 flowers covering 20,000 square feet of The Land). If the librarian gets stumped, she calls Disney's Burbank, California archives—which she says knows "evvvverrythinngg."*

Considering all the wonders of Disney World, what's the most-asked question? "How can I grow hydroponics?"

Besides computers, Epcot Outreach has librarians who will answer questions and provide brochures on various subjects. You'll find Epcot Outreach on the north end of CommuniCore West near FutureCom.

talking to on a 3-D video telephone. Every exhibit focuses on advanced technology and most feature "touch-sensitive" monitors where you control all the action by touching the screen. Preteens and teenagers love these monitors and will spend hours toying with the dozens of games. In fact, they usually opt for CommuniCore while their parents tour World Showcase (which kids sometimes call *borrrri-ing*). Adults, however, may want to visit the time-consuming CommuniCore exhibits on their second day at Epcot.

CommuniCore is divided into two crescent-shaped buildings:

CommuniCore East has computers that let you design a roller coaster (loops, drops and all), play trivia games and find out how to save money on home electricity. The Great American Census Quiz spits out fascinating figures, like the number of U.S. centenarians alive today (about 12,000), and which state should grow the fastest through the rest of the 1900s (Florida). Another exhibit, Backstage Magic, offers a behind-the-scenes look at Epcot's computer control room. Unfortunately, it's one of the few CommuniCore exhibits with perennial lines, and it's not worth the wait.

CommuniCore West is where you'll find the zany Fountain of Information, a communications collage of spinning signs and laser discs, revolving film reels, books, catalogues, stock certificates and much more. Nearby, a computer will provide the latest news from your home state; another monitor tells how, in coming years, you can order home videos via computer. One very engaging computer will snap a picture of your face, then let you change your features. A smaller nose? No problem. Sharper cheekbones? It only takes a second. The final products are always interesting and usually hilarious.

Tips: Other than Backstage Magic, there's rarely a long line at any of the CommuniCore exhibits.

FOUR

Disney–MGM

When Disney–MGM Studios opened in May 1989, it was hailed, at least in Florida, as nothing short of a world event. Here for the first time was a vehicle for attracting—indeed, *guaranteeing*—big-time movie and television productions while at the same time giving the public a close-up look at the entertainment industry.

To a state long thirsty for a taste of Hollywood, it was intoxicating.

Disney, too, was spanning new horizons. Though the company had for years been making movies and running theme parks, the two had never been joined in the same spot. Also, by bringing Metro–Gold-wyn–Mayer into the plan (a rare move for a company not traditionally inclined to share projects), Disney secured a lock on one of the biggest names in the motion picture business.

Built at a cost of $300 million, the 110-acre park is modeled after Southern California's highly successful Universal Studios tour. Despite its size, Disney–MGM at first view seems small and intimate because nearly two-thirds of the area is given over to motion picture and television production centers, which offer behind-the-scenes tours. The rest, for the most part, features rides, audience-participation attractions and movie stunt shows that capture virtually every facet of Hollywood-brand entertainment.

Like a movie set out of the 1930s or 1940s, the park is a colorful and nostalgic blend of art deco architecture, kitschy billboards, pop art, sculptured gardens, trendy restaurants, funky diners and curio shops. The whole area is comprised of five sightseeing clusters—each with only a handful of major attractions—and is easily walked in less than two hours.

Headlining the area is palm-lined Hollywood Boulevard, with its street actors, zany stores and ethereal pastel buildings. Just off the boulevard is Studio Courtyard, home to Disney's animation facilities. Here—for the first time in Disney history—visitors can see the company's cartoon artists at work on vintage and new characters.

Across the way is Lakeside Circle, punctuated by Echo Lake and its smoke-spewing Gertie, a life-size "dinosaur" that doubles as an ice cream shop. The adjacent Backlot Annex draws thousands of visitors every hour to its action-packed Indiana Jones stunt show. Along the park's northeast elbow are a jumble of tin-roofed warehouses and faux neighborhoods that form vast production centers and backlots. Here a two-hour (or longer) Backstage Studio Tour provides glimpses of the moviemaking business.

Unlike the Magic Kingdom or Epcot, Disney–MGM Studios is neither imposing nor overwhelming. There are only 11 major attractions, compared to 45 in the Magic Kingdom and 23 in Epcot. This means you can see the entire park (at a fairly leisurely pace) in a single day, even during busy times. This should continue to be true until Disney proceeds with plans to double the size of the place in the next decade.

Much of the park's beauty lies in the design subtleties and the fine tuning so typical of Disney attractions: streams of colors that unify the park, building facades so realistic visitors try to open the front door, out-of-work actors (playing out-of-work actors) who pitch pennies in the streets. Indeed, every place fits the Hollywood bill, from the Tune In Lounge and Starring Rolls restaurant to the Fototoons shop and Cover Story photo studio.

With few exceptions, each attraction is pumped with action, special effects and the kind of oddities that intrigue and delight anyone even remotely interested in the film industry. Sights, too, are more complex. As Disney learned that visitors often want more than just a "quick ride," it developed attractions that combine films, skits, educational narrative *and* rides.

Disney has also ensured that attractions here offer something for people of every age. While parents, teenagers and young children may often disagree on rides at Disney's other parks, here everyone should concur. In fact, the question won't be *which* attractions the family should see but *how many* it can experience in a day.

Of course, all the attractions symbolize the ultimate illusion. For if Hollywood is just one big act, then Disney–MGM is an act within an act. Every sight, sound and smell plays out the fantasies of Tinsel Town. The park, in effect, is the looking glass inside the looking glass.

Perhaps the park's premier act is it's signature, a monstrous 13-story water tower crowned with a 16-ton pair of mouse ears. Dubbed "Earffel Tower," the goofy-looking structure would surely in any other place or time be considered a spoof. But hey, this is Disney—and That's Hollywood!

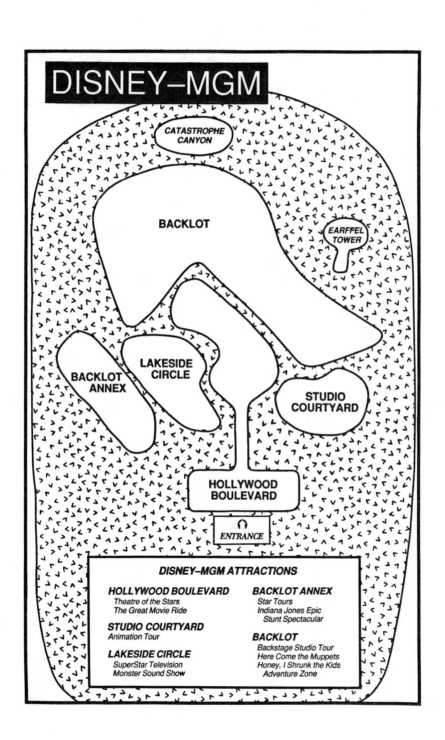

DISNEY–MGM

CATASTROPHE CANYON

BACKLOT

EARFFEL TOWER

BACKLOT ANNEX

LAKESIDE CIRCLE

STUDIO COURTYARD

HOLLYWOOD BOULEVARD

ENTRANCE

DISNEY–MGM ATTRACTIONS

HOLLYWOOD BOULEVARD
Theatre of the Stars
The Great Movie Ride

STUDIO COURTYARD
Animation Tour

LAKESIDE CIRCLE
SuperStar Television
Monster Sound Show

BACKLOT ANNEX
Star Tours
Indiana Jones Epic
    Stunt Spectacular

BACKLOT
Backstage Studio Tour
Here Come the Muppets
Honey, I Shrunk the Kids
    Adventure Zone

ARRIVAL

From the Contemporary, Polynesian Village and Grand Floridian Resorts: Take a Disney bus directly to Disney–MGM Studios.

From the Magic Kingdom and Epcot Center: Take a Disney bus directly to Disney–MGM Studios.

From the Disney Village Marketplace, Pleasure Island, Typhoon Lagoon or Fort Wilderness: Take a Disney bus directly to Disney–MGM Studios.

From the Disney Inn and the Caribbean Beach Resort: Take a Disney bus directly to Disney–MGM Studios.

By Ferry: Ferries provide scenic shuttles for guests of the Swan, Dolphin, Yacht Club or Beach Club resorts.

From area hotels outside Disney World: Most hotels offer shuttle service to Disney–MGM Studios. However, shuttles often run only on the hour or every two or three hours. In this case, it's more convenient to drive.

By Car: From Route 4, take the exit for the Caribbean Beach Resort, Disney–MGM Studios and the Disney Village Marketplace. The Studios are about a half mile from Route 4.

Anyone intimidated by the complex arrival system of the Magic Kingdom will rejoice when he sees Disney–MGM Studios. The 4500-space parking lot here seems minuscule compared to the Magic Kingdom's. Also, the Disney–MGM lot is located right at the park's entrance—no monorails or ferry boats to slow you down.

There's a parking fee (free for guests of Disney World hotels) and trams that whisk you from your car to the entrance, though many parking spots are within walking distance. It's crucial to *write down* your parking row number or you might not be able to find your car at day's end.

SIGHTSEEING STRATEGIES

Because of its newness and relatively small size, Disney–MGM Studios is rarely so jammed with visitors that it closes its gates. That's not to say it doesn't experience the occasional crowd crush, particularly during the summer and holidays. Thus, it's always best to arrive a *half-hour to an hour* before the park's "official" opening time. During the busy season, Disney sometimes opens the park before the advertised time, though there's no way to know when this will happen. You can, however, call 407-824-4321 the day before to find out the official opening time.

Just as important, Hollywood Boulevard, a sort of Main Street area, always opens a half-hour to an hour before the rest of the park. Here you can have coffee and pastries, get maps, brochures and entertainment schedules, and rent strollers, lockers and wheelchairs—before the hordes arrive. You can also be one of the first in line for the most popular rides—Star Tours and The Great Movie Ride.

By the same token, Hollywood Boulevard stays open a half-hour to an hour after the rest of the park closes. The official closing time, however, is rarely extended for the rest of the park.

The best news here: It's easy to sightsee at Disney–MGM Studios. Unlike the Magic Kingdom, Epcot and most other theme parks, the Disney Studios are so easily navigated that it's okay to skip attractions in one area and backtrack later. This will provide you with an opportunity to see everything without having to come up with an elaborate strategy.

If you are concerned about seeing the best rides early, however, then after you have seen Star Tours and The Great Movie Ride take a careful look through this chapter and pick out the four- and five-star attractions that interest you the most. After you have seen them it shouldn't be any problem getting on the less popular rides.

NUTS & BOLTS

Stroller and Wheelchair Rental: Available at Oscar's Super Service station just inside the main entrance.

Baby Services: Changing tables and nursing facilities are located at Guest Services at the main entrance.

Lockers: Located next to Oscar's Super Service station inside the main entrance. Note: Lockers cost 50 cents each time you open them.

Pets: Pets are not permitted into Disney–MGM Studios. There are no kennels here; however, you can board your pet at the kennel near the Magic Kingdom parking toll plaza. It's best to park at the Magic Kingdom, then catch a bus to Disney–MGM. This will cost you an extra hour or so, round-trip.

Lost Children: Report missing children to Guest Services or call 407-560-4654.

CHALKBOARD TOURING TIPS

You've just arrived at Disney–MGM Studios, and you can't decide where to start. Not to worry: Help is available in the studios' courtyard. Here the Disney folks set up a big chalkboard that lists major attractions with their approximate waiting times, and offers suggestions on when to see each one. Two employees regularly update the information and provide visitors with sightseeing tips for that day. I found most of the information accurate, although one attraction listed with a 25-minute wait had a 40-minute wait because the board advised everyone to "See it Now!" On those rare days when business is slow at the park, you won't find a chalkboard, but then, who needs it?

Package Pickup: To avoid toting your purchases around all day, ask the Disney–MGM store clerks to forward your packages to Guest Services. You can pick them up on your way out. The service is free.

Lost & Found: Report missing or found items to Guest Services.

Banking: There's no bank here; however, an automatic teller machine is located just outside the main entrance.

GETTING AROUND

Although Disney–MGM Studios encompasses 110 acres, nearly two-thirds is devoted to television and movie production centers and back-lots. Most of these areas are accessible only through guided tram tours or special observation walkways. The rest of the park is the real "walking" area where visitors are free to explore attractions at their leisure.

Shaped like an irregular circle, the park is divided into four small sightseeing areas plus the mammoth production facilities. Hollywood Boulevard travels up the front spine and is a good place to get oriented. The boulevard unfolds into a breezy brick courtyard that is more or less the center of the park. A place of oak trees and park benches, the courtyard is a good meeting spot if your party decides to split up or if someone gets lost. It's also a prime place to picnic; hot dogs, ice cream and popcorn are available from the vendors that dot the area.

Traveling counterclockwise from the courtyard, there's Lakeside Circle; Backlot Annex; the expansive production and back lot facilities; and Studio Courtyard, home to the Disney–MGM Animation Tour. The walking and tram tours of the production facilities are listed in the Disney guide as "Backstage Studio Tour." The walking tour starts at the top of the park near the Backstage Plaza; the tram commences on the park's east side near the Muppets theater. You can separate the two tours or enjoy them back-to-back for a two-hour experience.

Hollywood Boulevard

An ambitious facsimile of movie town's famous main drag, Hollywood Boulevard oozes panache. Streamlined moderne architecture forms a sassy contour of jutting ledges, gentle curves, pulsing neon and shiny chrome. Buildings washed in rose, turquoise, pale yellow and seafoam green thrust pastel palettes against an Aqua Velva blue sky. Glass block plays catch with the sun's rays, and store windows reflect the faces of mouse-hatted visitors.

Edging the boulevard are old-fashioned street lamps, black-and-white striped stop signs and pole-mounted street lights that sound a quirky *ding!* when they change colors. Magnificent palms soar upward from the concrete, their spiked fronds performing little twists in the wind. Strains from the soundtrack of *Doctor Zhivago* sift through the sun-warmed air.

Funky shops and businesses crowd along the sidewalk, drawing visitors in with playbills that announce their fortes. Most are great places to browse, even if you don't like to shop, because they paint a rosy portrait of days gone by.

To complete this tinsel-tinged picture, wannabe actors and actresses roam the boulevard with painted faces and outrageous costumes. There's marble-skinned Marilyn Monroe and trench-coated Dick Tracy, as well as some "typical" Hollywood characters—a gum-chewing cabbie, a nosy television reporter and a pesky guy selling maps of movie stars' homes.

Before you stroll Hollywood Boulevard, stop by the **Crossroads of the World** kiosk. It's the first thing you see after entering the park, and it's stocked with guides, maps and schedules of the day's filmings and performances. Disney employees are also here to help you get organized.

If you're touring first thing in the morning, opt for a quick walk down the boulevard and head for attractions that become crowded later in the day. I recommend first riding Star Tours—usually *the* most popular attraction—then The Great Movie Ride, and then taking the Animation Tour (which is most crowded in the afternoon). This will bring you to lunchtime, when you can return to Hollywood Boulevard and see it at a leisurely pace while the rest of the park becomes packed.

Across the street, a 1947 grape-colored Buick has pulled up to **Oscar's Classic Car Souvenirs & Super Service Station**. Vintage auto buffs will love this service station-cum-museum and shop, which

MOVIE STAR MEMORABILIA

One place not *to miss on Hollywood Boulevard is* **Sid Cahuenga's One-of-a-Kind** *antiques and curios. The plank-floored shop brims with Hollywood peculiarities and memorabilia: Brenda Vaccaro's shawl, a program from John Belushi's memorial service, Liberace's table napkins, and racks of original playbills and autographed stars' photos. Look for Sid on the porch, rocking in his wooden chair and spreading Hollywood gossip.*

Gene Kelly personally inspected his robot lookalike for The Great Movie Ride.

is lined with fuel pump bubble-gum machines and photos of great antique cars. Moms and dads will love the "real" service here: stroller and locker rentals, as well as infant goodies (for sale) such as bottles and diapers. Wheelchairs are also for rent.

Feeling famous? Step into **Cover Story**, where friendly Disney employees will doll you up, snap your picture and put it on the cover of your favorite popular magazine (for a fee, of course). Kids love this place, but their favorite spot is nearby **Sights & Sounds**. Here they can play singer and musician and record their own music video, MTV-style.

Toward the crest of Hollywood Boulevard are its two headline attractions:

Theatre of the Stars ★★★ Fashioned after the famed Hollywood Bowl, this concrete amphitheater is propped on a broad brick promenade dotted with maple trees. The "stars" are a crew of loony Disney characters, leggy dancers and pearly-teethed guys who stage a witty and sentimental chronicle of the silver screen. During the 25-minute "Hurray for Hollywood!" show, Goofy plays Rudolph Valentino, Tigger does John Travolta in *Saturday Night Fever* and Minnie cavorts in giant coins to the tune of "We're in the Money." A fine orchestra and array of costumes and props—including minidresses in fruit colors and ten-foot bananas—make this an extravaganza the whole family will enjoy.

TIPS: Shows are held five to six times a day. Most fill up, so it's best to arrive about 15 minutes before starting time. The last show of the day, usually after 4 p.m., is the best because it's the least crowded, and the coolest in summertime.

The Great Movie Ride ★★★★★ This ride easily ranks as "great," but what truly sets it apart is its building—a superb replica of the gorgeous Grauman's Chinese Theater. Situated at the crown of Hollywood Boulevard, the 95,000-square-foot theater boasts spectacular pagoda roofs and an ornate facade with glossy red columns and stone carvings. Scattered across its plaza are foot and hand prints of some Hollywood stars: Bob Hope, Jim Henson, Danny DeVito and Rhea Perlman, among others. Through the threshold are soaring ceilings, elaborate painted panels and massive Chinese lanterns. And that's only the beginning.

The lobby, which is really a massive queue area, features a mini-museum with goodies such as a space suit from the movie *Alien*, ruby slippers worn by Judy Garland in *The Wizard of Oz* and the tiny piano played by Sam in *Casablanca*. If lines aren't long (which is rare), visitors tend to hurry through the lobby and miss all the treasures. Take my advice: Relax and enjoy the exhibits—these are worth seeing.

Once inside, visitors board open-air box cars and are immediately plunged into the spirit of moviemaking. Murals of the 1930s Hollywood Hills paint a nostalgic picture with cascading hillside villas and an original "Hollywoodland" sign lit by the sunset. Most of the 20-minute ride, though, uses sound stages to provide a dazzling, dynamic and incredibly realistic trek through Hollywood's most celebrated films. Rain streams down on Gene Kelly in *Singin' in the Rain*, Mary Poppins floats with her magical umbrella to the lyrics of "Chim Chim Cher-ee" and *Public Enemy's* James Cagney turns on his throaty drawl to tell a gangster, "Oh, you dirty, double crossing. . . ."

One of the most powerful scenes is a gangster shootout (using pop guns) where visitors get stuck in the line of fire. Amazingly, it's tough to tell the difference between the Audio-Animatronics robots and the real Disney employees in this gunfight. Just around the corner, poker-faced Clint Eastwood is waiting at the Monarch Saloon and rifle-toting John Wayne is astride his horse on a sunwashed prairie. Wayne is after some bank robbers who blow up a safe and send flames hurtling from the building. Visitors can feel the fire's warmth in their box cars.

In one eerie movie snapshot, the *Alien* monster drips goo while smoke pours through metal chambers; in another, Indiana Jones struggles to remove the Lost Ark in a snake-filled tomb. (Warning: Both scenes can frighten young children.) But perhaps the most fantastic scene is from *The Wizard of Oz*, featuring hundreds of lovable munchkins, Dorothy and her crew of quirky friends, and the beastly wicked witch.

Each scene enthralls with intricate costumes, visual details and Audio-Animatronic figures whose features and mannerisms are remarkably real. Indeed, with few exceptions, every figure, ensemble and prop was designed *precisely* as its real-life counterpart, down to the witch's spindly broom and John Wayne's horse and rifle.

TIPS: One of Disney–MGM's most popular rides and therefore most crowded. A hint for estimating length of wait: When the inside queues are full, there's at least a 25-minute wait. If lines are spilling outside onto Hollywood Boulevard, you're talking an hour or more. Also, posted waiting times usually *overestimate* the wait by 10 to 15 minutes. For instance, if a sign says "Approximate wait from this point: 40 minutes," it's more likely to be 30 minutes. One exception: Sometimes, particularly toward the end of the day, Disney employees will "stack" this ride, which means queuing visitors *outside* to clear up lines *inside*. So before you let long lines outside scare you off, check for inside lines.

Another important note: Though this ride will appeal to people of all ages, it has several scenes that sometimes frighten small children. Not to be missed.

Lakeside Circle

Stashed off the west side of Hollywood Boulevard, Lakeside Circle is Disney's vision of California Cool: trendy restaurants splashed with pink and aqua and trimmed in chrome, lounges and cafés where televisions outnumber waitresses, and a shop where most souvenirs sport the face of a star.

The main "star" here, of course, is the lake, a glimmering sweep of water the color of Paul Newman's baby blues. On one side of the lake rests Min and Bill's Dockside Diner, a Disneyesque freighter that serves fast food. On the other side is Gertie, a funky-looking reproduction of a dinosaur. Gertie serves ice cream and Disney souvenirs, and occasionally sends up a puff of smoke.

Lakeside Circle is so small it's difficult to get lost. Once you've traveled around the lake, you've seen it all.

SuperStar Television ★★★ If you've ever wanted to be on a popular television show, this is your big chance. Actually, you won't be on a real show, but the simulations are so superb it will keep you and the audience laughing almost continuously.

The attraction starts in an outdoor area filled with television monitors and Disney employees searching for audience participants. Employees must select people of varying ages, from preschoolers to grandparents.

Once guest stars are chosen, visitors enter a comfortable, 1000-seat theater with eight six-foot-wide monitors and a stage that has several sets. For the next 30 minutes, the sets feature fast-paced footage of scenes from some of television's best-loved shows. The only catch is, audience participants replace some of the stars in each scene. Each guest—in full makeup and costume for the role—is filmed live on the set and then "dubbed" into the television scene, which is played on the

---

CURTAIN CALLS ANYONE?

It's not easy to be chosen as a guest star for SuperStar Television (only about 12 of 1000 make it), but following these tips will increase your chances: Arrive 15 to 30 minutes before the show starts and go to the front of the waiting area. Stand near an employee and let him or her know you're dying to be in the show. Dressing outrageously should get you extra points.

Remember that SuperStar Television is not a real television show but a Disney–MGM attraction. Shows are held 8 to 12 times a day; check the schedule outside the attraction.

monitors. The results, depending on the participant's degree of craziness, can be hilarious.

In what is probably *the* most famous "I Love Lucy" scene, Lucy and Ethel Mertz attempt to wrap chocolates that whiz along a conveyer belt. The scene is first played for the audience as it originally appeared on television, then replayed with a guest star, usually a teenage girl. Dressed in a white baker's hat and apron, the girl fumbles with the candy as the conveyer moves faster and faster and the audience laughs louder and louder.

Other clips are just as amusing, including a sappy "General Hospital" love triangle where two guest stars duke it out, and a pie-in-the-face scene from a Three Stooges film. There's also the great "Cheers" episode where dim-witted Woody gives everybody free drinks when they convince him it's their birthday. Kids get plenty of roles, too, such as the castaways on "Gilligan's Island" and a New York Yankees home run hitter (often a girl) interviewed by Howard Cosell.

The special effects, the unpredictability and the nostalgia of vintage television make this a top attraction for all ages. At the same time, it offers a cool, relaxing break from crowds.

TIPS: Though popular, the show's theatre accommodates 1000 people and rarely fills up. See it between 11 a.m. and 4 p.m., when the rest of the park is most crowded. Shows are every 35 to 45 minutes.

Monster Sound Show ★★★★ Despite its name, this show is not scary. Rather, it's a clever, multifaceted lesson on the genius behind motion picture sound. Like SuperStar Television, it uses audience guests to create a humorous, impromptu performance that entertains as well as educates.

The main show, held in an intimate, 275-seat theater, is hosted by a pert man who selects audience volunteers at random (sorry, only luck and possibly good looks will help you get picked). He first rolls a short spook film, starring Chevy Chase and Martin Short, that features a series of birdbrained mishaps. Things get hairy the second go-around when the audience sound crew has to fill in the movie's sound effects. On the emcee's cue, the amateurs "whiz" barrels, "zip" sandpaper and perform various other loony sound duties that have them racing frantically across the stage.

When the movie is shown a third time, it's surprising to note some differences: Doors creak when chandeliers are supposed to fall, thunder booms *after* the storm and Chase gets a good boink on the head *before* Short ever hits him.

Interestingly, many of the show's sound-making gadgets are originals created by sound-effects guru Jimmy MacDonald. During his 45 years at Walt Disney Studios, Macdonald made over 20,000 sound devices. Most qualify as doodads and gizmos—things made with nails, straw, mud, leather and other humble components.

After the presentation, guests are treated to splendid hands-on exhibits called **SoundWorks**. Filled with all sorts of gadgets that go squeak, creak, bonk and buzz, the place is a child's dreamland. There are panels you touch to "boing" a drum and knobs you push so your voice will sound like a gargoyle's. There's Movie Mimics, which lets you dub your voice over Mickey Mouse, Roger Rabbit and other Disney heros. And there's Earie Encounters, where you create flying saucer sounds for a scene from the 1956 flick *Forbidden Planet*.

Then there's **Soundsations**, a "3-D audio" experience that's nothing short of otherworldly. After entering a dim, soundproofed booth and donning earphones, you close your eyes and suddenly. . . . . .You're a movie executive at his first day of work. You get briefed on your new job, greet boss Michael Eisner (Disney's head honcho) and then meet the really big cheese—a familiar tenor voice with mouse ears. It's all wonderfully realistic, but the most bizarre part is when you get your hair cut and blow-dried: The hair on the back of your neck *stands up*.

TIPS: Because this is an attraction to delight all ages, the show's small (270-seat) theater makes for long waits, much of it in the hot sun. Try to see it about an hour before the park closes. Also, notice that when nearby SuperStar Television releases its audience (often 500 to 800 people), most head for the Monster Sound Show. This is *not* a good time to get in line. Instead, wait until SuperStar Television is *almost* over and then head for the Monster Sound Show.

Another hint: It's possible to visit the SoundWorks portion separately. This is especially good for parents with children who need to release some energy, and for people like me who return twice in one day just to hear Soundsations.

Backlot Annex

Little more than an offshoot of Lakeside Circle, Backlot Annex is a corner niche whose sum parts equal three: two attractions and one restaurant. Despite its seemingly small size, the area usually teems with

---

LETTERMAN ON SOUND

Don't miss the prelude to the Monster Sound Show. It's a video of David Letterman doing his "Top 10 Good Things About Sound." In classic Letterman style, he pitches a pencil against the window to demonstrate the "breaking" sound. He also hosts Jack Foley, a master of movie sound effects, who demonstrates a few secrets: crunching his empty wallet to make the dwarf steps in "Snow White," and clunking coconut halves for the sound of horses' hooves in various Disney movies.

To create one 24-minute film, Disney–MGM's 70-plus animators must produce 34,650 drawings with at least 300 background scenes.

thousands of people. Many are clamoring to get on Star Tours, a *Star Wars*-style ride that is the park's most popular attraction. Others are hanging around the Indiana Jones Epic Stunt Spectacular trying to find out what all the commotion is about. Every few minutes, the stunt show sends off a loud explosion or earth-shaking rumble that reverberates across the park.

Like a futuristic banana republic, the annex is a weird mix of metal and jungle. Looking like a giant bug on stilts, a steel *Star Wars* creature guards the front of Star Tours; nearby, a thick web of palm trees and vines masks the entrance to the stunt show. In between the two attractions is Backlot Express restaurant, an exposed tin warehouse filled with ramshackle objects and arid plants.

Though there are only two attractions here, it's important to experience them in the correct order. Rule No. 1: If there's a short line at Star Tours, GO FOR IT! Rule No. 2: If the stunt show has just finished, DO NOT attempt to ride Star Tours. Most of the stunt show crowd (up to 2000 people) will be heading for the ride, so you should not. And, because the stunt show holds so many people, you can see it nearly any time.

Star Tours ★★★★★ This is one fast and furious ride where you—quite literally—take a trip and never leave the room.

Technically, it's a ride in a flight simulator like the ones used to train military and airline pilots. Realistically, it's the ultimate trick on the senses: Your mind says you're not whirling through space, yet your eyes, ears, fingers and pounding heart say you are.

Using themes and scenes from the movie *Star Wars*, the ride features several small rooms, called StarSpeeders, where you are belted into a seat. Eyes planted on a video screen, you plunge through space at lightning speed, dodging planets and ice crystals and battling laser fighters. All the while, your seat is turning, your stomach is churning, and the whole room seems to float.

Piloted by the bumbling but lovable *Star Wars* characters R2D2 and C3P0, the ride is supposed to be a leisurely voyage to Endor Moon. Things quickly go awry, though, when the novice pilots veer off course. After seven minutes of spins and loops and near misses, everyone is returned safely (but shakily) home.

Designed very much like Epcot's Body Wars ride, Star Tours uses spectacular video images and other high-tech effects to induce sensations that most first-time riders have never felt before. Unlike a roller coaster, you don't "go" anywhere; unlike a standard 3-D film show, you do get tossed around. Put simply, there's nothing else like it.

TIPS: Pregnant women and children younger than three are not allowed to ride. Some youngsters old enough to ride will find Star Tours rough and frightening. Not recommended for people with bad backs or weak stomachs.

The park's most popular ride, Star Tours is plagued by long lines (40 to 60 minutes) virtually all day. Try to ride during the first half hour after the park opens or shortly before it closes. Like the Great Movie Ride, Star Tours is often "stacked" to clear lines inside (for more on stacking, see "The Great Movie Ride"). Not to be missed.

Indiana Jones Epic Stunt Spectacular ★★★ This fast-paced, special effects escapade takes place in a 2200-seat amphitheater that seems hunkered beneath the jungle. In traditional *Raiders of the Lost Ark* style, the 25-minute show reels off a series of near-death encounters in an ancient Mayan temple: Indiana plummets from the ceiling, drops in a hidden hole, dodges spears and flames, and barely avoids being squashed by a gargantuan boulder.

In the middle of all the blazes and rumbles, the set crew calls time out and casually wheels away the entire stage. Behind is a re-creation of a busy Cairo plaza where tumblers and acrobats, dressed as Egyptians, frolic along the street. A bunch of Nazis soon show up looking for Indy, and a riot ensues. During the fist fighting and falling, jeeps and motorcycles buzz around and a Nazi airplane roars up. There's one terrific scene where a truck gets blown up and flipped, its flames warming the first few rows of the audience.

Directed by Glenn Randall, stunt coordinator for the Indiana Jones films as well as *Poltergeist* and *E.T.,* the show also provides some insight into the filming of stunt scenes. Professional stunt actors and actresses demonstrate using doubles for dangerous scenes, how cameras are tucked behind imitation rocks, and how "pickup" action shots are filmed. Some of these shots are done with audience guests who are randomly chosen about ten minutes before the show. Watch carefully, though, because some participants are actually stunt men *playing audience guests.*

TIPS: This quick-moving presentation captures the interest of all ages. The eight to ten daily shows often fill up well before show time. Your best bets are the first two and last two shows of the day. These almost never fill up. Another important note: The Disney people will tell you it's mandatory to line up (in the blazing sun) at least 30 minutes before show time. This is not necessary. Be at the show ten minutes early, and you should be able to walk right into the theater. If it's full, return for a later show. Make sure you check the *side aisles in the very front.* These often fill up last.

Warning: Restrooms are available only at the start of the Backstage Studio Tours.

Backstage Studio Tour

This vast piece of property forms the nitty gritty of Disney's Florida-turned-Hollywood: soundstages that change faces every day; backlots strewn with old cars and airplanes; fake skylines and fake neighborhoods; and warehouses jammed with bizarre props and costumes.

These production facilities make up the East Coast counterpart to MGM Studios in Burbank, California. They're also the "working" part of Disney—the only place where visitors can regularly witness dozens of employees in action. Virtually every day a camera is rolling somewhere. Television commercials are shot, movies filmed, game shows played out. In between all the filming, costumes and props are created, styrofoam buildings are thrown up and extras are gleaned from throngs of hopefuls.

Most of the area is accessible only through the shuttle and walking tours. You can take the tours separately or back-to-back for a one-and-a-half-hour-to-two-hour experience. The best time to visit is after 3 p.m., though it's important to note that *both tours close at dusk.*

The production facilities also offer a few attractions that can be toured at leisure (provided crews aren't filming) and are especially designed for families. Young children love the Here Come the Muppets stage show, and preteens flock to hourly street appearances by the Teenage Mutant Ninja Turtles. There's also the Honey, I Shrunk the Kids Adventure Zone, a cleverly-designed, oversized yard where you can stroll through 20-foot blades of grass.

Shuttle Tour ★★★★ This tour's expansive queue area can seem formidable, and it should. If it's packed with people (which is likely), you're facing a minimum 45-minute wait. There is, however, plenty to entertain you along the way, including Disney movie memorabilia and video clips of Clint Eastwood films and the making of *Jaws*.

Visitors board canopied shuttles, which resemble pastel caterpillars as they coil around tall buildings and backlots. Affable and sometimes humorous guides season the ride with anecdotes and notable details. At the greenery department, there's the faux tree trunk used in *Honey, I Shrunk the Kids*. At the prop warehouse are roadsters from *Dick Tracy*. And in the costume warehouse—home to over two million garments—there are outfits worn by Madonna and Warren Beatty in *Dick Tracy*, Bette Midler in *Big Business*, and Julie Andrews in *Mary Poppins*.

Catastrophe Canyon's flash flood is created by air cannons that blow 25,000 gallons of water over 100 feet.

Here, through big windows, visitors can also watch seamstresses at work on costumes for upcoming movies.

Next is the scenic shop, where sets are built, and the camera and lighting departments. The former are labyrinths of high-tech equipment, blinking lights and tangles of cords. Interestingly, the equipment is so state-of-the-art that it's used by visiting camera crews to film the space shuttle launches some 75 miles away.

The shuttle also winds along what could be termed Hollywood's "Street of Dreams"—a road lined with make believe houses. From the front you see trimmed lawns and pretty facades; from the back, the buildings are hollow. Notice the midwestern-style home where Vern lived in *Ernest Saves Christmas* and the pink cadillac used in *Tin Men* parked in a driveway. Down the way is a "boneyard," eternal resting grounds for rusty airplanes, crushed cars, airplanes and other *objets d'Hollywood*. There's an orange-and-red Pacific Electric trolley car from *Who Framed Roger Rabbit?*, spaceship modules from *E.T.* and Mother Goose's house.

From here it's all wet and woolly—at least for passengers sitting on the shuttle's left side. As the driver pulls into a barren cavern called Catastrophe Canyon, an oil tanker explodes, the road splits and a deluge of water comes hurdling toward the tram. The fallout is a lot of shimmying, a lot of soaked people and a few screams of "Let's-get-the-hell-out-of-here." The idea, of course, is a simultaneous simulation of a fire, thunderstorm, earthquake and flash flood. Later, passengers learn that the "canyon" is actually a mammoth steel coop wrapped in copper-colored cement. The water—all 70,000 gallons—is recycled over 100 times a day, or every three-and-a-half minutes for each shuttle group.

Desert scenes soon give way to urban ones as the shuttle veers down simulated New York City streets. Brownstones merge with red brick, marble and stained glass in a remarkable illusion of the Big Apple. Look closely and you'll see that the buildings are merely facades of fiberglass and styrofoam that have been expertly painted. Notice that, at the end of the street, the Empire State and Chrysler buildings are two-dimensional painted flats. Both buildings, by the way, can be removed if film crews want to portray a different U.S. city.

Tips: Though the tour appeals to all ages, some preschool children may be frightened by special effects at Catastrophe Canyon. The tour closes at dusk.

Kids love climbing through the Roger Rabbit-shaped hole near the start of the Backstage Walking Tour.

Walking Tour ★★★ From the shuttle exit, follow Roger Rabbit's purple footprints into **The Loony Bin**. Children (and many adults) invariably get sidetracked here, so plan on spending at least ten minutes in this wacky store. There are gizmos and gag gifts from favorite cartoons, including Acme boxes that cackle and go *choo choo* and *kaplooie!* Notice the air freight cartons from Hobart, Tasmania, which have labels that say "wabbits."

The first official stop is a special-effects area where an audience member dons a yellow raincoat and takes the helm of a ship at battle. The helmsman soon gets lost at sea, then is doused with 400 gallons of water. The nutty scenario is captured on video and played back for the audience.

A nearby special-effects workshop is also a favorite of kids, who love spotting props from popular movies. There are ferry boats, a drawbridge and train from *Dick Tracy,* pods from *Cocoon* and Maximilian's costume from *The Black Hole.* To show how the miniature props are filmed to look life-size, Disney employees use three children from the audience to shoot a scene from *Honey, I Shrunk the Kids.* One child plays director while the other two soar through the air on a hairy bumble bee. It's a hilarious take that also demonstrates stop-frame animation and other film techniques.

Visitors then file along a dim, soundproof catwalk to view three soundstages. Past filmings include "Let's Make a Deal," the long-running game show that was temporarily revived, and *The Lottery,* a funny, four-minute flick starring Bette Midler. The Midler flick, which is shown on overhead monitors, follows the crazy capers of a woman with a winning lottery ticket. Guests tour the sets and props used in

NEW YORK NOSTALGIA

The New York backlot can also be toured on foot as long as crews aren't filming. Anyone with a passion for detail should return and peruse the storefronts. Check out the old Smith-Corona behind the dusty window of Sal's Pawn, and the 1950s hair nets and foam curlers in the Rexall window. A rusty old stamp machine on the street corner is out of stamps—but will keep your coins.

the movie, and gain some fascinating perspective on the use of camera angles, editing and special-effects filming.

Next is the Post Production area, where informative and humorous videos reveal more moviemaking secrets. George Lucas, R2D2 and C3PO give a funny spiel on editing and computer effects, while Mel Gibson quips about soundtracks.

Last stop is the Walt Disney Theater, which previews upcoming Disney and Touchstone films. Narrated by Disney Company Chairman Michael Eisner, it's an entertaining but obvious push for "what's just around the corner."

TIPS: The tour closes at dusk.

Here Come the Muppets ★★ Small children are mesmerized by this playful song-and-dance show starring their favorite Muppet characters. Hosted by the gracious Kermit (who sings "It's Not Easy Being Green"), the 14-minute musical features a solid performance by dolled-up Miss Piggy. Dr. Teeth and his rock 'n roll Electric Mayhem Band are a hoot.

TIPS: Not recommended for adults without children. There's rarely more than a half-hour wait, so visit during midday when other attractions are packed. Another note: In the preshow waiting area, everyone is usually scrunched together. If you're easily claustrophobic (or don't want to lose your kids), stay on the perimeter of the crowd near the building's entrance.

Honey, I Shrunk the Kids Adventure Zone ★★★ Based on the popular 1990 Touchstone movie, this "zone" is a giant playpen of distortions. As you wander through a family's yard, blades of grass loom two stories above and a lawn sprinkler seems like a menacing spaceship. Kids love scaling the 40-foot bumble bee and other colossal insects that tower everywhere.

SO YOU WANT TO BE IN THE MOVIES

Depending on what's filming at Disney–MGM Studios, you could get a part in a movie or television show. In the past, visitors have dressed outrageously for contestant roles on the game show "Let's Make a Deal." And for most of the year, kids can try for parts on the "Mickey Mouse Club."

Being chosen for a role requires advance planning, waiting in line (sometimes several hours)—and a lot of luck. Two days before you visit, call 407-824-4321 for a filming schedule and instructions on when and where to get in line. It's a first come, first served situation, so those closest to the front of the line have the best chances. If you're not chosen for a role, you could be part of a studio audience.

TIPS: A fantasyland for all ages. Because it's tucked away in a backlot area (near the New York City street scene) and because it opened in spring 1991 this attraction has minimal lines. However, as more visitors find out about it, I predict it will become a very popular place.

Teenage Mutant Ninja Turtles ★★ Every time these guys make an appearance, it's like Michael Jackson showing up: The street becomes a sea of shrieking kids who compete for autographs, photographs and up-close looks. The infamous turtles—Raphael, Michelangelo, Leonardo and Donatello—come roaring down Mickey's Avenue in their bright yellow buggy, deliver a 15-minute song-and-dance show and shout a lot of "Cowabunga, dudes!" If you're serious about getting a good view, pick up a performance schedule (available from most shops) and be there 15 minutes before show time. Performances are held about 12 times daily.

TIPS: If you're a ninja turtle fan, don't miss it. If you're not, stay clear during show time: The gridlock extends about two blocks.

The Animation Tour's hilarious film starring Walter Cronkite and Robin Williams was tough to film because Cronkite kept cracking up.

Studio Courtyard

A short stretch of concrete off Hollywood Boulevard, the courtyard is an art deco enclave with buildings washed in turquoise, yellow and rose. It's usually thronged with people waiting to get into its only attraction, the Animation Tour. There's also the Catwalk Bar and the Soundstage Restaurant, a clever place that looks part plaza, part hotel. The food's nothing special, but stop anyway to check out the dozens of chairs and chandeliers dangling from the ceiling.

Animation Tour ★★★★★ Housed in a piano-shaped building, this multifaceted tour provides the first-ever look at Disney's animation process. One of the park's most popular sights, it ranks as one of the best attractions in all of Disney World. From the history and techniques of animation to a look at working artists, the tour is truly a nostalgic and enlightening voyage.

The prelude is a gallery lined with original cels, or frames, from some of Disney's best-loved films, including 1937's *Snow White* and 1953's *Peter Pan.* There are also papier-mâché, wood and plaster models of characters from *Pinocchio, Beauty and the Beast* and *The Little Mermaid.* The room's centerpieces, though, are glistening reproductions of Disney's 32 Oscars—the most won by any film studio.

Between its theme park and movie costumes, Walt Disney World boasts the largest working wardrobe in the world.

From the gallery, visitors enter a cool theater for a delightful eight-minute film on animation. Called *Back to Neverland,* the crowd-pleaser stars maniacal Robin Williams and straight-faced Walter Cronkite. Williams is drawn into *Peter Pan* as a cartoon character, survives a skirmish with Captain Hook and the alligator, and gets rescued by Tinkerbell. Between Williams' hilarious one-liners and Cronkite's constant admonishing, you learn about cel making, layout artists, background artists, sound effects and much more.

Next is a stroll through studios where you watch Disney animators at their drafting tables. Particularly for first-timers, it's a fascinating sight: Headphones turned up and funky artwork everywhere, the artists sketch cels of familiar and yet-to-come cartoon characters. The tour progresses through each phase of animation, from clean-up (where rough sketches become line drawings) to effects (lightning, water, fire) and backgrounds (backdrops for the characters). To create a 24-minute film, the park's 70-plus animators must produce 34,650 drawings with at least 300 background scenes. For those worried about missing the animators on Saturdays and Sundays, there's always a group pulling the weekend shift.

The tour's finale is a dynamic, sentimental vignette of Disney's premier animated films. Shown in the plush Disney Classics Theater, the movie features great scenes from *Bambi, Snow White, Cinderella, Lady and the Tramp* and many others. Anyone who has ever enjoyed those enduring classics can't helped but be moved by this film.

Tips: If at all possible, take this tour before 10:30 a.m. After that, the wait is rarely under 45 minutes. Lines do typically shorten after 5 p.m.—but by then most of the animators have gone home. Not to be missed.

FIVE

The Rest of The World

Some people say the rest of Disney World is the best in the world. **115** Considering what "the rest" is, who could argue?

You have thick pine forests for pitching a tent and broad, clear lakes for taking a plunge. There are big and brassy nightclubs and tranquil rivers, drop-off water slides and one of the biggest swimming pools in Florida. And there's more: whimsical shops and backwoods hayrides, even an island for a zoo, a place so pristine and remote it's overlooked by most visitors.

There's so much to see and do you could easily spend a whole week taking in these six themed attractions that are truly the icing on the Disney cake. Spanning over 800 acres "the rest of the world" boasts Fort Wilderness, a vast, forested campground and outdoor play-ground. Nearby are River Country, a Tom Sawyer-style swimming hole, and Discovery Island, a lush zoological park where beautiful birds and animals roam. South of this natural isle is a *faux* tropical island, Typhoon Lagoon. Fashioned like a sand and palm tree paradise, the lagoon is a waterslide fantasyland. Then there's Pleasure Island, a pulsing pad of nightclubs, restaurants and shops on the edge. Next door, Disney Village Marketplace offers a lakeside menagerie of more shops and restaurants.

No doubt, the Disney Company has added these attractions over the years to capture even more of your time and money. But really, they give you more (and sometimes better) options. After an exhaust-ing day at the Magic Kingdom or Epcot, you can decompress at one of the smaller parks the next day. Many places put you out-of-doors and away from the computerized attractions of the big theme parks. And at two places, you get to wear your swimsuit. These minor parks also cost* less than the big parks and—with the exception of River Country and Typhoon Lagoon—don't stick you in long lines.

This easy-on-the-mind-and-wallet approach has attracted many locals who rarely venture into the big parks. Like them, once you discover the flip side of Disney World, you won't want to miss "the rest."

Fort Wilderness

Spread across 740 acres, ribboned with streams and canals, teeming with small animals and places to swim, bike, run and hide, this wooded wonderland is the best. Here at Fort Wilderness, fences are made of pine poles, bus stops are wood shingled, and trash cans look like tree stumps. Paved lanes, with names like Possum Path and Cottontail Curl, cut through miles of campsites surrounded by spidery slash pines. All the lanes lead to Bay Lake, where still, picturesque waters are rimmed in cypress trees and marshy reeds.

Fort Wilderness is the only attraction that looks a lot like it did when Disney bought it three decades ago. Unfortunately, the only reminders of the forest's first settlers, Seminole Indians, are a few totem poles outside a trading post. Inside the post, youngsters can buy coonskin caps and toy rifles. Fort Wilderness bus drivers add to the backwoods mood by talking with a twang and cracking corny camping jokes.

For families on a budget or who love the outdoors, the campground is a perfect place to stay (see Chapter Eight). After all, where else can you sleep under the trees, then have breakfast with Chip and Dale? And even if you don't camp here, be sure to visit. There are many activities for kids and spots where parents can take it easy. And everything is tuned to nature, from horseback riding and canoeing to just beaching it along the lake.

ARRIVAL

Whether you arrive by Disney bus or in your own car, it takes some time to get to the heart of Fort Wilderness. Driving a car, however, is the fastest and easiest way to go. Here are the various ways of getting there:

From the Magic Kingdom and Contemporary Resort: Take the scenic, 30-minute boat launch. Or, take the monorail to the Ticket and Transportation Center, then catch a Disney bus to Fort Wilderness. The monorail-bus trip takes 40 to 50 minutes.

From Epcot Center and the Grand Floridian Resort: Take the monorail to the Ticket and Transportation Center, then ride the Disney bus to Fort Wilderness. Traveling time: 40 to 50 minutes.

From all other Disney World locations: Take a Disney bus to the Ticket and Transportation Center, then transfer to the Fort Wilderness bus. From the Ticket and Transportation Center, the ride is 30 to 40 minutes.

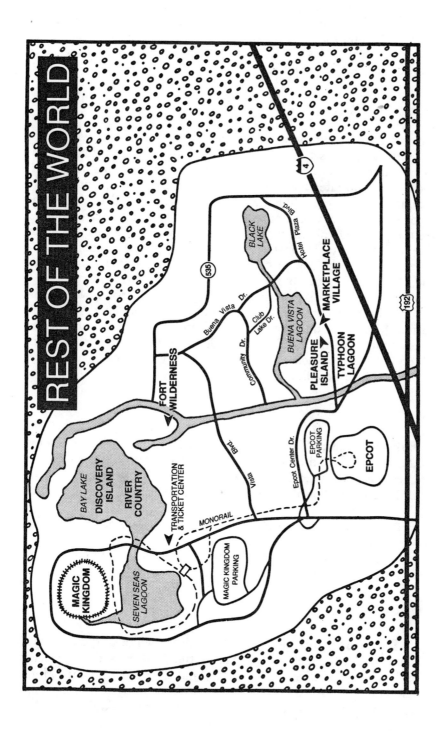

From area hotels not in Disney World: Most hotels provide a shuttle to the Ticket and Transportation Center. From there, take the bus.

By Car: From Route 4, take the exit for the Magic Kingdom (also Route 192) and follow the signs to Magic Kingdom. As soon as you pass through the Magic Kingdom toll plaza (and pay a parking fee), bear to the right. From here, you can follow the signs.

SIGHTSEEING STRATEGIES

Now that you're out in the woods, you might as well stay awhile. Stop by Fort Wilderness Lodge (407-824-2900) for maps, schedules and touring information. From here you'll take a bus to the main sights. It's about a ten-minute ride through the woods, with frequent stops for camping loops. Fort Wilderness is never really crowded, so you can enjoy the activities in any order at your leisure. Two musts for families are the petting farm and the horse stables, where you can join a trail ride. A few events (Hoop-Dee-Doo Revue, hayrides, campfires, etc.) are scheduled each day, so check the times before you go. Hayrides and campfires are open only to guests of Disney World resorts.

While you're here, you can take a one-hour excursion over to Discovery Island and/or visit River Country next door. There's a combination ticket for both attractions. One important note: River Country offers limited swimming for small children. If your kids are still in the water-wings stage, stick to the beach at Fort Wilderness. The water is shallow and, best of all, free.

NUTS & BOLTS

Baby Services: Changing tables are at the Pioneer Hall restrooms. Diapers, formula and other baby supplies are available at the Meadow and Settlement trading posts. Strollers are *not* available, so bring your own.

Babysitting: Available at the fort's KinderCare Learning Center. For reservations, call 407-827-5444.

Pets: Not allowed. However, you can leave yours at the kennel at the Fort Wilderness parking lot.

Lost Children/Lost and Found: Report lost children and lost and found articles to the Fort Wilderness Lodge.

WHAT TO SEE AND DO

Fort Wilderness Beach—A swath of silvery white sand edged with tall pine and oak trees, this is one of the prettiest spots in Disney World. The view of Space Mountain and the Contemporary Hotel across the water is spectacular. There's a shallow, sandy swimming area, playground and picnic area and shady hammocks for taking a snooze.

Marina—Right off the beach, here's where you hire a bass fishing guide or rent boats. If you're headed to Discovery Island, launches leave from the marina every ten minutes.

Petting Farm—Children can't get enough of these barnyard animals. All day, you'll see them chasing goats, ducks and peacocks, dirt and grass flying everywhere, until their little legs give out (the kids' legs, that is). Nestled under broad shade trees, the petting farm also features pony rides.

Tri-Circle-D Ranch—You know those neat horses that pull the streetcars down Main Street U.S.A.? They live here in a great big stable surrounded by pastures. A smithy, or blacksmith, cares for over a hundred Percheron and Belgian Draft horses and lets visitors take pictures while he works.

Horseback Riding, Bicycling and Canoeing—All three activities make great family excursions. If your children are at least nine years old, you can take the Fort Wilderness Trail Ride, a 45-minute guided walk through the woods. For reservations, stop by Pioneer Hall or call 407-824-2803.

Fort Wilderness has super bike paths. You can rent bicycles by the day or hour from the Bike Barn, located behind the Meadow Trading Post. If you're looking for an easy ride, rent an electric golf cart. The Bike Barn also has canoes for those anxious to explore Fort Wilderness' vast labyrinth of canals and streams.

Hayrides—A long, hay-stacked wagon, pulled by a pair of black Percherons, winds through the woods twice each night. It's the quintessential family outing, where kids bound around in the hay and parents share the day's ups and downs. At the end of the 45-minute ride, you've made good friends.

THE TREE THAT TAMED THE LAWN MOWER

At the foot of a spiraling pine tree, not far from the Fort Wilderness marina, rests a bizarre poem:

> *Too long did Billy Bowlegs*
> *Park his reel slow mower*
> *Alas, one warm and sunny day*
> *Aside a real fast grower*

Beside the poem, the rusted blades of a lawn mower are entwined in the trunk of the pine tree. It's a strange sight, for sure, but even stranger is that no one knows how the tree and mower got that way. Some cynics speculate that when Walt Disney bought the forest, the tree—fearing it would be bulldozed to make way for a theme park—snared the offensive machinery.

The food sold at River Country tastes bad with a capital B. Pack your own lunch; it's a lot cheaper anyway.

River Country

Any attraction where you can wear your swimsuit rates high in my book. River Country is, indeed, such a place. One of the best dern swimming holes around, it looks like a spot where Tom Sawyer and Huck Finn might have taken a dip. A six-acre cove of Bay Lake, rimmed in pine forest and white beach and cooled by breezes, it offers a sandy lagoon with boulders you actually can dive or slide from. A barrel bridge cuts across the lagoon to a lush island swirling with waterslides. All day, kids (and plenty of adults) rocket down the slides and—arms and legs flailing—cannon ball into the moss green water.

Next to the lagoon is one of Florida's biggest swimming pools: 330,000 gallons of crystal blue water flanked by more boulders and waterslides. There also are a toddler pool with a soft sand bottom, knee-deep water and four slides that go from super tame to kind of scary (for a tot). Just off the pools, a myriad of shady retreats let parents relax while keeping an eye on the kids.

ARRIVAL

River Country is adjacent to Fort Wilderness. To get there, follow the same instructions in Fort Wilderness Arrival and remember that it's not a quick trip from anywhere.

SIGHTSEEING STRATEGIES

It's a hefty walk from the bus stop to the heart of River Country. But once you're there, getting around is a breeze. The most important thing to know is when to go (and when not to). If possible, avoid River Country on summer weekends, when locals and tourists pack the place. The best time to visit is during fall or spring. If you do go during summer, arrive after 4 p.m., when crowds have thinned and admission is reduced. The park stays open until 7 or 8 p.m. in summer. Another tip: On crowded days, River Country often closes its doors by mid-morning. However, you'll still be admitted if you've purchased a ticket in advance. Also, be advised that aside from the toddler pool, swimming is limited for small children.

River Country's big swimming pool is heated in winter, though the park usually closes in January and February for a tuneup. Call 407-824-4321 for closing dates.

NUTS & BOLTS

Towels: You can bring your own or rent one. If you're staying at a hotel and don't want to hassle with wet towels, I recommend the rentals.

Showers, Dressing Rooms and Lockers: Showers and dressing rooms are provided. Lockers can be rented.

Coolers: Coolers are allowed, and highly recommended by this veteran visitor. Pack a lunch and plenty of thirst quenchers. Alcoholic beverages are prohibited, but beer is sold inside the park.

Pets: Not allowed. However, you can board them for at the nearby Fort Wilderness Kennel.

WHAT TO SEE AND DO

Mostly what you do at River Country is swim, read and bask in the sun (who can get enough?). For the more adventurous, there are also:

Waterslides and Raft Rides—Bay Cove has two water flume rides, including a short trip down 100 feet and a longer spiral down 260 feet. Starting at the top of a ridge called Whoop 'n Hollow Holler, you corkscrew around trees and boulders before blasting into the lagoon. If relaxation is your goal, ride Bay Cove's White Water Rapids, a leisurely inner-tube journey through foliage and calm pools.

Over at the big swimming pool, two slides do a 90-plus degree drop (you can't see the bottom from the top) and torpedo you into the water from seven feet up. Though not as scary as Typhoon Lagoon's slides, they'll still put your stomach where your throat is.

Unfortunately, River Country slides suffer the same disease as most Disney rides: LINES! The wait ranges from a few minutes during slow times to 60 minutes on summer weekends. In my opinion, anyone

---

THE LOW-DOWN ON RIVER COUNTRY ROCKS

If River Country's boulders look familiar, they should. Their creator is the same man who designed Big Thunder Mountain, the caves on Tom Sawyer Island and other Magic Kingdom rock wonders. Fred Joerger is his name, and fake rocks are his game. One exception is the pebbles strewn across River Country's boulders. Those babies come from Georgia and Carolina stream beds.

who waits an hour for a 30-second slide should have his head examined. Go when it's slow.

Swings, Climbs and other Fun Times—Smack in the middle of Bay Cove lagoon are a tire swing, boom swing, rope climb and cable ride. When you first get to River Country, they look so inviting that many people do a mad dash across the lagoon. There's rarely a long line for any of these, so play here when the slides back up. Kids love it when Goofy shows up in his long john swimsuit and starts swinging and climbing.

Nature Walk—If you long to hear the birds chirp, take a stroll along the short but scenic boardwalk. (The chirps, by the way, are coming from Discovery Island). The trail winds through a cypress swamp and along Bay Lake, with superb views of the Contemporary Hotel and Space Mountain in the distance.

Warning: Fort Wilderness and Discovery Island mosquitoes bite hard and often. Don't forget your repellent.

Discovery Island

Too often, visitors complain Discovery Island is too quiet compared to Disney's high-tech, high-volume attractions. But that's just the point. The lovely nature preserve offers a soothing reprieve from theme-park overload, a place to unwind and contemplate the "real" world. Instead of mechanical birds, you have real ones here that poke around thickets, flit between trees and carry on their lives almost as if you weren't around.

Ironically, the zoological haven was envisioned as a haven for the human species. When Disney bought the island in the 1960s, it was cleared and planted with palms, bamboo and other tropical vegetation from around the world. Lagoons were dredged and a wrecked ship was parked on the shore. The idea was to re-create the setting for *Treasure Island*, a sun-and-fun paradise for tourists. The plan was eventually abandoned, but the shipwreck and lush scenery remain. Now, the 11-acre island, framed by white sand, is etched with shady trails and damp hollows, fragrant flowers and ponds streaked by sunlight.

Most of Discovery Island's 120 animals are birds; the rest are quirky tamarins and lemurs (primates), Florida alligators and mighty Galapagos tortoises. The birds include flaming orange flamingos, bright scarlet ibis and others of flamboyant color. All day they chirp, caw, hoot, honk and purr, as if giving the world's funkiest musical recital. Perhaps the oddest sound comes from the kookaburra, an Australian kingfisher that lets loose a raucous laugh. Some of the feathered creatures live in aviaries or cages, but many roam free. Albino peacocks, for instance, parade about with lacy, white tails that look like bridal trains.

Like any zoo, Discovery Island is particularly exciting for children. One six-year-old visitor, enthralled by the dense foliage and bird noises, kept a lookout for "George of the Jungle." The many signs identifying plants make good tools for teaching children. And, the island is so small that older kids can explore on their own, giving parents a much-needed breather.

Discovery Island's aviary boasts one of the nation's largest breeding colony of scarlet ibis.

ARRIVAL

From the Magic Kingdom, Contemporary Resort, Polynesian Village, Grand Floridian Resort, River Country and Fort Wilderness: Take one of the canopied riverboat shuttles directly to Discovery Island.

If you're coming from anywhere else, the trip to Discovery Island will not be fast or easy. First you have to get to Fort Wilderness (see Fort Wilderness Arrival). Then take a Fort Wilderness bus to the Fort Wilderness Marina, where you purchase tickets and board a launch to the island. Launches leave every ten minutes.

SIGHTSEEING STRATEGIES

Because Discovery Island is small and rarely crowded, you can pretty much do as you please. Go anytime, though in the morning the island is cooler and practically empty. (Call 407-824-3784 for operating hours.) Pick up a map and guide at the Discovery Island Dock. There's only one trail (with a couple of side branches) that winds across the island. Along the way are lots of ponds, roosts and other nooks and crannies to explore. All are well-marked and on the map.

NUTS & BOLTS

Baby Services: Changing tables are provided at the two Discovery Island restrooms.

Stroller and Wheelchairs: Free strollers and wheelchairs are available at the dock.

Pets: Discovery Island's animals may welcome your pets, but the humans in charge won't. Leave your pets at the Fort Wilderness Kennel.

Picnicking: The island beach is an ideal place. You can bring a cooler, but you'll have to tote it around all day. Either pack a small knapsack or pick up sandwiches from the island's Thirsty Perch refreshment window. Ice cream and beer are also available at the Perch.

WHAT TO SEE AND DO

Bird Exhibits—Macaws, toucans, cockatoos and other big brilliant birds live in large cages sprinkled across the island. One of the most bizarre-looking is the rhinoceros hornbill, whose giant orange bill protrudes *above* its eyes. If you have small children, find the moluccan lorries: The most colorful of all parrots, the Australian birds are red and purple and black all over.

Discovery Island Bird Shows—Two different shows are offered several times daily. The first is a wacky parrot presentation where the birds do flips, stand on their heads, whistle tunes and wave bye-bye. The second explores the mysteries of birds of prey. Hawks, owls and king vultures are the stars. For show times, check at the dock.

Trumpeter Springs—Loud trumpet music (or is that a bird call?) signals you've reached Trumpeter Springs. Here you'll find trumpeter swans that, true to their name, honk like there's no tomorrow.

Avian Way—Covering a half-acre, this aviary is so big you forget you're enveloped by mesh (hopefully the birds do, too). It's a lush place zigzagged with streams and vines and filled with birds of dazzling color. The scarlet ibis is such a penetrating red that explorers once mistook it for blood on the trees. And the roseate spoonbill, whose bill is in fact spoon-shaped, has a long, white neck, pink body and rose-colored wings and tail.

Tortoise Beach—Children are fascinated by these giant creatures that seem plucked from the Stone Age. They lumber across the sand and munch on melons, apples and other garden delights. Long endangered, tortoises grow to 500 pounds and live as long as 150 years.

Typhoon Lagoon's surf and wave pools hold 2.75 million gallons of water.

Typhoon Lagoon

On a typical day at Typhoon Lagoon, you will drift along a slow river and whirl down a twisting, turning slide. You will bodysurf some waves and snorkel with sharks, then dry out on a palmy beach. You will climb a mountain called Mayday and ride a slide called Humunga Kowabunga. This will scare the smithereens out of you, but you will

THE REST OF THE WORLD

insist on riding again. You will climb many steps and wait in many lines. And you will get tired, very tired.

And so it goes at Typhoon Lagoon, whose tranquil setting belies its frenetic activity. The Disney-proclaimed "world's ultimate water park" is truly the ultimate, certainly when it comes to fast slides, wet times and lovely surroundings. The 56 acres are a glorious oasis of jungly hills, sugar white sand, thatched huts, wooden bridges, meandering creeks and swimming pools that could cover two football fields. Add to that the seemingly endless special effects, right down to the thunderous whitecaps created by wave machines. And then there are the slides: corkscrew slides and whitewater slides, storm slides and speed slides that put you airborne at 30 mph.

The idea behind Typhoon Lagoon is that the island is recovering from a terrible storm. Surfboards poke through palm trees, buildings are half-cocked, and a shrimp boat named Miss Tilly is impaled on a volcano. The ragged boat and the 85-foot "volcano," called Mount Mayday, form the showpiece of the lagoon. Every half hour Mayday releases a torrent of water, supposedly trying to eject ole Tilly.

There is a terrific energy at Typhoon Lagoon. The whitewater rapids and heaving waves, shrieks of children and pound of steel drums, and screams of surfers and sliders create a maelstrom of constant activity. Of course, whether you choose to roar down a slide at breakneck speed or toast on the beach and swill a drink is completely up to you.

At Typhoon Lagoon, the big trees sporting bright yellow blooms are called scrambled egg trees.

ARRIVAL

If at all possible, drive to Typhoon Lagoon. It's much faster and easier than Disney transportation, and parking is free.

From the Magic Kingdom, Epcot Center, Contemporary Resort, Polynesian Resort or Grand Floridian: Take the monorail to the Ticket and Transportation Center, then transfer to a bus going directly to Typhoon Lagoon.

From Fort Wilderness or the Caribbean Beach Resort: Take a bus directly to Typhoon Lagoon.

From any other Disney World location: Take a Disney bus to the Ticket and Transportation Center, then transfer to the bus to Typhoon Lagoon.

By Car: From Route 4, take the exit for Epcot Center. Follow the signs to Typhoon Lagoon. The park is about half a mile from Route 4.

SIGHTSEEING STRATEGIES

Typhoon Lagoon is easy to navigate, once you pick up a map. The real problem is that Typhoon Lagoon gets unbearably crowded. To me, rubbing elbows in a water park is the pits. The best time to go is the spring or fall, or on Mondays during the summer. Sunday mornings, when locals are at church, is also crowdless. If you must go on a summer weekend, arrive 30 minutes before opening time. This gives you time to park, buy tickets and rent an inner tube before mass water mania starts. And for the first hour, slides and other rides have minimal lines. You should also know that, during summer and holidays, Typhoon Lagoon often reaches capacity (7200) and closes by mid-morning. When this happens, lines at all the slides and raft rides have an hour-plus wait.

Once you're there, set up camp. If you have toddlers, the beach near Ketchakiddee Creek children's area is best. For a mix of sun and shade, seek out the grassy areas around Getaway Glen. The glen is fairly quiet and has picnic tables. If you're into people-watching, plant yourself front and center of the surf pool. With teenagers and grandparents competing for body surfing action, you'll get quite a show.

Your first Typhoon Lagoon ride should be Castaway Creek. The inner-tube cruise rambles around the park, providing an excellent orientation. After Castaway Creek, you can enjoy the pools and rides in any order.

ADVENTURES FOR KIDS

*What child would pass up a chance to ride in a boat, trudge through the woods and pet friendly animals? At **Kidventure**, children can do all this—plus be with other kids. The guided tours, for ages 8 through 14, take children behind-the-scenes at Fort Wilderness and Discovery Island. The four-hour excursions include lunch and a souvenir photo and cost $30 per child. They're held daily during the summer and sporadically the rest of the year. Call 407-824-3784 for tour times and reservations.*

*Disney World also offers full-day tours for kids ages 10 to 15. Called **Wonders of Walt Disney World**, they feature three excursions: (1) Exploring Disney's 7500-acre nature preserve (2) Studying Disney architecture, landscaping, costumes and animation (3) Taking a backstage look at Disney entertainment, including tours of rehearsals and makeup and costume rooms. Tours cost $75 per child and include picture manuals, lunch and use of a camera all day. Days and times vary; call 407-345-5860.*

River Country and Typhoon Lagoon usually close on rainy days. Call 407-824-4321 to make sure.

NUTS & BOLTS

Baby Services: Restrooms are equipped with changing tables. Strollers are not provided, so bring your own.

Wheelchairs: They're available, free for the day, at Guest Relations.

Towels and Life Jackets: You can bring your own towel, but it's more convenient to rent one. After paying over $18 to get in, I say towels should be free. If you're not a good swimmer, life jackets are provided free (there is a refundable deposit).

Showers, Dressing Rooms and Lockers: I love the showers here; they're under a thatched roof. So are the dressing rooms and lockers; lockers can be rented.

Shoes: Even if you don't have tender feet, it's a good idea to wear shoes. There's a lot of concrete inside the park, and some of the footpaths are rough on the soles. Flip flops will do just fine.

Coolers: Bring a cooler filled with thirst quenchers and eats (sliced fruit tastes great when you first come from the water). Glass containers and alcoholic beverages not permitted. However, beer and frozen rum drinks are sold at several spots.

Inner Tubes: You should only rent an inner tube if you want to use it in the wave and surf pools. Otherwise, tubes are provided for all the raft rides. To avoid long lines, be at the rental counter first thing in the morning. You cannot bring your own tube into Typhoon Lagoon.

Pets: Not allowed.

WHAT TO SEE AND DO

Castaway Creek—Parents, this inner-tube ride is for you. A long, slow float along a picturesque creek, it's relaxation at its best. The water is three feet deep and crystal clear, and the scenery is imaginative. You'll wind through caverns and tropical greenery, bypass shipwrecks, barrels and abandoned coolers (from the typhoon, remember?) and cruise right under two waterfalls. Along the way, you'll get a great overview of Typhoon Lagoon. There are several spots where you can bail out for a break, then get back in again. Without any stops, the trip takes about 30 minutes.

Surf and Wave Pools—Sprawled across the heart of Typhoon Lagoon, these swimming pools are where the action is. Technically, there are three pools: (1) Typhoon Lagoon, a surf pool that sits right in the middle (2) Blustery Bay, a wave pool on the left of the lagoon (as you

Wanna go really fast on a waterslide? Lay flat and cross your ankles, then cross your arms over your chest and arch your back. Happy flying!

face Mount Mayday) and (3) Whitecap Cove wave pool, to the right of the lagoon. Serious surfers hang out in Typhoon Lagoon, waiting for the ten-footers that come barreling out every 90 seconds (no surfboards allowed—it's bodysurfing only). For those who like their waves less ferocious, Blustery Bay and Whitecap Cove offer four-foot swells where you can swim or bob in an inner tube.

Ketchakiddee Creek—A water version of a schoolyard playground, Ketchakiddee has dozens of places to romp and get wet. Children can climb barrels, explore damp caves, slide down a whale (he even toots water from his spout) and ride baby inner tubes down baby rapids. A favorite spot is the bubbling sand ponds, where kids can sit in gurgling waters. To play, children must be four feet or shorter and be accompanied by an adult.

Humunga Kowabunga—When people talk about Typhoon Lagoon, the first thing they mention is Humunga Kowabunga. Little wonder, since these two speed slides are meant to scare the living daylights out of you. Situated side by side, they each plummet from Mount Mayday, a vertical fall through caves and into the deep blue yonder. Average speed is 30 mph. And average length of ride? Three seconds. To ride, you must be at least four feet tall and not be pregnant.

Storm Slides—What great names these three slides have: Jib Jammer, Rudder Buster and Stern Burner. Designed for the chickens who won't go on Humunga Kowabunga, they offer a sinuous journey through caves, under waterfalls and around boulders. Each 300-foot ride is fairly fast—20 mph—and offers some nice scenery.

Raft Rides—These are incredibly fun. All three raft rides—Gangplank Falls, Mayday Falls and Keelhaul Falls—corkscrew down the face of Mount Mayday and send you swishing and twirling through caves and around rocks and trees. None are really scary, though Mayday has the most twists and turns. Mayday and Keelhaul are one-person inner-tube rides, while Gangplank is a three- to four-person ride in inflatable rafts. Gangplank is ideal for families, though if you don't have enough people, the attendants will pair you with other riders. You must be four feet tall to ride Mayday and Keelhaul; Gangplank has no height restrictions. Pregnant women are prohibited from all three rides.

Shark Reef Snorkeling Tank—What a drag this place is. First you have to wait in a crummy line, and then be rushed through a tank swarming with other snorkelers (the attendants practically time your swim). On rare occasions when Shark Reef is not crowded, it's worth a dive. The reef is fake, but the thousands of colorful fish—including small leopard and nurse sharks—are very real. With no lines, you can spend as long as you like chasing the fish and exploring the pool's sunken tanker. Landlubbers can view the pool from porthole windows inside the tanker.

Special notes: Free snorkeling gear is furnished; you cannot bring your own. Attendants provide a quick snorkeling lesson. For those who want proof of their dive, underwater cameras are available for rent. To keep the algae out, Shark Reef is kept at a chilly 72 degrees—18 degrees colder than the rest of "Typhoon Lagoons" waters. The Reef is usually closed from November through April.

Pleasure Island

Pleasure Island is where you go to get wild—at night, anyway. During the day, when nightclubs are closed, the six-acre entertainment mecca is a serene spot to shop, eat and stroll with the kids. But come 7 o'clock, it cranks with rib-rattling music, brilliant lights and a sea of people jammin' in the streets. A mod mix of painted metal, brick streets, neon signs and trendy dressers, Pleasure Island is Disney's hip zone, its outer edge. The place boasts six nightclubs, four restaurants, ten shops and ten movie theaters.

One of the best things about Pleasure Island nightlife is there's just as much happening outside as inside. Waiters sling drinks at curbside bars, and street vendors hawk outrageous gifts. Rock 'n roll bands and

---

WHICH IS WETTER?

While at Disney World you want to visit a water park. But Disney has two: River Country and Typhoon Lagoon. Which one is better? Or perhaps you should ask: which one is wetter?

If you have small children, River Country is. There's a spacious toddler's lagoon here, and the atmosphere is more laid-back. However, River Country can't compete with Typhoon Lagoon when it comes to thrilling waterslides and elaborate scenery. Built back in 1976, the six-acre River Country is homier and less crowded. Typhoon Lagoon, which opened in 1989, is seven times the size of River Country. Plus, it's high tech and happenin'. (In other words, older children and teenagers will insist on going to the lagoon.)

If the family splits on where to go, try this: Spend an afternoon at River Country, and save Typhoon Lagoon for a nightcap after a big day at a theme park. (Both are included in Disney's five-day plus super pass). With the water and mountain illuminated, the lagoon is beautiful in the evening—and less crowded.

lithe dancers—wearing next to nothing—perform on outdoor stages. Here's where locals and tourists really mix—the high schoolers and grandparents and yuppies. And here's where nightly New Years Eve street parties are held. Fireworks blast above the island, confetti fills the air and laser strobes sear the night sky, sending flying colors for miles around. For further information, see Chapter Eight.

Although there are no rules against it, Pleasure Island at night is no place for kids. Those 18 and older are allowed in all the clubs, but you must be 21 to drink. Some clubs do permit those under 18 to enter if they are accompanied by an adult.

ARRIVAL

By car, it's easy to get to Pleasure Island. There's plenty of free parking, but it's a hike from your car to the main gate. If you're arriving by Disney bus, allow at least 30 minutes from your Disney hotel.

From the Magic Kingdom, Epcot Center, Contemporary Resort, Polynesian Resort or Grand Floridian: Take the monorail to the Ticket and Transportation Center, then transfer to a bus going directly to Pleasure Island.

From Fort Wilderness or the Caribbean Beach Resort: Take a bus directly to Pleasure Island.

From any other Disney World location: Take a Disney bus to the Ticket and Transportation Center, then transfer to the bus to Pleasure Island.

By Car: From Route 4, take the exit for Epcot Center and follow the signs for Pleasure Island. The island is about three-fourths of a mile from Route 4.

BOATING, ANYONE?

No one should come to Florida without getting in a boat, and Disney World has plenty of 'em. Most cruise the 200-acre Seven Seas Lagoon (the one you always see from the monorail) and the lovely 450-acre Bay Lake, which borders Fort Wilderness. Depending on your fancy, you can rent anything from a water sprite (small speedboat) or pedal boat to a canoe or sailboat. Motorized pontoon boats, also called flotebotes, are ideal for families. They hold either 6 or 12 people, are easy to drive and have bench seats and a canopy for shady, relaxing sightseeing.

Boats are rented by the half-hour or hour and are available at several locations. **Fort Wilderness Marina** *and* **Disney Village Marketplace Marina** *have water sprites, flotebotes and pedalboats. Fort Wilderness also rents sailboats and waterski boats, including driver and equipment. In addition, several Disney resorts rent boats. Call 407-824-4321 for rental locations and prices.*

SIGHTSEEING STRATEGIES

One Pleasure Island ticket gets you in all the nightclubs, so you can come and go as you like. The nightclubs, restaurants and shops are all on one street, but the movie theaters are located off the island, across a short bridge. It's easy to get around, but pick up a map at the ticket window or from any club or restaurant.

Trumpeter swans, the largest swans in the world, were once hunted to near extinction.

Disney Village Marketplace

I hope you're not going to Disney World just to shop. But for those who can't resist a quick spree, there's the Disney Village Marketplace. Next to Pleasure Island, it's a fanciful place with wood-shingled buildings draped along a lake. Little speedboats zip across the water, and lyrical music floods the whole area. The 17 shops feature a slew of items, from pricey toys and Christmas decor to surfing duds. Mickey Mouse has his own store and restaurant and naturally roams the village every day.

Even if you're not a shopper, the market is a good place to relax. During midday when the theme parks are most crowded, it's quiet here. You can window-shop, have a cocktail along the lake or rest on a waterfront bench. When the kids get antsy, there's a nice playground in front of Chef Mickey's Restaurant. For further information, see Chapter Eight.

To help you explore, pick up a map and directory from any shop.

ARRIVAL

To get to the marketplace, see Pleasure Island Arrival. The same Disney buses make stops at both places. Also, for those driving to the marketplace, parking is free.

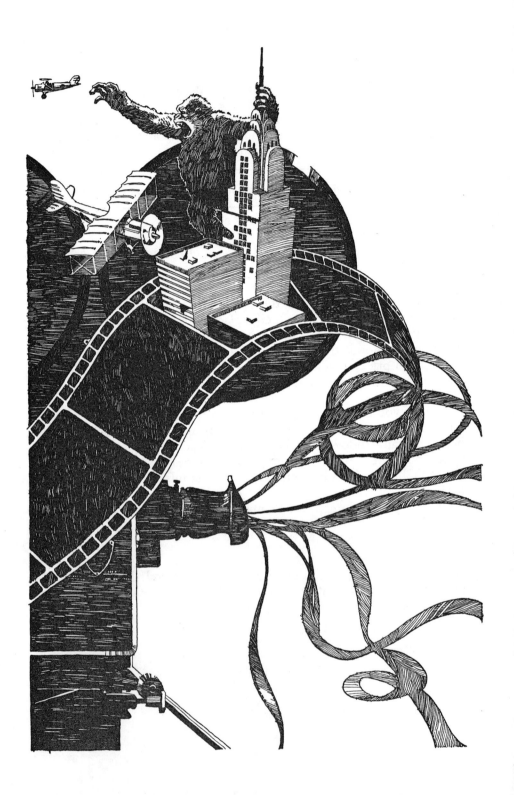

SIX

Universal Studios

With a cast of characters such as Mickey Mouse, Cinderella and **133** Shamu the killer whale, it was only logical that Orlando would eventually go Hollywood. Disney–MGM Studios got the film rolling when it opened in 1989, but it was Universal Studios that a year later staged the savviest movie coup outside Tinsel Town.

In classic Hollywood style, the film giant scooped up a patch of Orlando pasture and sand pits and cast it with mythical characters and places and electrifying scenes from great American movies. Sprawled across these 444 acres is a $600-million movie mecca of imitation earthquakes, murder mysteries, cartoon capers and time travels all reeled into one sizzling special-effects bonanza.

If Hollywood is one big fantasy, Universal Studios is one big set within the fantasy. For here virtually everything happens on a set. There's the seaside town straight from *Jaws*, the gritty 1930s Manhattan terrorized by King Kong and the damp forests roamed by E.T. There's also Norman Bates' *Psycho* house, Louisiana's bayou, L.A.'s chic Rodeo Drive and the streets of San Francisco.

More than four times the size of Disney–MGM Studios, Universal is the largest motion picture and television studio outside Hollywood. It boasts 40 elaborate set streets, six sound stages, 14 rides and shows, 17 eateries and 25 shops.

Technically, the park is split into six different theme or backlot areas, though to the eye they appear as a single fluid stroke of an artist's brush. The glass block, buff-colored stucco and gilded marble of Hollywood mix with the painted metal, circus-style canopies and grand palms at the adjacent Expo Center. The Expo buildings rim a Pacific-blue lagoon shared by San Francisco's floating tin shacks and weathered wharfs. The city by the bay spills into the New England seaside town of Amity, dotted with shuttered cottages and carnival vendors.

Sea scenes easily give way to a New York cityscape of brownstone walkups, Broadway billboards and high-toned shops. A nearby warehouse district, called Production Central, is a minimalist's vision of blank streets and slate-gray buildings with cinema billboards parked on the front. Around the corner is The Front Lot, a parade of pastel-washed facades, art deco curves and arches and glass-front eateries that welcome visitors to Universal Studios Florida.

Snazzier and slightly bigger than its Hollywood counterpart, Universal Studios Florida owes at least some of its sparkle to moviemaking genius Steven Spielberg. As the studios' creative consultant, Spielberg helped craft rides fueled with action, shows offering insight into moviemaking, and a landscape shaded with surrealism. Universal owes most of its kid appeal to Nickelodeon, the children's television network that moved its headquarters here in mid-1990. All day every day, the network produces clever and zany kids' shows and offers peeks at its state-of-the-art facility.

Since Universal Studios opened in 1989, its rides have become notorious for their long lines. But anyone who has felt the mystique of *E.T.*, the wackiness of Yogi Bear, or the white-knuckle thrill of *Back to the Future* knows Universal's rides are worth the wait. And though the rides and shows are the main events here, it's the street sets that prove to be the true flights of fantasy. Like Hollywood footprints, they offer a nostalgic journey from one film to the next.

Universal's magical street sets put visitors behind and in front of the camera. Virtually every day, it's possible to witness a motion picture or television show being filmed somewhere in the park. It's also possible (though not as probable) to land a role as an extra or an audience guest. For most people, though, simply absorbing all the Hollywood imagery and nuances is truly intoxicating enough. There's a certain excitement, a childlike elation, in knowing that the line between illusion and reality runs very thin here indeed.

WHAT SHOULD WE RIDE NEXT?

It's midday, and you've ridden Back to the Future, E.T. and Hanna-Barbera. What next? To find out which attractions have the shortest (and longest) lines, check the billboard in front of Mel's Drive-In in Hollywood. The marquee lists each Universal Studios attraction with its approximate waiting time and advice on when to see it. I found that several posted times underestimated the real waits by five to ten minutes, though in all fairness it's tough to keep up when line lengths can change drastically in a matter of seconds.

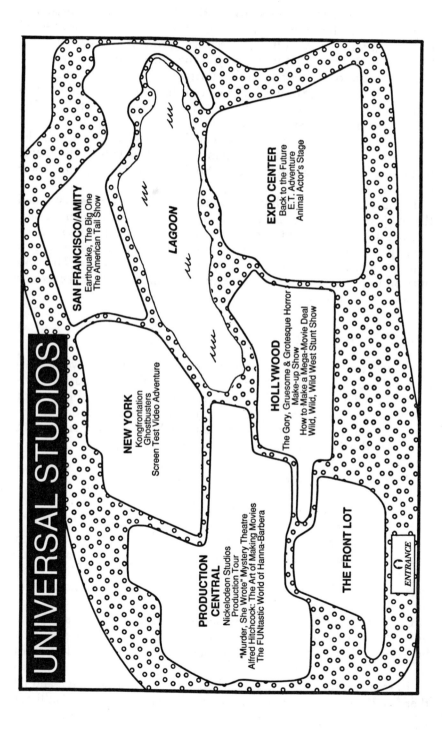

UNIVERSAL STUDIOS

SAN FRANCISCO/AMITY
Earthquake, The Big One
The American Tail Show

LAGOON

EXPO CENTER
Back to the Future
E.T. Adventure
Animal Actor's Stage

NEW YORK
Kongfrontation
Ghostbusters
Screen Test Video Adventure

HOLLYWOOD
The Gory, Gruesome & Grotesque Horror
Make-up Show
How to Make a Mega-Movie Deal
Wild, Wild, Wild West Stunt Show

PRODUCTION
CENTRAL
Nickelodeon Studios
Production Tour
"Murder, She Wrote" Mystery Theatre
Alfred Hitchcock: The Art of Making Movies
The FUNtastic World of Hanna-Barbera

THE FRONT LOT

ENTRANCE

ARRIVAL

From area hotels: Most hotels provide shuttle service to Universal Studios, either on the hour or every two or three hours. Disney World hotels, naturally, don't offer this service. However, **Mears Motor Shuttle** (407-423-5566) will take you there from any Disney resort. Universal Studios is about ten miles northwest of Disney World.

By Car: Universal Studios is just east of the intersection of Route 4 and Florida's Turnpike. From Route 4, take exit 29 or exit 30B. The studios' main entrance is off Kirkman Road.

You'll pay a parking fee and be directed to one of 7100 spaces in the studios' parking lot. From here, trams will deliver you to the scenic main gate where a giant Universal Studios globe gently spins over erupting fountains.

Because of its mammoth size, Universal Studios is rarely so crowded that it closes its doors. Still, getting there early can save several hours standing in line. It's best to arrive 30 minutes before the park's scheduled opening time so you can park your car, purchase tickets (if you don't already have them) and pick up maps and brochures. This will put you in perfect position to see Universal's most popular attractions as soon as the park opens.

SIGHTSEEING STRATEGIES

In an ideal touring situation, you would leisurely enter Universal Studios and linger along the picturesque Front Lot, then stroll down Hollywood Boulevard. But such is not reality in the jungle of theme-park ride warfare. If you're going to avoid megalines, you have to get there early, hightail it past all the scenic stuff, and catch a few rides right away. Based on popular appeal and location of each attraction, I recommend riding in the following order:

(1) Back to the Future
(2) E.T. Adventure
(3) The FUNtastic World of Hanna-Barbera

If you ride these three before 10 a.m., pat yourself on the back: You've just saved two to three hours standing in line. Now you can relax and explore the rest of Universal. To orient yourself, head over to Production Central and take the Production Tour. It provides a good overview of Universal Studios and is a relaxing way to spend the late morning.

Other touring tips: It's best to see all of one theme area (Hollywood, New York, etc.) before moving on to the next. The park is so big you won't want to backtrack, particularly with small children and a stroller in tow.

To save valuable time, decide where you want to eat lunch and be there by 11:30 a.m. Likewise, plan to eat dinner at 4:30 p.m. You'll not only miss the 5:30 dinner traffic jam but you'll be ready for the 7 p.m. Dynamite Nights Stunt Spectacular boat show in The Lagoon. If you plan to dine at Studio Stars or Lombard's Landing, Universal's most popular restaurants, make reservations early in the day. Or you can call 407-363-8000 up to several days in advance.

NUTS & BOLTS

Stroller and Wheelchair Rentals: Available just inside the main entrance, next to Southeast Bank.

Baby Services: Located at Guest Relations, just inside the main entrance, and at First Aid, behind Louie's Italian Restaurant between New York and San Francisco. Diaper changing tables are available in every restroom.

Lockers: There are two sets of lockers: inside the park next to the exit area and outside the park next to the group entrance. Lockers cost 50 cents each time you use them.

Pets: Pets are not allowed in Universal Studios. However, for a daily fee you can board them at the kennels just outside the main entrance, next to the parking toll plaza.

Lost Children: Report lost children to Guest Relations, located just inside the main entrance.

Package Pickup: This convenient, free service lets you send all your purchases to Guest Relations, then pick them up at the end of the day. Just notify the sales clerk at any Universal store that you want package pickup.

Lost & Found: Located at Guest Relations.

Banking: Southeast Bank, located just inside the main entrance, provides credit-card cash advances, travelers-check services and currency exchange. You'll also find an automatic teller machine. Open 9 a.m. to 6 p.m. Monday through Saturday, 9 a.m. to 3 p.m. on Sunday.

CHILD SWAPPING

When you see a sign that says "Child Swapping," don't panic: It's just Universal's way of letting both parents ride the scary rides. This clever system offers an area outside each attraction where one parent stays with the kids while the other experiences the ride. The parent who has just ridden then "swaps" with the other parent so he or she can ride. And, since the first parent already waited in line, the second goes right to the front!

Child swapping comes in handy on attractions such as Back to the Future, where children shorter than 46 inches aren't allowed to ride, and The Gory, Gruesome and Grotesque Horror Make-Up Show, which sometimes frightens small children.

GETTING AROUND

By far the largest individual Florida theme park, Universal Studios sprawls. Even during low season when lines are minimal, it takes at least two days to see everything these 444 acres have to offer. Unlike Disney–MGM Studios, where two-thirds of the park is accessible to visitors only by guided tour, nearly all of Universal can be explored at leisure.

On a map, Universal Studios looks like a boxy letter C getting ready to take a gulp of water. The water is The Lagoon, and the C is made up of six different theme areas that gather around The Lagoon. At the bottom crook of the C is The Front Lot, punctuated by the palm-lined main entrance with its grand Universal Studios archway. The bottom of the C curves out into Hollywood and then the Expo Center. Along the back of the C is Production Central, where vast buildings house movie and television production stages and rides. New York and San Francisco/Amity make up the top of the C.

It's a good idea to establish a meeting place in case your party gets split up. The best spot is in front of Mel's Drive-In, a flashy art deco eatery on a corner of Hollywood Boulevard in (where else?) Hollywood.

The Front Lot

What better way to dive into film fantasy than through rose-colored scenery? This small but sassy place offers a host of chrome and glass block, crimson balloon awnings, bleached gray buildings and ledges that snake across facades. Straddling a street corner, The Boulangerie alfresco café tempts bypassers with whiffs of espresso and fresh-baked croissants. At the nearby Fudge Shoppe, women in pinafores stir huge vats of gooey chocolate and advertise "variety platters" of the sweet stuff.

But behind all the niceties, The Front Lot is mostly business. There are no attractions here; rather, the place is a catch-all for visitor affairs such as stroller, wheelchair and locker rentals, lost and found, foreign-language interpretation and banking. Before you start touring, stop by Guest Relations for brochures, maps and schedules of the day's entertainment and filmings.

Hollywood

From The Front Lot, Hollywood Boulevard angles off into dreamland. Here in this fantasy factory called Hollywood are star-studded sidewalks, hat-shaped shops, posters of cheeky movie stars and elaborate facades that seem styled by a magician. Soaring palm trees cast

Each year, the Horror Make-Up Show uses about 365 straight-edge razors, 912 quarts of stage blood and 547 gallons of blood and guts (employing a secret recipe that mixes shrimp sauce, oatmeal and red dye).

leafy shadows across the rosy pavement, and strollers step in tune to the theme song from "Mr. Ed."

Many Southern California trademarks have been dreamily reproduced, including the Beaux-Arts-style Beverly Wilshire Hotel and Schwab's soda fountain with its timeworn penny scale parked out front. From the legendary Sunset Strip there's Ciro's nightclub and the Garden of Allah, a tranquil cluster of red-tiled stucco buildings rimmed in silky soft grass and flowers in fat clay pots. Chic shops boast names such as The Dark Room and It's a Wrap, and the spaceship-shaped Mel's Drive-In boasts a slew of gleaming '50s "cruisin'" cars. All day long, family members take snapshots in front of these snazzy locales.

Of all Universal's street scenes, Hollywood's seem to evoke the most passion and intrigue. It's not unusual to hear comments such as "Is it really like this?" or "Take a long look—this is as close as *you'll* ever get to Hollywood!" Maybe it's the human psyche reveling in the ultimate world of make-believe. Or perhaps it's because everyone— regardless of age or background—wants a piece of the camera.

Unfortunately, the attractions in Hollywood are Universal's worst. My advice is to explore Hollywood's street sets, take in the Wild, Wild, Wild West Stunt Show, skip the duds and head over to the Expo Center.

The Gory, Gruesome & Grotesque Horror Make-Up Show ★★
Guts and gore have always had a way with American filmgoers, so you'd expect this to be a hit attraction. Sadly, unless you're between 8 and 18 and love gross-outs, this show is less entertaining than a B horror flick. Presented in a comfortable theater and hosted by a zealous Universal employee, the show aims to imaginatively divulge the special effects in some of Hollywood's grisliest scenes. Instead, it offers a dull and disjointed series of failed shock-attempts: wrist slashings, bullet hits, torsoless heads and headless torsos. You learn how an actor's mouth became a roach motel in the movie *Creep Show*, how heads spun 360 degrees in *The Exorcist*, and how man turned wolf in *American Werewolf in London*. The best parts of the show are the classic clips from these movies and others such as *Gorillas in the Mist* and *The Fly*. And, though it all sounds rude and crude, most of the demonstrations are done in cornball fashion.

Tips: Some preschoolers are frightened by the show's gory details, while older kids love this gross stuff. For infants, the cool, dark theater is a good place to take a quick snooze.

How to Make a Mega-Movie Deal ★ This ripoff show would be better named "How to avoid spending a boring and insulting 15 minutes in a theme park." In a blatant case of corporate advertising parading as a theme-park attraction, AT&T has concocted a story about a guy who works his way from mail boy to corporate executive at Universal Studios. The young man, played by a Tom Cruise lookalike, does this by convincing Universal's head honcho to use various AT&T services. Guests see several short films that tell this hackneyed rags-to-riches fable, then visit video kiosks that hype AT&T.

TIPS: If you're a glutton for punishment, visit this banal attraction during the middle of the day when other rides are jammed—this one's never crowded. One to be missed.

Wild, Wild, Wild West Stunt Show ★★★★ Here, a cowboy named Clod Hopper and his brother Cole are testing their gun-slinging, bar-brawling skills. The Hoppers do pull some outrageous stunts, like hurtling off highrises and blasting a town with dynamite. Stunt secrets and clips from classic westerns are featured in this 15-minute, hair-raising show, held continually each day.

TIPS: Small children may be frightened by gunshots and explosions, but teenagers generally love the show.

With box office and video rental receipts topping $500 million, E.T. is the biggest movie money maker of all time.

Expo Center

This brilliant, bubbling place is a vision of vast metal buildings with candy-cane stripes, circus-style canopies, thick stands of palms and fat columns painted like barber's poles. Despite its moniker, the area's only real reference to a World's Fair Exposition is a strand of international flags and a food bazaar peddling Greek gyros alongside Asian egg rolls and German bratwurst. Most of the scenery here looks colorfully futuristic, though some sights are a study in contrasts. The broken down Psycho House, for instance, broods atop a spooky hill right next to the flashy, guitar-shaped Hard Rock Café. At night, heavy metal music pours through the pitch black house tainted by memories of Hollywood-brand murders.

But it's the rides, not the scenery, that keep the Expo Center thronged with people virtually every second. Many visitors are clamoring to see Back to the Future, a time-travel ride lodged in a warehouse-like building splashed with piercing color. Others are streaming into E.T. for a poignant journey through shadowy woods. Kids love

Before you hop into your DeLorean in Back to the Future, *notice the license plate: It reads "Outatime."*

this ride, as well as the nearby Animal Actor's Stage, where lovable creatures stage clever tricks.

Indeed, the Expo Center is a favorite of families. There's the Animal Crackers restaurant for young picky eaters, E.T.'s Toy Closet shop and the Animal House store lined with stuffed Pink Panthers and Bugs Bunnies. Best of all, there are plenty of umbrella-topped resting places where parents can unwind after waiting in line for all those rides.

Back to the Future ★★★★★ In the cutthroat world of theme-park one-upmanship, Universal has one-upped everybody with Back to the Future. This flight-simulator-style ride is a super symphony of speed, fantasy, terror and mind-blowing special effects. When it's over, your throat aches because you've unwittingly screamed so long and hard. It's the kind of ride where 12-year-olds do high-fives at the end, then turn to Mom and announce: "We're going again!"

Based on the *Back to the Future* smash-hit trilogy, the four-minute journey hurls you through centuries at supersonic speed. The action begins in a briefing room where bug-eyed scientist Doc Brown tells guests that Biff (the movie's bully) has come back from the past. As a "time-travel volunteer," you must find him and send him back to 1955. Biff dares you, his big-oaf face filling a video screen and taunting: "What are you looking at, butt head!" Eight riders then climb into a fancy DeLorean Time Machine, which spews liquid-nitrogen fog that looks like ice on fire. Your car eerily floats out of its garage, and suddenly you're enveloped by a room-size video screen that takes you on a brain-blasting visual trip: You tumble down waterfalls, soar off cliffs, ricochet around caverns and canyons, and get chomped and spit out by a growling Tyrannosaurus Rex. In the meantime, you're getting bounced around the car and desperately trying to focus on the person next to you.

E.T.'S SPECIAL CAST OF CHARACTERS

Truly an elaborate special-effects feat, E.T. features 80 animated figures, 558 simulated trees and bushes and 306 dancing plants. The sprawling Earth city has 3340 miniature buildings, 1000 streetlights and 250 cars, while its galactic ceiling boasts 4400 stars.

Most of the dogs and cats in the Animal Actor's Stage show came from the pound.

What Universal did here was take the state-of-the-art simulators used in Disney's Star Tours and Body Wars—and turn up the juice. The sounds, feelings and visuals are all more intense, almost like a fourth dimension. Much of this 4-D realism is created with a 70mm film that's projected on seven-story "hemispherical" screens around each DeLorean. The ride's electrifying soundtrack comes from a "multichannel surround-sound" system, and the DeLorean's perfectly timed jolts are fueled by hydraulics. The Back to the Future building itself—a crazy crisscross of orange, aqua and mustard-color metal—is a real piece of work. After Back to the Future opened in May 1991, reviews hinted it might be the theme-park ride of the '90s.

TIPS: Signs outside Back to the Future call it a "dynamically aggressive ride simulating aerial acrobatics," a convoluted way of saying this is a *very* rough ride! Children shorter than 46 inches are not allowed to ride. Not recommended for expectant mothers, people prone to nausea or claustrophobia, or those with bad backs. Take it from me: If you have even a slightly queasy stomach, think twice about riding.

Just about everyone who visits Universal wants to ride Back to the Future (even those masochists with queasy stomachs and bad backs). Given this fact, know that unless you ride *as soon as the park opens*, you'll face a wait of 45 minutes to (incredibly) 2 hours. In this writer's opinion, no ride no place is worth a two-hour stint in a boring line.

E.T. Adventure ★★★★ Steven Spielberg's celebrated and wildly successful film sets the scene for this airborne bicycle tour through misty redwood forests and to faraway planets. The story line closely follows the movie, with E.T. stranded on Earth three million light years from his beloved Green Planet. E.T. (actually his computer image) hops aboard your bicycle for a trip back home, where he must save his planet from ruin. City lights sparkle below as you peddle away from Earth and across showers of stars. On the Green Planet you encounter enchanted waters, rainbow colors, dancing baby E.T.s and plants that seem right from the pages of a fairy tale. No doubt the most endearing moment comes at the ride's end, when E.T. bids you goodbye by your first name!

TIPS: E.T. gets my vote for having the best waiting area of any ride in the universe: a cool, dim forest where tree trunks are broader than cars and the air is scented with evergreen. As you inch toward the front of the line, a lifelike E.T. glows atop a knoll and speaks to you. Considering these surroundings, the typical 45-minute wait for this ride isn't so bad after all.

Animal Actor's Stage ★★★ The mod purple and green stairwells outside this building give no clue to the interior: a stage fashioned with ancient ruins and a tropical rain forest. The jungly backdrop is ideal for Jerry Lee, Chelsea, Mr. Ed and the rest of the critters who star in this wacky animal comedy. Set in a covered 1500-seat stadium, the show is hosted by trainers who demonstrate just how human animals can be. There's a parrot who steals money from your hand, a canine who waves, limps and hides his eyes with his paws, and a fat-lipped chimp who imitates Mick Jagger. Many performers are former movie and television stars. Einstein was the shabby pooch of *Back to the Future,* and Benji starred in his own three movies as well as *Oh Heavenly Dog* with Chevy Chase. Jack the parrot was on "Fantasy Island," and Jerry Lee the German shepherd starred in *K9.* The 25-minute show does have some slow spots and occasionally animals who muff their parts. But that's half the fun of a show that—unlike programmed attractions with computer robots—shares the spontaneous side of life.

TIPS: This show rarely has long waits, so see it between 10 a.m. and 4 p.m. when other attractions are packed. Eight to ten shows are held daily; check the show schedule (available from Guest Services or any Universal store) and be there ten minutes before show time. You should be able to walk right in and have a seat.

San Francisco/Amity

In all of Universal Studios, no place is so inviting as San Francisco/Amity. These two towns converge along a rippling lagoon lined with boulders and dotted with sloops and soot-covered tugboats. This is a festive maritime place, with tin warehouses, street jugglers, ruddy

---

"SAN FRANCISCO VICE"

The sun has just begun to slip behind San Francisco's dock houses when the seaplane dives into the bay and explodes. Seconds later, a cigarette boat roars across the water and collides with a seawall of flames. Two more boats tear across the water, turning lightning-fast to avoid a wharf as the crowd groans with relief.

In the end, the good guys catch the drug dealers and everybody goes home happy—and a little dazed by this **Dynamite Nights Stunt Spectacular** *boat show. Universal's action-packed scene-stealer is held most nights at 7 o'clock in The Lagoon. To get a front-row spot, show up along the waterfront about 20 minutes before show time.*

Earthquake's flash flood recycles 60,000 gallons of water every six minutes.

brick buildings, carnival vendors, shingled cottages, banjo and trumpet players, and lighthouses all tossed into one vibrant, merry cultural collage.

It's tough to know just where San Francisco ends and Amity begins, though naturally each place maintains its own flavor. San Francisco has stone streets, wood-plank buildings, old gas pumps and D. Ghirardelli Co., the trademark brick chocolate factory near Fisherman's Wharf. Docks are piled with lobster traps and fish nets, and cable-car tracks cut through the middle of the street (though there's no car in sight). Details here are so precise that even the rusty "No Fishing" signs are written in Chinese.

Farther along the waterfront, Amity smells and looks like a carnival. This New England seaside village, meant to imitate the town victimized in *Jaws*, is a jumble of popcorn and ice cream vendors, street artists, Cape Cod-style homes and game stalls strung with stuffed animals. A suntanned man with a pony tail does "salty sketches," while a burly woman clutching a microphone will guess your age or weight. Near the wharf's end stands a corny billboard of a bikini-clad woman on a raft stalked by a giant fin. The big guy himself, a 24-foot great white shark with spiked teeth, dangles from a rack in the middle of town.

Earthquake, The Big One **★★★★** The subway train is packed with people when the first tremor hits. Slowly, the mild earth twitch escalates to full-blown shaking so violent you can't get your grip. Lights blow and it's pitch black. The burning city above comes tumbling down as flower pots and chunks of roadway land near your train. A propane tanker slips through the crack in the earth and explodes, the heat warming your face. But the fire is instantly doused by a tidal wave

TRICK PHOTOGRAPHY

If you've ever wanted to shoot some movie-style trick photography, here's your chance. Using miniature cardboard sets and distorted glass, you can make your subjects look like they're in the Hollywood hills or bustling Manhattan—or like the crew of a NASA shuttle. Here's what you do: Go to one of the three special-effects photo spots located in Hollywood, New York and San Francisco/Amity. Position your subjects underneath the cardboard set, put your camera on the adjacent metal stand, line up your lens with the distorted glass, and shoot! (If you get stuck, follow the directions on nearby panels.) For best results, shoot between 1 and 6 p.m.

Get a good whiff of King Kong's breath and you'll smell bananas!

that surges toward you. You're saying your "Hail Marys" when suddenly a man yells: Cut! Then—like a videotape being rewound—the whole scene strangely goes back to normal. Your subway train continues on, as if nothing happened.

Universal's masterful earth-quaking, stomach-shaking ride does register on the Richter Scale—at a sobering 8.3. Based on the movie *Earthquake* and narrated by Charlton Heston, the attraction offers fascinating insider looks into catastrophe filming. A pre-ride movie reveals how miniature sets, matte painting, blue screen and stunt actors can make something so fake seem so real. To make this ride seem graphic, Universal hired special-effects ace John Dykstra to design the dramatic film sequence. Many props are the real McCoys, including the 20-ton subway train (purchased from the city of San Francisco) that holds 200 passengers and the falling roadway slab that tips the scale at 45,000 pounds.

TIPS: Children under three are not allowed to ride. Some older ones may be frightened by the special effects. Not recommended for those with a low fright threshold.

And, although the ride is quite popular, one thought disturbs: It is ironic that Universal portrays San Francisco in such a striking way, then offers an attraction that mimics the city's most tragic catastrophes. Though technically the ride is modeled after a movie about an earthquake, I bet those who've felt the real earth move would settle for strolling the area's beautiful street sets.

The American Tail Show ★★★ Kids, get ready for that lovable rodent Fievel Mousekewitz and his pals Tony, Bridget and Tanya. The stars of Steven Spielberg's hit movie *An American Tale* match wits in a song and dance show. During the merry toe-tapping revue, the foursome strikes out in search of a place where the streets are paved with cheese and cats are only a myth. It's presented throughout the day.

TIPS: Small children adore these characters; older kids may be bored.

New York

At Universal Studios, all that separates San Francisco from New York is 50 feet. In this short stroll, salty bay scenes give way to wall-to-wall brownstones, silvery brick streets, ornate theaters and roadside fruit boxes piled with the orangest oranges and reddest apples. A rusted barber pole punctuates a narrow alley lined with crinkled metal signs and filmy store windows crammed with cheap merchandise.

There's a certain charisma, a saucy veneer, about this place that emulates the East Coast's cultural dynamo. Billboards flash the latest on Broadway, and carved facades paint a swanky picture of the Upper East Side. Just outside Macy's, a Marilyn Monroe lookalike leans against a cab, her image reflecting across the glassy yellow hood. Wrapped in a clingy gold dress and sapphire feather boa, she aims her painted lips at bypassers and coos demurely. A man in a zoot suit and spats stops in front of her, checks his gold pocket watch and continues down the street.

Some famous Big Apple addresses have been nostalgically duplicated, including Greenwich Village, Grammercy Park and the Queensboro Bridge. There's a Coney Island arcade, a faux thrift shop called Second Hand Rose and a real Italian restaurant named Louie's. A place called Fotozine will put your photo on the cover of a well-known magazine. And Safari Outfitters, in the spirit of Hollywood corniness, supplies jungle duds in case you meet up with King Kong. Considering this is a Hollywood version of New York, who knows when you might spot the big ape. . . . .

Kongfrontation ★★★★ One of Universal's most elaborate and compelling attractions, Kongfrontation pits a tram full of poor, innocent visitors (in other words, you) against the savage, mountain-size King Kong. The terror starts just seconds after you board an aerial tram for a routine trip from Manhattan to Roosevelt Island. As you inch through the New York air, you see the beast's telltale signs: crumpled buildings, severed water lines and trams (like your own) crushed like toys. Remembering that "where there's smoke there's fire," you round a corner to face one very ticked off gorilla. He yanks telephone poles from the sidewalk and bats your tram around like a discarded banana. During the ensuing battle of the beast, helicopters fire bullets and

---

DANCIN' IN THE STREET SETS

New York's 42nd Street is quiet on this sunny afternoon when suddenly. . . . .six suave dudes in street clothes start jammin'. Like a scene from Michael Jackson's "Beat It" video, electric rhythm ricochets off skyscrapers and the men's bodies whip around, submitting to the beat.

*New York's breakdancers are just some of the superb **street performers** you'll see every day at Universal Studios. The Blues Brothers perform on New York's Delancey Street, and jugglers and mimes show up on San Francisco's wharf. There's a Dixieland jam in Amity and a '50s a cappella quartet at Mel's Drive-In in Hollywood. For show times, pick up a schedule from Guest Relations or any Universal Studios store.*

Over 2000 computer cues and 11 tons of liquid nitrogen create the ghastly effects in Ghostbusters.

Kong hurls your tram to the ground for a stomach-loosening plunge (actually measured at 1.75 Gs, or gravitational forces).

Keep your eyes peeled or you'll miss all the street life that's been graphically re-created. There's grimy subway graffiti, ripped cellophane trash bags and crutches that poke out of a dumpster. There's also the bag woman who looks so lifelike visitors sometimes double-check with the tram driver. These oh-so-real props help decorate more than 50 Manhattan facades that make up Kongfrontation's set. They're housed in a sound stage that—at 71,000 square feet and six stories—is one of the world's biggest. Then there's the big ape himself: A four-story, six-ton phenomenon, he's the largest computer-controlled robot ever built. His arm span is 54 feet, and his fur alone weighs 7000 pounds. Now that's no small banana.

TIPS: Expectant mothers and children under three are not allowed to ride. Adults must accompany children younger than nine or shorter than 48 inches. Though some think this ride genuinely scary, I found it was more exciting than frightening. This top attraction has long (45 to 60 minutes) midday lines. Try to see it after 6 p.m., when the wait should be no more than 15 minutes. Not to be missed.

Ghostbusters ★★★★ This spook sensation, based on the *Ghostbusters* action comedies, cranks with special-effects wizardry. Laser lights, strobes, video images, fire and fog fuel this theatrical show, which headlines a cast of demons, gargoyles and banshees who stalk the Temple of Gozer. The temple—a spectacular set that looms above the audience—is ruled by Goza, a she-devil with a tight white pantsuit and a bad attitude. When Goza threatens to wreck havoc on the place, four ghostbusters blast her with their neutrana wands. During the skirmish, a 100-foot Stay-Puff Marshmallow Man inflates on stage and shoots neon currents from his eyes. Things get more bizarre when Marshmallow Man, zapped by the ghostbusters, roasts in a ball of flame. If the story line sounds nearly invisible, it is. No matter: The electrifying effects make this show's 15 minutes seem like five.

TIPS: Hurray! This 500-seat auditorium is big enough to keep lines at a minimum. Even during midday, there's rarely more than a 20-minute wait.

Screen Test Video Adventure ★★★ Arguably the cleverest new theme-park endeavor, this "adventure" puts visitors in front of a real camera with a real director, costumes and cue cards. It's the only attraction that costs extra bucks, but keep reading and chances are you'll find it's worth it. Here's how it works:

Guests choose to star in either (a) a "Star Trek" scene or (b) A Day at Universal, a movie recounting your escapades at the park. Star Trekkies slip into Federation uniforms, get prepped on dialogue, then step into the "blue room," where filming takes place. As recent graduates of the Federation Academy, you beam to the Starship Enterprise for training. Unfortunately, Captain Kirk and Mr. Spock are away when you receive a distress call from a fellow ship hijacked by Klingons. You beam over to their ship, battle the bad guys and save the day. During the action, you get a quick lesson on reading cue cards, talking to video images of "Star Trek" crew members and following the director's orders. (Sorry, if you bungle your lines there's no second take. Mistakes are edited out.) The screen test takes about 15 minutes, and the videotape is ten minutes long.

For A Day at Universal, visitors wear their own duds (Mickey Mouse hats frowned on). When the camera rolls, you fight off King Kong, bike across the moon with E.T. and direct a stunt show. When the ten-minute video is played, it looks like a cameraman followed you around Universal all day. Funny thing, he never filmed you waiting in any lines.

TIPS: Good news: The extra charge for this attraction ($30 for one to six visitors) has a crowd-killing effect. It's definitely worth the money, however, if you're in a group. Show up any time; there's rarely a line.

Production Central

Like a warehouse district that's been spit-shined, Production Central is a maze of mammoth, unadorned buildings laid out in neat rows. These are Universal's muscles, its production pad of sound stages, technical equipment, wardrobes and props.

HEY, THERE'S FRED AND BARNEY!

What could be more exciting to a child than bumping into Fred Flintstone and Barney Rubble? The nutty buddies usually hang out at Universal Studios' main entrance, posing for photos and signing autographs. Other favorite cartoon characters show up, too, including George Jetson, Scooby Doo, Woody Woodpecker and Yogi Bear and his lovable pal Boo Boo.

Children should know that characters don't talk but communicate through body language. Also, they often seem larger in "real life" than on television, which can sometimes startle unprepared toddlers.

The bathrooms outside Nickelodeon Studios have green slime soap, Nickelodeon toilet paper and toilets that sound a siren when you flush!

One exception to this spartan setting is Nickelodeon Studios, the children's television network. Not surprisingly, this building looks wonderfully dabbed with fingerpaint in a kaleidoscope of colors. The area is sprinkled with cardboard castles for picture taking and park benches shaped like hands making an okey-dokey sign.

Unlike San Francisco, New York or other theme areas, Production Central has no street sets. Instead, sights here are concentrated inside five attractions that delve into both new and fabled Hollywood productions.

Nickelodeon Studios ★★★★ It's easy to find Nickelodeon Studios: Simply follow the bright orange zigzags to the building that's swarming with dozens of squealing, frolicking, ecstatic children. This must be Universal's happiest place, where kids get to lose themselves in some of their favorite television programs. Everything seems like one big game, right down to the building—a postmodern design with yellow stairwells, red triangles, black squiggles and blue amoebas. Just outside the front door, a Green Slime Geyser spews green goo out of shower heads. A sign explains that the slime, used on the show "Super Sloppy Double Dare," is "purified" until "only the nastiest parts remain." Inside the building, guests get a tour of the world's only television network designed for kids. About 90 percent of Nickelodeon shows are shot here on two sound stages, so guests almost always get peeks of a filming. A space-travel adventure called "Launch" and the sitcom "Clarissa Explains It All" are regularly filmed. You'll also see hair, makeup and dressing rooms used by the kid stars and the wardrobe room—a child's dream world of fanciful masks, costumes and shoes. The tour culminates (where else?) in a room filled with elated children and even more elated parents. (For details, see "Calling All Game-loving Kids!")

Tips: Though several Universal attractions show film and television clips in their waiting areas, Nickelodeon (incredibly) does not. I say, let's see some of those nostalgic Nick reruns—it sure would make the time pass faster. Another note: The broad grassy areas outside Nickelodeon are ideal for family picnics. You can pick up hot dogs, potato chips and other kiddie eats from a nearby vendor.

Production Tour ★★★ If you're looking for action, skip this tour. But if you want a slow, relaxing overview of Universal Studios, step in line behind Nickelodeon Studios. There you'll see a short film in which Robert Wagner reveals a few ins and outs of moviemaking. Next you'll tour the Nickelodeon sound stages, then board an open-air tram that slithers up and down Universal's street sets. Comical narrators point out all the important sights, providing the low down on how the park's 40 street scenes were designed. You'll learn that brick facades are really wood, and wood facades are really styrofoam. You'll also hear great Hollywood anecdotes, like how Alfred Hitchcock put his critics' names on tombstones in his last movie.

TIPS: The tour of Nickelodeon sound stages repeats part of the Nickelodeon Studios tour. Unfortunately, there's no way to skip this portion of the Production tour. On the positive side, parents will find the tram portion a great way to rest tired bones. Smaller kids may find it dull, though most like seeing the sights.

"Murder, She Wrote" Mystery Theatre ★★ The idea of this show sounds just dandy: Take an audience and walk them through an episode of "Murder, She Wrote." Along the way, they'll learn about story development, sound effects, lighting, improvising and film editing. Unfortunately, the lesson turns out to be information overload. Worst yet, you spend half your time traipsing from theater to theater as the film crew explains all the technical stuff. A few audience members do get to create sound effects and voiceovers for the film clip, but even that's a little disorganized. By the end, the only murder you're plotting is of this show's creators.

TIPS: Naturally this below-average show holds lots of people and rarely has more than a ten-minute wait. If you must see it, go between 10 a.m. and 2 p.m.

Alfred Hitchcock: The Art of Making Movies ★★★ In a touching tribute to the king of silver-screen suspense, this attraction whisks you through some of Hollywood's most chilling scenes and introduces you to the genius behind them. The three-part show features re-enactments of several classic scenes, including the one in *Vertigo*'s bell tower

---

CALLING ALL GAME-LOVING KIDS!

The small bleacher is crowded with excited parents when the first child takes off across the stage. Crouched on all fours, she rolls a ripe orange along the floor—with her nose. Minutes later, another kid wobbles penguin-style across the stage with a rubber chicken lodged between his knees.

These are just two of the wacky antics in store for contestants at **Nickelodeon Studio's Game Lab.** *During the daily sessions, the television network tries out new games for upcoming children's shows. (For game lab times, check with Guest Services in The Front Lot or ask a Nickelodeon attendant). Besides playing games, contestants can visit Nickelodeon's kitchen to taste new recipes for goodies featured on kids' programs. The most popular menu item? Green slime.*

Alfred Hitchcock's Psycho *is based on the same real-life serial killer as the movie* Texas Chainsaw Massacre.

---

and the *Psycho* murder in the shower. Fans of the portly, dry-humored producer will love all the Alfred trivia, like how he used 78 camera angles to portray that infamous shower attack. You'll also hear that *Dial M for Murder* was supposed to be a 3-D film—and now it is. For the show's finale, guests slip on funky 3-D glasses to witness a bizarre collage of scenes from that movie and many others. All the scenes are vivid, but the 3-D effects of *The Birds* are so intense the audience gasps. Hitchcock would be pleased.

   TIPS: Many scenes may be frightening and inappropriate for small children. Because of this, it's possible to skip the show's first two parts and just see the 3-D film. If you're pressed for time, do this even if you don't have preschoolers: The movie is the best part.

   The FUNtastic World of Hanna–Barbera ★★★★★ There you are, strapped in your spaceship and soaring through Bedrock with Fred and Wilma when some old man next to you hollers: "Yabba-Dabba-Doo!" It's just the kind of thing to happen on this ride that makes you feel like you dove into Saturday morning cartoons. Bill Hanna and Joe Barbera, creators of the Flintstones and many other animated legends, combined wits to invent this fantastic junket through cartoonland. Set in a theater that seems created by a berserk Andy Warhol, the flight-simulated ride combines a 70mm movie, 3-D characters and surround-sound that produce realism-plus. The story has the Jetsons' boy Elroy kidnapped by the diabolical dog Dastardly. You ride with Yogi Bear on a maniacal rescue mission and meet up with the Flintstones, Scooby Doo and Shaggy, and dozens of ghosts and goblins. There are plenty of surprises, including theater rows that lift up, separate and become little spaceships. The best surprise comes after the ride, when you're led to a room stocked with cartoon toys and exhibits. Kids go nuts here making pterodactyl squawks on a Flintstones' piano, romping around Pebbles' dollhouse and creating their own "Jetsons" episode.

   TIPS: This remarkable ride also has remarkable lines (an hour is standard). See it first thing in the morning or after 6 p.m. Not to be missed.

SEVEN

Sea World

It's only fitting that a state virtually surrounded by water would harbor a manmade aquatic wonderland. Covering 135 acres, Sea World is a mere drop in the ocean, yet it packs a gulf-size dose of shows and exhibits that probe the puzzles of the deep.

The 8,000 creatures who call Sea World home hail from as close as Tampa Bay and as far as Antarctica. Here at the best-known oceanarium on earth are house-size whales and toe-size clownfish, slick black seals and pink-fringed invertebrate. There are clever porpoises and endearing penguins, whiskered sea lions and mischievous otters. There are less familiar characters, too, such as puffins and buffleheads, unicorn fish and slithering sea snakes.

Many of the critters hang out in big, blue swimming pools that dot Sea World's lush landscape. Every day thousands of people file into stadiums around these pools to watch the fascinating animals play while they work: whales who whistle and do somersaults, seals who slap each other on the back, and dolphins who swim the backstroke.

Amphibious actors (plus a few human performers) steal the shows that have made Sea World world-famous. But this place is much more than shows. The $150 million theme park and research center boasts over 20 exhibits that dive into underwater mysteries. From the mammoth coral reef aquarium and snow-filled house of penguins to the den of scary sharks, they paint a poignant portrait of the sea.

Outside the exhibits, the park looks like a seaside painting in motion. Seagulls shriek overhead, and salty breezes shift across lawns of soft grass. Rock ponds weave through palmy gardens, and bubblegum-colored flamingos make clawprints on patches of sand. Speedboats roar across a rambling lagoon earmarked by the 400-foot Sky Tower.

Sea World's frame of reference, the tower resembles a blue needle pricking the shore.

Within this briny setting you can watch swivel-hipped Polynesian dancers or a sandcastle sculptor. You can ogle live Florida gators, then have one for lunch at Al. E. Gator's restaurant. Or you can lounge on the lagoon beach—frozen rum drink in hand—and eye the water skiers buzzing by.

If this sounds like quintessential Florida touristing, it is. Since Sea World opened in 1973, it has offered marine life education with a kick-back-and-take-your-shoes-off attitude. Today, Sea World endures as an old-style Florida theme park. Concrete walkways are nicely worn, and theaters and stadiums have a "lived-in" look. Flower beds are lush but lack that meticulous Disney quality. And unlike the big mouse house next door, Sea World offers little in the way of high-tech attractions.

But those are really the best things about Sea World. Life here is more relaxed, more tuned to the out-of-doors. This is a place where you can downshift into slow gear and think about what happens below sea level. A place that, for many people, is the only real thread to that strange, liquid cosmos.

ARRIVAL

Hurray! Sea World is easy to find, and parking is free. It's located right next to the intersection of Route 4 and the Bee Line Expressway, about ten miles south of downtown Orlando. From Route 4, take the Sea World exit and follow the signs to the main entrance. You'll park and board a boxy tram that ferries visitors to the front gate. Remember to *make a note of where you park* (rows are named after Sea World characters such as Oppie Otter) so you'll be able to find your car at the end of the day.

IT'S CHOW TIME

*Do you want to get close to Sea World's animals? Just feed them. Buy a box of herring or smelt and head over to the **Sting Ray Lagoon, Dolphin Community Pool** or the **Sea Lion and Seal Community Pool**. The sting rays and dolphin will eat right out of your hand, and you can even pet them. The Sea Lions and Seals put on a real show, barking for food and rolling on their backs. Get there late in the day and you'll see the whiskered fellows all fat and happy and snoozing in a big heap.*

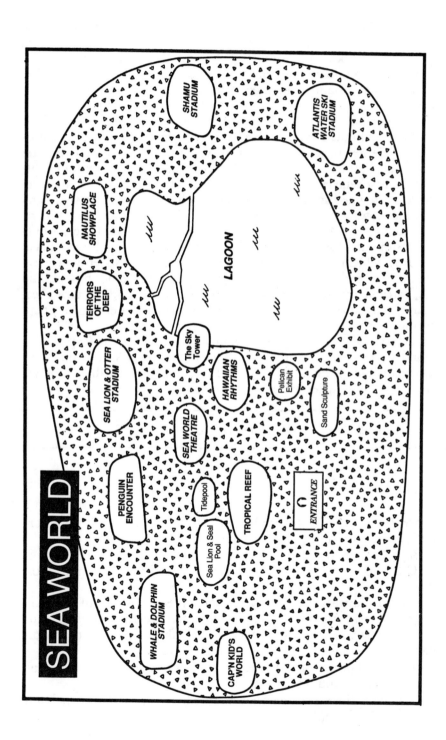

SIGHTSEEING STRATEGIES

As a first-time visitor, you may expect the same crowd craze faced at Disney World and Universal Studios. Don't. Laid-back Sea World rarely has gridlock and is so well-planned it hardly ever has lines. The main thing to know is that most attractions are shows, so you should plan your day around showtimes. You can't see every one, but you can see the majority.

Sea World helps you decide what to see and when to see it with an up-to-the-minute **Map and Show Schedule**. Available at the Information Center near the main entrance, the schedules are computer customized for each new visitor. The computer keeps count of people requesting schedules and which shows it sends them to, then recommends the least-crowded attractions. No matter what the computer says, don't miss the shows at the Sea Lion and Otter Stadium and at Shamu Stadium.

Allow at least 45 minutes between shows. This gives time for restroom stops and for enjoying smaller, "walk-through" exhibits such as the Tropical Rain Forest and Penguin Encounter. It also lets you arrive ten minutes early for each show so you get a seat. Some shows fill up fast, particularly during midday. If you have small children, take a seat near an aisle so you can easily make restroom or other emergency trips during the shows.

Parents also will want to schedule a midday stop at Cap'n Kid's World playground. Children love all the nifty activities, and you'll love taking a break in the shade. Above all, don't rush. Half the joy of Sea World is taking the leisurely way around.

Sea World strollers are shaped like baby porpoises.

NUTS & BOLTS

Stroller and Wheelchair Rental: Both are available at the Information Center just inside the main entrance.

Baby Services: Nursing facilities are next to the Penguin Encounter Gift Shop. Changing tables are provided inside or next to most restrooms.

Loaner Cameras: Forgot your camera? Sea World will lend you one for the day. All you need is a cash or credit card deposit (refundable when you return the camera) and a valid driver's license. Most loaners are the one-step, 35mm variety.

Lockers: Located near the exit area. Lockers cost 50 cents to one dollar each time you open them.

Pets: Not allowed. However, there are free, self-service kennels just south of the main entrance.

Penguins have 70 feathers per square inch.

Lost Children: Report lost children to the Information Center inside the main entrance.

Package Pickup: This free service lets you shop without having to tote the bags around all day. Just inform any Sea World store clerk you want package pickup, and they'll send your purchases to Shamu's Emporium. You can pick them up there on your way out of the park.

Lost & Found: Located just inside the main entrance.

Banking: Automated teller machines are located at the main gate. To exchange foreign currency, visit the Special Services window at the main gate from 10 a.m. to 3 p.m.

GETTING AROUND

Sea World is a breeze. Just think of it as a lopsided doughnut. The doughnut's hole is a sweeping lagoon bridged by a Y-shaped walkway. Just off the lagoon are shops and eateries, small marine life pools and the Sea World Theatre. Along the doughnut's outer edge are eight major attractions. Traveling clockwise they are Cap'n Kid's World, Whale & Dolphin Stadium, Penguin Encounter, Sea Lion & Otter Stadium, Terrors of the Deep, Nautilus Showplace, Shamu Stadium and Atlantis Water Ski Stadium.

If you're in a wheelchair, Sea World is easy to navigate. Walkways are broad, and ramps are abundant and gently sloped. Stadiums and theaters offer plenty of wheelchair seating (often front-row) that's a snap to get in and out of.

A SEA LION OR A SEAL?

How can you tell a sea lion from a seal? If you don't know, sign up for Sea World's **Behind-The-Scenes** *tour. The 90-minute guided excursion features oodles of sealife trivia and a backstage look at Sea World attractions. You'll see animals that were injured and rescued by the park, and the place where penguins incubate. You'll also get reserved front row seats at a Shamu show.*

The tour costs $5.95 for adults and $4.95 for children three through nine (plus park admission), and is offered several times a day. To sign up, visit the Information Center near Sea World's main entrance.

(P.S. A sea lion is a seal with earflaps.)

Sea World's 12 manatees eat 800 pounds of romaine lettuce every day.

The Shows

Whale & Dolphin Stadium ★★★★ Remember that Sea World television commercial where the dolphin rockets into the air and does a really great triple flip? It was a teaser for this "Whale and Dolphin Discovery" show that reveals just how clever dolphins can be. For 25 minutes the jovial creatures perform gracefully on command, doing backstrokes, acrobatics and even the hula. The crowd oohs and aahs at just the right times, like when a child from the audience does a flipper shake with a dolphin. Beluga whales do some pretty neat things too, such as dancing to reggae music and giving their trainer affectionate shoves. If you ever doubted the intelligence of whales or dolphins, this show will change your mind.

TIPS: If you'd like to be an audience participant, be there 30 minutes before showtime. Go to the front of the stadium and ask for an operations employee. There is, of course, no guarantee you'll be chosen, but this gives you a big head start.

Sea World Theatre ★★★ Many people think of Sea World as Shamu the killer whale and a bunch of aquariums. Sea World folks let you know it is much more in "Window to the Sea." Presented in a cool, dark theater, this show features Jules Verne-style footage of deep ocean dives, animal rescues and interviews with trainers and researchers. Some of the scenes are slow-moving, but most are intriguing. There's a killer whale attack on a blue whale, the only known footage of such an assault. You'll also see splendid scenes of a killer whale birth (a 300-pound baby) and of a male seahorse squirting out hundreds of pinhead-size eggs.

TIPS: A favorite of grandparents, this show usually bores young children. Infants use the dark surroundings for a quick snooze.

Hawaiian Rhythms ★ Where is it written that a marine life park must have an island revue? Probably nowhere, which is why this sluggish show should be taken out to sea and sunk. At Sea World, it's on a lakeside "beach" of dirt and sand where spectators sit on stumpy benches. A three-man band plays rat-a-tat-tat for a trio of barefoot Hawaiian women who swing their hips and change costumes way too often. Unfortunately, the performers seem bored and the show lacks energy. Fortunately, audience members can easily exit during the 25-minute revue—which they do. At least kids like the show because they get to play in the dirt.

Killer whales have no natural enemies.

TIPS: Check the schedule and plan to be *next door* at Al. E. Gator's tiki bar during a show. Hawaiian Rhythms makes ideal background sound for downing a tropical drink.

Sea Lion & Otter Stadium ★★★★ Psychedelic scenery, funky tunes and great animal shenanigans make this the liveliest, zaniest show at Sea World. It stars Clyde and Seamore, a sea lion duo who disco dance, pat each other on the back and cover their eyes when embarrassed. They're assisted by an otter who—Pepsi can in paw—rocks to Michael Jackson's "I'm Bad." The animals duck in and out of caves tattooed with flowers and mushrooms and play tricks on cavemen named Zodd and Ugg. They continually pick up after a litterbug caveman, conveying an environmental message to the audience. Everyone seems to enjoy this fast-paced show, but it's the preschoolers who can't get enough of the adorable animals.

TIPS: Avoid seats on the far sides of the stadium; the view is lousy.

Nautilus Showplace ★★★★ At last, humans get to be the stars at Sea World. And not just any stars. The Chinese Golden Dragon Acrobats who perform at this indoor theater are beautifully costumed, lithe and talented. They do handstands on chairs stacked over two stories high. They walk on tall skinny poles and dance on hair-thin tightropes. They even twirl plates on their noses. It all takes place on a dramatic stage where an ornate temple is flanked by gold dragons.

TIPS: Living proof that we can be as entertaining as creatures with fishy breath. Don't miss it!

MISCHIEVOUS MIMES

The pot-bellied man from Boise, Idaho never had a chance. No sooner had he wandered into the stadium than a mime was tailing him, mimicking the man's jelly belly. Every time poor Boise took a step, the mime would shake his gut in perfect unison. The crowd in the stands erupted with laughter and Boise glanced around, confused.

Sea World's mimes poke fun at unsuspecting guests who come to see the show at Sea Lion & Otter Stadium. They're so funny they've become the hit of the whole theme park. The mimes' forte is picking out the tacky in tourists: sun scorched legs in pink socks, long-eared Goofy caps, high heels and shorts up to here. You get the picture.

To see the mimes, be at the stadium 15 minutes before showtime. And don't forget to look behind you.

The underwater singing of beluga whales nicknamed, "sea canaries," is heard several miles away.

Shamu Stadium ★★★★★ Outside the Disney domain, no theme park character has gotten more hype than Shamu the killer whale. Not to worry: Everything you've heard is true. Sea World's best loved mammal—all 8,000 pounds of him—lives up to his reputation in this splendid attraction called "Shamu: New Visions." Black and white and glossy all over, the big guy does a graceful underwater ballet and waves to the crowd with his tail, then sends a mini tidal wave over the first few rows. He also parks himself on a platform so audience members can pet him and a child can climb on his back. The action is captured on state-of-the-art cameras that broadcast Shamu's feats (and the crowd's reactions) on a 15-by-20-foot video screen above his tank. In one exhilarating scene, a trainer straddles Shamu as he barrels full-speed toward an underwater camera. Just before impact, the pair soar out of the water, separate and dive back into the pool. Watching the action through the trainer's own camera adds to the thrill.

TIPS: This is the only attraction that regularly fills up well before showtime. Of the three daily shows (noon, 2 p.m. and 4:30 p.m.), plan to see the 4:30 show and get there 30 minutes early. If you must see the noon or 2 p.m. show, arrive at least 45 minutes ahead of time. There is an interesting preshow video, narrated by James Earl Jones, on the exploration of whales. (P.S. If you'd like to be an audience participant, see "Tips" for Whale & Dolphin Stadium, in this chapter). Not to be missed.

Atlantis Water Ski Stadium ★★★ The Wild West and waterskiing make strange bedfellows, but maybe that's what gives this attraction its

SANDY SCULPTURES

He is Sea World's earth mover, a man with a shovel in his hand. All day long he toils, sifting and shifting grains of sand until they take delightful shape—a smooth whale, perhaps, or even a child's innocent face.

*Meet Richard Varano, Sea World's resident **sand sculptor**. Every week Varano creates a new and elaborate figure from his big sandbox along the lagoon. And every day spectators stop to study the intricacies of his designs, which include 12-foot sandcastle cities. Varano enjoys talking sandcastle business and invites aspiring sculptors to make their own castles in a small sandbox next to his.*

Look for Varano near the Pelican Exhibit. You'll be glad you found him.

delightful lunacy. Set along Sea World's lagoon, the "Gold Rush Water Ski Show" stars a crew of bare-chested cowboys, womenfolk in checkered skirts and rail-thin miners with names like Elwood and Billy Bob. When they ski across the water, they jump, spin, wave and sometimes crash into buildings. You'll hear lots of cornball jokes, catchy phrases like "dangnabbit!" and a snappy, little tune called "Who gives a heck?" Better yet are the covered wagons that bob across the lagoon. The show's cardboard western sets, adobe hut and cactuses don't mesh with the beachlike surroundings, but who cares? This *is* theme park la la land.

TIPS: The performers like to ski right up to the audience, completely drenching the first two rows (this is your only warning).

Five tons of manmade snow falls at The Penguin Encounter every day.

In Between the Shows

The Penguin Encounter ★★★★ Sea World's most charming creatures live here in a $13 million den of snow-capped rocks, icy waters and blustery breezes. As visitors drift by on a 120-foot moving beltway, the little guys waddle across the floor, dive into their seapool and zoom around underwater. Occasionally they cock their heads at you through the viewing window as if to say, "What's the big deal?" To many people, the Penguin Encounter *is* a big deal. The simulated polar world is the largest penguin home away from home. Hundreds of the flightless birds live where the light is arctic dim and the air is a penguin-comfy 32 degrees. Next door in a similar room are dozens of alcids, arctic birds who look like a cross between a parrot and a duck. Unrelated to penguins, alcids have wonderfully bizarre names such as buffleheads, puffins, smews and murres. If you have small children, take them to the alcids: They'll love seeing the strange creatures and learning to pronounce their names.

TIPS: After stepping off the beltway, guests can take longer looks at the birds from a separate viewing area. There's also a Learning Hall where exhibits and videos detail penguin research and exploration.

Cap'n Kid's World ★★★★ "I wish you hadn't shown them this. I'll never get them out," lamented one mom after dad brought the kids here. Getting small fry to leave is a common problem, and little wonder: It's filled with stuff kids love best. There are tunnels to roam and water muskets to fire, bells to clang and wheels to turn. There are shallow pools and rigging net ladders, and rooms where children can wade thigh-high in plastic balls. All day, jubilant kids pour across the two-and-a-half-acre playground, testing one gadget after another. The

Sharks smell a single ounce of blood in a million ounces of water.

crowd favorite is a 55-foot pirate galleon with zillions of places to run, climb and hide. For parents, there's a sheltered area with good views of the kids and (yes!) plenty of seats for resting aching feet.

TIPS: Open from 10:30 a.m. to 5:30 p.m. To play, kids must be between 37 and 61 inches tall. However, there's an infant ball crawl room and a wading pool for children one to ten years old. P.S.: The woman's restroom nearby is usually jammed. Use the one at Whale & Dolphin Stadium instead.

The Sky Tower ★★★ Often called "the needle in the sky," this ink blue tower rises a skinny 400 feet from the lip of Sea World's lagoon. A round, windowed elevator ferries people back and forth to the summit and looks like a top in slow motion spiraling up and down a string. It's the only real ride at Sea World, and the only attraction that costs extra. The 15-minute vertical voyage is quiet, leisurely and scenic, and the view from the top is enough to make your day. Whether it's worth the extra bucks is, of course, a matter of opinion. Frankly, I think the scene from the top of Disney's Contemporary Hotel is just as stirring—and it's free.

TIPS: Some preschoolers are frightened when they see the ground start to shrink below. Older kids, however, think it's the greatest thing since Shamu.

Terrors of the Deep ★★★★ There's nothing too terrifying about this exhibit, except for the toothy barracuda, prickly puffer fish and six-foot sharks that slink around you. And oh, did I mention the surgeon-fish whose scalpel-sharp barb can saw right through a wetsuit? These sea scaries and more prowl the aquariums in this large exhibit that is all the more fascinating because you view it from a tunnel—with the demons as well as 500 tons of seawater *above you.* Traveling on a moving walkway, you are very much the stranger in this watery Oz of deadly underwater creatures. Many are immediately intimidating, but others are more subtle. The gorgeous lionfish, for instance, injects a venom that kills a human in six hours. And camouflaged scorpionfish are nicknamed "three steppers" because, after walking across the fish, victims take three steps before recoiling in pain. Ready for a quick swim?

TIPS: Children of all ages give this attraction high marks because, as one 8-year-old said, "it's like being inside a big aquarium." They also like being able to easily walk through again. . .and again. . .and again. . .

Tropical Reef ★★★★ A stroll through aquariums swarming with weird and wonderful creatures, Tropical Reef is truly a walk on the watery wild side. Unlike the sunny outdoor settings of most attractions, this exhibit offers pitch-black hollows ignited by neon coral the size of a semi-truck. The coral looms inside a 160,000-gallon tank, the nation's largest South Pacific coral aquarium. Thousands of oddities thrive here, including moray eels and raccoon butterflyfish, surgeonfish and giant lobsters. Bright orange clownfish flutter against underwater waves, and purple anemones do a silent ballet on the sandy aquarium floor. Preschoolers line up along the bottom of the tank, pressing their faces against the floor-to-ceiling glass. Smaller tanks are sprinkled everywhere, each home to some peculiar brand of sealife. There's also a standard Florida alligator den, and a pretty special tank where fanged baby sharks swim about.

TIPS: One of my favorite things about this attraction is the big, luminous signs that point out various sealife and help explain the riddles of the ocean.

EIGHT

Staying, Eating and Playing

Among the many tough decisions Disney vacationers face is where to **165** sleep and eat. To help you make good choices, this chapter provides lodging and restaurant suggestions inside Disney World and just outside Disney's boundaries. The "Playing" part of the chapter takes you sightseeing and shopping in the Disney area, and also offers prime nighttime spots.

Lodging

Ever since Mickey Mouse came to town, hotels have sprouted more profusely than orange blossoms. Disney World alone boasts 19,000 hotel rooms and campsites, and another 11 major resort hotels are planned before the year 2000. Just outside Disney's door are some of Florida's most luxurious accommodations, as well as motel rows that stretch into distant cow pastures. These chain lodgings were slapped up so fast it has taken awhile for the demand to catch up. Consequently, you can find some deals here, especially in the off-season (May 1 to December 15).

Perhaps the most-asked lodging question is the toughest to answer: Should we stay inside Disney World? Staying at a Disney resort is one of your most expensive options, but it's *the* most convenient. And when it comes to a Disney vacation, convenience cannot be stressed enough. Particularly for families with young children, proximity to the theme parks and Disney transportation can save *hours* of travel time (and aggravation) every day.

If your budget prohibits Disney resorts (or they're all booked up), consider staying at Disney's Fort Wilderness campground or one of the several campgrounds nearby. If you prefer a motel or family-style

Notice that the Dolphin hotel's fish statues aren't dolphins; rather, they resemble the fish from The Little Mermaid.

apartments, stick to those within a few miles of Disney. You may save money at a motel out in the boonies, but you'll spend hours fighting traffic to and from the Disney World area. No matter where the accommodations are, most let children stay free with parents.

Unless otherwise noted, the following price categories include two adults and two children under 18 staying in a room. *Budget* hotels are generally less than $50 per night; *moderately* priced hotels run $50 to $90; *deluxe* hotels are between $90 and $130; and *ultra-deluxe* facilities price above $130.

Lastly, if your children are older and you have plenty of time and money, I recommend staying at the Hyatt Regency Grand Cypress or Marriott World Center. Located about five minutes from Disney World, they both offer superb Florida lodging experiences.

DISNEY WORLD HOTELS

Certainly one of the biggest benefits of staying on Disney property is that you can put away your car keys as long as you're here. Monorails, ferries and buses provide free transportation to all the Disney sights, restaurants, shops and nightclubs. You also can take midday breaks from the theme parks, retreating to your hotel for an afternoon swim or nap—a big plus if you're traveling with children.

But that is only the beginning, particularly if you have kids. Most resorts here were designed with families in mind. Sleeping in Disney's world means Mouseketeer Clubs, teen programs, cartoon wallpaper and Mickey Mouse roaming the lobby. Also, there are a host of other

OUT ON THE TOWN

*For parents who want a day or night out on the town, Disney resorts offer 24-hour in-room babysitting through its **KinderCare** service. Reservations must be made at least eight hours in advance by calling 407-827-5444. KinderCare also operates two bonded babysitting centers inside Disney World. In addition, the Grand Floridian, Contemporary Resort Hotel, Polynesian Village, Yacht Club and Beach Club have their own supervised activity centers.*

*If you're not at a Disney resort, there are a number of bonded child care services in the area. Try **Super Sitters** (407-740-5516) or **Mother's Babysitting Service** (407-857-7447); both will send a babysitter to your hotel room.*

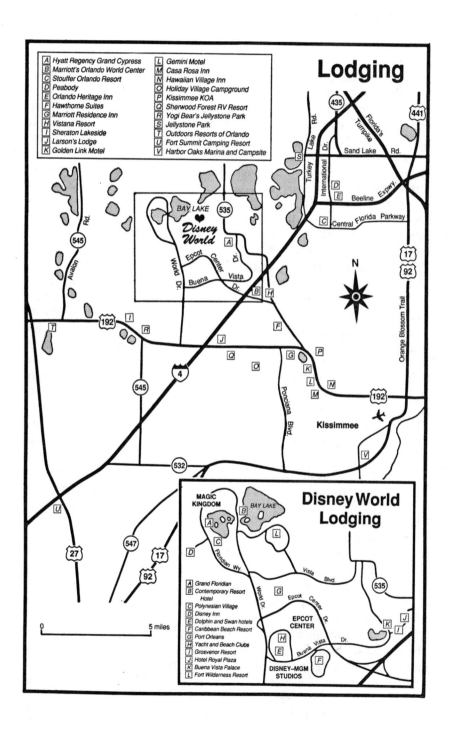

Lodging

A	Hyatt Regency Grand Cypress
B	Marriott's Orlando World Center
C	Stouffer Orlando Resort
D	Peabody
E	Orlando Heritage Inn
F	Hawthorne Suites
G	Marriott Residence Inn
H	Vistana Resort
I	Sheraton Lakeside
J	Larson's Lodge
K	Golden Link Motel
L	Gemini Motel
M	Casa Rosa Inn
N	Hawaiian Village Inn
O	Holiday Village Campground
P	Kissimmee KOA
Q	Sherwood Forest RV Resort
R	Yogi Bear's Jellystone Park
S	Jellystone Park
T	Outdoors Resorts of Orlando
U	Fort Summit Camping Resort
V	Harbor Oaks Marina and Campsite

Disney World Lodging

A	Grand Floridian
B	Contemporary Resort Hotel
C	Polynesian Village
D	Disney Inn
E	Dolphin and Swan hotels
F	Caribbean Beach Resort
G	Port Orleans
H	Yacht and Beach Clubs
I	Grosvenor Resort
J	Hotel Royal Plaza
K	Buena Vista Palace
L	Fort Wilderness Resort

Kissimmee

0   5 miles

The Contemporary Resort Hotel's lobby mosaic portrays stylish flowers, trees, birds and one five-legged goat. Can you find the goat?

advantages, such as being able to make Disney restaurant reservations up to three days in advance. And since imagination is at the heart of Disney World, it is only natural that this extends to the accommodations (including camping!) as well. From elegant to zany, Polynesian to New England, each Disney resort has a style all its own. When finding a place, you really can wish upon a star.

Does all this sound swell? Well, join the crowd. So many people want to stay inside Disney World that reservations are needed several months in advance. In season, booking a year ahead of time is not uncommon. Reservations at all Disney properties can be made through the **Walt Disney World Central Reservations Office** (Box 10000, Lake Buena Vista 32830; 407-934-7639).

The **Grand Floridian** (Walt Disney World, Lake Buena Vista; 407-824-8000) is the *grande dame* of the Disney resort area. Though fairly new, it has the look and feel of elegance enjoyed by the 19th century privileged class. Victorian verandas, red gabled roofs, brick chimneys and delicate gingerbread lend the exterior a grand appearance. Inside are stained-glass domes, crystal chandeliers and ornate balustrades. The 900 rooms are dreamily decorated with Victorian wallpaper, plush carpets, armoires and marble vanities. Parents who want a night out alone can let the kids join the Mouseketeer Club (for a fee, of course). Ultra-deluxe.

The **Contemporary Resort Hotel** (World Drive, Lake Buena Vista; 407-824-1000) is the most faceless of the Disney properties. Meant to look futuristic with a monorail through the lobby, lots of glass and a 15-story atrium housing shops and restaurants, the concrete ziggurat comes off as stark and sterile. Of its 1052 spacious rooms, those facing the Magic Kingdom offer the best view. For an additional charge there's the Mouseketeer Club for children featuring activities from 4:30 p.m. to midnight. Teenagers gravitate to the Fiesta Fun Center, a mammoth video gameroom just off the lobby. The whole family can enjoy Disney flicks daily in the Contemporary's theater. Ultra-deluxe.

One of the first Disney World resorts, **Polynesian Village** (Seven Seas Drive, Lake Buena Vista; 407-824-2000) creates a South Pacific ambience. The two-story longhouses lie on South Seas Lagoon and its sandy, palm-strewn beaches. In typical Disney fashion, the public areas feature a bit of manufactured Polynesia, complete with volcanic rock fountains and gardens thick with banana trees, orchids and sweet-smelling gardenias. Of the Polynesian's two jungle-like swimming pools, the one near the beach is the absolute favorite of kids. Here they can duck under waterfalls and zoom down waterslides that cut through boulders. For toddlers, there are shallow areas in both pools and a good-size playground nearby. There's also the Neverland Club, which offers supervised activities for children at night. The resort's 855 ultra-deluxe rooms accommodate up to five people each (or a sixth under three years old).

More remote from the Mickey Mouse rat race, **Disney Inn** (1 Magnolia Palm Drive, Lake Buena Vista; 407-824-2200) is favored by golfers and families looking for seclusion. Fashioned with a Snow White theme, the resort sits between two golf courses and features two swimming pools and 288 oversized rooms with a contemporary country flair. Ultra-deluxe.

People either love or hate the **Dolphin** and **Swan** hotels (1500 Epcot Resort Boulevard and 1300 Epcot Resort Boulevard, respectively; 407-934-4000). Inside and out, the coral and turquoise resorts look like they were dreamed up by a Disney animator. Seahorses dangle from chandeliers, lamps resemble birds, and hall carpets have painted-on beach blankets and palm trees. Headboards zigzag, pineapples and bananas are sketched on the dressers. To admirers, this is imagination gone wonderfully wild. To critics, it's decorator overload, tacky city. Designed by architect Michael Graves as prototypes of "entertainment architecture," the whimsically flamboyant hotels face each other along a lake and are connected by a flower-lined cord of pavement. Nearly twice the size of the Swan, the pyramid-shaped Dolphin has 1509 rooms and a vast lobby rotunda draped with ballooning canvas. Water plunges down the face of the Dolphin, cascading into terraced scallop shells for a crowd-ahhing effect. Smaller but certainly not subdued, the 758-room Swan is fashioned like a gentle arch painted with aqua waves. Both places boast sprawling swimming pool areas, fitness centers, gamerooms, *beaucoup* restaurants and bars, and day and evening camps for children ages 4 to 12. Prices are, needless to say, ultra-deluxe.

In recent years, Disney has taken pity on the poor souls who can't afford $200-a-night hotel rooms. The result: **Caribbean Beach Resort** (900 Cayman Way; 407-934-3400) and **Port Orleans** (1661 Old South Road; 407-934-5000). Both cost about half as much as the other Disney resorts but still offer the advantages of staying "on property." Villas at the Caribbean Beach Resort are named and color-coded for different Caribbean islands, such as pale peach for Barbados and ocean blue for Martinique. Each island has its own swimming pool, and each hugs a 42-acre lake rimmed with sand. There's also a lively street market laced with Caribbean food and colorful wares. The Caribbean Beach Resort's 2112 rooms make it one of the largest hotels in the United States. On the downside, the hotel restaurants are all fast-food, and they're usually packed. Despite its billing as a family

The Swan statues perched on the Swan hotel weigh a whopping 28,000 pounds each.

resort, it has no child-care facilities. There are, however, a beautiful playground and plenty of water sports. Opened in June 1991, Port Orleans represents the Disney vision of the Crescent City. Wrought iron balconies and clapboard shutters decorate the resort's three-story rowhouses perched along a river much cleaner than the Mississippi. The elaborate pool area, with its Mardi Gras character sculptures and giant sea serpent statue, looks New Orleans funky. Kids like to slide down the serpent's tongue and land in the pool. Like its Caribbean Beach buddy, the 1008-room Port Orleans is extremely popular and should be booked *at least six months* in advance. Both are moderate.

Two other new kids on the block, the **Yacht Club** (1700 Epcot Resort Boulevard; 407-934-7000) and **Beach Club** (1800 Epcot Resort Boulevard; 407-934-8000), re-create New England. The oyster gray clapboard buildings converge on a 25-acre lake outlined with magnolia and pear trees and punctuated by a lighthouse. The more formal of the two, the Yacht Club boasts a lobby of millwork and brass, naugahyde sofas and shimmering oak floors. Its 635 guestrooms are navy and white and nautically themed and have French doors that open onto lanais. The Beach Club lobby features white, wicker furniture and cool, limestone floors. Jars of seashells garnish its 580 pastel-colored guestrooms. The hotels share Stormalong Bay, a fabulous three-acre water playground with tons of treasures: a life-size shipwreck with waterslides (including one that plunges down a broken mast); hot sand baths and a bubble pool; a snorkeling lagoon teeming with bass, crappie and other native fish; and a kiddie pool that's sunk into a treasure ship. The hotels also offer the Sandcastle Club, which features supervised games for ages three through twelve. Both ultra-deluxe.

Several resorts on Disney World property are not owned by the Disney Company and have slightly lower rates. Located in the Walt Disney World Village, these hotels offer free transportation to the theme parks as well as Epcot restaurant reservation privileges. You can reserve rooms through the Walt Disney World Central Reservations Office.

For a taste of old England, try **Grosvenor Resort** (1850 Hotel Plaza Boulevard, Lake Buena Vista; 407-828-4444). Its 614 rooms are pleasantly decorated in a modern style with British flair and are equipped with a refrigerator and VCR. Guests have access to a gameroom, tennis courts, two pools, and an evening babysitting center. Deluxe to ultra-deluxe.

The **Hotel Royal Plaza** (1905 Hotel Plaza Boulevard, Lake Buena Vista; 407-828-2828) plays the other side of the street. Modern with Spanish highlights, this 400-room contemporary facility offers two restaurants, tennis courts, sauna, swimming pool and putting green. The hotel's pride and joy is the celebrity rooms: one is a two-bedroom suite with memorabilia from Burt Reynolds, the other has Barbara Mandrell's personal belongings and family portrait. Ultra-deluxe.

The **Buena Vista Palace** (1900 Buena Vista Drive, Lake Buena Vista; 407-827-2727), the Royal Plaza's sister hotel, houses 841 rooms and features even snazzier decor. Situated on 27 acres, the $112 million mega-resort looks like a sleek tower poised on a huge pedestal. The lobby soars sky-high and is crowned with stained glass and is streaming with water. Rooms are modern affairs with plush carpets, light oak furniture and private balconies. For families, the adjacent Palace Suites building has spacious one- and two-bedroom accommodations with kitchens, living and dining rooms and Mickey Mouse telephones. In between the two buildings are three heated swimming pools, children's wading pools, a Jungle Gym and tennis courts. You'll also find three 18-hole golf courses and four restaurants, including one family-style eatery with quality fast-food. Ultra-deluxe.

JUST OUTSIDE DISNEY WORLD HOTELS

A mouse hop from Disney's gates are more places than you can possibly, yes, imagine. Most every chain motel known to mankind can be found here—sometimes two or three times in only a few miles. In between are cheap sleeps with high-camp names like Adventure Motel, Viking Motel and Maple Leaf. At the opposite end, several addresses rank as some of the state's finest accommodations.

Several lodging services can help you find a room. Call **Kissimmee-St. Cloud Central Reservations** (800-333-5477), **Holiday Vacations of America** (800-447-4333) or **Central Reservations Service** (800-548-3311).

If I could stay at any hotel in Florida, with money no object, I would choose the **Hyatt Regency Grand Cypress** (1 Grand Cypress Boulevard, Orlando; 407-239-1234). Set on 1500 acres, this shimmering tower with tiered roof and spectacular 15-story glass atrium is truly a showplace. The $110 million world outside Disney World has it all: a tri-level fantasy swimming pool cascading with waterfalls, pretty lakeside beaches, lush hills and bridges, and winding footpaths laced with bronze sculptures and herb gardens. Flowing streams, flourishing tropical flora and more than $1 million in stylized artwork accent the lobby. And there's more: a 45-acre Audubon nature preserve, tennis courts, horseback riding, jogging trails, 45-hole Jack Nicklaus golf course, 21-acre lake with sailing center, health club and five superb restaurants. The rooms have such special touches as wicker settees, love seats and pastel color schemes. There's a children's pool and playground, and children age 3 to 15 can join Camp Gator for supervised activities. The Hyatt offers in-room babysitting and a day care center.

Folks traveling with children can take advantage of "Camp Hyatt," a rate plan that provides a second room at half price. Ultra-deluxe.

Besides its distinction as one of Florida's largest hotels, **Marriott's Orlando World Center** (One World Center Drive, Orlando; 407-239-4200) is also one of the most dramatic. The 143,000-square-foot resort rests on 200 acres adorned with swimming pools and fountains, rock grottoes and golf greens, and ponds filled with neon fish. The main building is a series of tiered towers that unite in a dazzling atrium lobby with marble floors, waterfalls and Chinese artifacts. At night, braids of light trace the hotel's tiers and are striking from miles away. The 1503 guest rooms, decorated with rattan furniture and soft hues of rose and champagne, feel relaxed and airy. Included in the myriad of amenities are a health club, four swimming pools (including one indoor), a dozen tennis courts, 13 restaurants and lounges, children's day camp and the Lollipop Lounge evening sitting service. Ultra-deluxe.

When the **Twin Towers Hotel** (5780 Major Boulevard, Orlando; 407-351-2311) opened in the mid-1970s, it was the largest convention hotel between Miami and Atlanta. Today, after a $30 million renovation, it is only one of many sleek hotels catering to the theme park millions. Parked at the main entrance to Universal Studios, the hotel's double spires house 760 oversized rooms outfitted with wicker furnishings, pastel designs and two queen beds. There's a heated swimming pool, health club, game arcade and children's playground. Deluxe.

From the outside, the **Stouffer Orlando Resort** (6677 Sea Harbor Drive, Orlando; 407-351-5555) looks like a stark concrete block. But inside is the world's largest atrium lobby, a vast and opulent space styled with lush gardens, fish-filled ponds, Victorian aviary and balconies strung with vines. The grandeur continues into 778 oversized rooms where the decor is rich green and plum, the vanities are marble and the carpets are super plush. Located next door to Sea World, the

---

PARENTS NEED NOT APPLY

*Few hotels anywhere cater to families like the **Holiday Inn Lake Buena Vista** (13351 Route 535, Lake Buena Vista 32830; 407-239-4500). Kids have their own restaurant (sorry, no parents allowed) and check-in desk where they're presented with a "Fun Bag" of microwave popcorn and microwave S'mores. The goodies can be popped into the microwave ovens featured in each of 507 guestrooms, which also come with refrigerators, VCRs and oversized bathrooms. In addition, guestrooms adjoin so parents can rent the room next door for half-price. Outside there are three swimming pools, while inside next to the lobby is Max's Magic Castle—an enormous child care center where kids can enjoy movies, puppet shows and magicians. The best news is, kids under 12 eat free (in their restaurant) and the rates are moderate.*

Stouffer features a big swimming pool, tennis courts and playground for kids. There are children's daytime activities, a teen gameroom and free coffee and newspapers every morning. Deluxe to ultra-deluxe.

Ducks are the unique attraction at the **Peabody** (9801 International Drive; 407-352-4000). They parade through the soaring lobby, across a red carpet especially laid for their daily procession to the pond. There's even a Dux Restaurant and a Mallard Lounge. The hotel's 900 rooms are as elegant as its lobby. On the fourth floor you'll find a recreation center with four tennis courts and an Olympic-sized pool. Ultra-deluxe, with discounted rates during "Summer Sizzler Days."

Orlando Heritage Inn (9861 International Drive; 407-352-0008) is fancy without ultra-fancy prices. Flavored with antebellum decor, its 150 rooms are done up with lacy curtains, quilted bed covers and paddle fans. The lobby is a vision of floral wallpaper, stretch windows and antique chandeliers. Food and dinner theater entertainment are provided in this open yet intimate spot. Moderate to deluxe. Children under 12 stay and *eat* free.

During recent years, a new brand of family-style lodging has popped up around Disney World. Fashioned like apartment and townhouse complexes, these resorts offer spacious units with full kitchens, bedrooms and washers and dryers. Grocery shopping service is usually available for a small fee, and on-site restaurants cater to young picky eaters. These are three of the best:

Hawthorne Suites (8800 Meadow Creek Drive, Lake Buena Vista; 407-239-7700) was built in 1983 as an apartment complex, but now the modern, two-story buildings host vacationing families. Spread across 50 quiet, woodsy acres, the 688 villas have contemporary appointments, full kitchens and either one or two bedrooms. Many have washers and dryers, and they all have two televisions and a VCR (a lobby library is stocked with videos). Ask for a room near one of the three swimming pools or you'll have a bit of a walk. Deluxe rates, with moderate prices available through the "Family Room" plan.

The first thing most people notice about the **Marriott Residence Inn** (4786 West Route 192, Kissimmee; 407-396-2056) is its woodburning fireplaces (a rarity for a Central Florida hotel). What families should notice are the inn's spacious suites (many with kitchens) and swimming pool, kiddie playground and picnic areas with gas grills. They're all nestled in the woods along pretty Lake Cecile, where you can sail, water ski, canoe or fish off a dock. Deluxe rates include a generous family-style continental breakfast buffet.

Tennis players with generous vacationing budgets might like **Vistana Resort** (8800 Vistana Center Drive, Lake Buena Vista; 407-239-3100). The 629 units can accommodate large groups in their spacious designer villas and townhouses, all with full kitchens. Fourteen tennis courts are framed in 50 acres of lush landscaping. A swimming pool and health club are other extras. Ultra-deluxe.

Another group with modest rates is the "Maingate Hotels" named for their location at Disney World's northern entrance. Most are of the generic chain variety and offer lower rates than Disney hotels.

A few stand out:

The most reasonable prices near Disney World can be found at the string of chain hotels on Route 192. The **Sheraton Lakeside Inn** (7711 West Route 192, Kissimmee; 407-828-8250) boasts its own private lake, tucked in a 27-acre throng of pine trees. Accommodations are motel-style with plenty of added touches: three swimming pools plus two kiddie pools, two children's playgrounds and video gamerooms, putt-putt golf, tennis courts and a late-night deli and ice cream parlor. Herbie's Kids Club hosts daytime games and meals for ages 5 through 12. Moderate.

Besides good prices and proximity to Disney, **Larson's Lodge** (6075 West Route 192, Kissimmee; 407-396-6100) has a big plus: It sits way back off the road, away from the endless noise of Route 192. The four-story lodge features tidy motel rooms, a small pool and playground, and coin washers and dryers. Kids make a beeline next door to Water Mania, where a labyrinth of waterslides waits. Budget.

The two-story brick front **Golden Link Motel** (4914 West Route 192, Kissimmee; 407-396-0555) sits on Lake Cecile. A swimming pool and fishing pier come with 84 clean and adequate rooms. Budget.

Arches and red brick trim lend **Gemini Motel** (4624 West Route 192, Kissimmee; 407-396-2151) a touch of Mediterranean flavor. Large, modern rooms are complemented by a restaurant next door and swimming pool. Budget.

Another hotel that deserves mention along this route is the **Casa Rosa Inn** (4600 West Route 192, Kissimmee; 407-396-2020). The 54 rooms offer quiet rest and a small pool. The motel itself shows a little character with its blushing Iberian facade. The rooms are thankfully clean and not gimmicky. Budget.

Fresh as a hibiscus, **Hawaiian Village Inn** (4559 Route 192, Kissimmee; 407-396-1212) decorates its 114 rooms in tropical tones and offers family convenience. Some rooms include kitchenettes, and the inn also has a restaurant. The swimming pool and playground are kidpleasers. Budget.

Camping

Few experiences put you closer to the "real" Florida than camping. Dozens of campgrounds, right outside Disney's door, offer sleep among mossy slash pines and palmettos or on wide-open fields dotted with lakes. You can arrive in your own RV or pitch a tent, or rent those provided by many campgrounds. In addition, there is a splendid campground in Disney World itself.

For families, camping can be an ideal alternative to the hotel–motel scene. Children have plenty of room to run (no more zipping down hotel hallways and waking up the neighbors) and a myriad of activities. There are hayrides, campfires, canoeing, swimming, bicycling, trees to climb, trails to explore and lakes to fish. Of course, camping is usually cheaper than staying at a hotel. You get to cook your own food and often bring your pets. And no fancy room service can replace the camaraderie of campers, particularly among families. All in all, a welcome change of pace from theme-park mania.

For discount hotel packages near Disney World, check the Sunday travel section of almost any major newspaper.

DISNEY WORLD CAMPING

Not unexpectedly, Walt Disney World boasts the most elaborate campground. **Fort Wilderness Resort** (407-934-7639) offers every amenity imaginable, from a nature island and petting zoo to nightly Disney movies and a water theme park. The shower facilities are so complete, says one mother, that "we could get real dressed up for dinner every night." And you can even hear the birds sing. Among the many Disney perks are:

❖ Boat shuttles to the Magic Kingdom and bus service to everything else inside Disney World.

❖ Air-conditioned "comfort stations" with restrooms, hot showers, spacious changing areas, ice machines and coin laundry.

❖ Several delis and snack shacks and two moderate-priced restaurants.

❖ Pioneer Hall, home of the Hoop-Dee-Doo musical revue and Chip and Dale character breakfast.

❖ Riding stables, nature trails, tennis courts, swimming pools, arcades, playgrounds, a picturesque lake with a beach and swimming, canals for canoeing and a marina with sailboat and water ski rentals and bass fishing charters.

❖ River Country (admission), a sprawling, Tom Sawyer-style swimming hole next door, and Discovery Island (admission), a nearby zoological center.

Despite all this, many people incredibly won't stay at Fort Wilderness because they think they'll be roughing it. What a mistake. The 740-acre wooded retreat has trailer homes that make motel rooms look like closets. Nestled in shady pines, the 363 air-conditioned trailers come with full kitchens and bathrooms, bedroom, televisions, telephones and daily maid service. They're ultra-deluxe-priced, but they sleep up to four or six people, depending on the model. Outside, there's a little yard with a picnic table and barbecue grill.

For those who bring their own RV, pop-up camper or tent, Fort Wilderness offers 830 campsites buried in the trees. They all have electrical outlets, picnic tables and charcoal grills, and many provide water and sewer hookup. Prices range from budget to moderate, depending on how close you are to the Fort Wilderness lake.

During the summer, Fort Wilderness is often booked solid by Easter. If you're going in-season, make reservations several months in advance. (For more on Fort Wilderness, see Chapter Five.)

JUST OUTSIDE DISNEY WORLD CAMPING

From vast RV parks and tiny backwoods fish camps to nudist resorts, there is a wide range of ways to camp outside Disney World. When booking a site, check the distance from Disney: It's best to stay within a few miles or you'll waste time getting to and from the theme parks. Most campgrounds will arrange shuttles to the parks (for a fee), though it's more convenient to drive. For an extensive listing of campgrounds, write or call the **Kissimmee-St. Cloud Convention and Visitors Bureau** (P.O. Box 422007, Kissimmee, 34742-2007; 407-847-5000) or the **Florida Campground Association** (1638 North Plaza Drive, Tallahassee, 32308-5364; 904-656-8878).

Some of the prime camping grounds for families are:

Holiday Village Campground (2650 Holiday Village, off west Route 192, Kissimmee; 407-396-4595) is one of the biggest campgrounds, featuring 800 sites for RVs, pop-up campers and tents. Some sites are right out in the open, while others rest amid the tall oaks and palms that dot the park. Only four miles from Disney World, the village is next to the Old Town shopping and entertainment complex. There's a swimming pool and grocery and some unusual amenities such as cable television hookups, video and car rentals and outdoor concerts. Budget.

Besides 380 RV and tent sites, **Kissimmee KOA** (4771 West Route 192; 407-396-2400) has 13 primitive wood cabins with double and bunk beds. Kids can sleep in the bunks or pitch a tent right next to the cabin. Every campsite in the 40-acre park is grassy and shaded, and there are *beaucoup* amenities: three swimming pools (two for children), playground, tennis courts, bicycle rentals, coin laundry and grocery. A fancy miniature golf course sits next door. Five miles from Disney World, the park offers free bus service to the major theme parks. Budget.

Despite its name, **Sherwood Forest RV Resort** (5300 West Route 192, Kissimmee; 407-396-7431) is not thick with trees but has a modern spick-and-span look. Over 500 RV and tent sites are available, as well as a heated swimming pool, miniature golf, tennis courts

Pluto signs the "o" in his name with a paw print.

and two lakes for fishing. Families frequent the park during summer, but seniors are the primary winter customers. Budget.

Yogi Bear's Jellystone Park (8555 West Route 192, Kissimmee; 407-239-4148) is a rustic, scenic place about five miles from Disney World. Many of the 612 campsites border picturesque Raccoon Lake, where you can fish off docks or rent paddleboats. There are a few wooded tent sites, as well as RV sites with water, sewer and electric hookups. Yogi Bear has his own boulevard, but he usually hangs out around the children's playground and wading pool. For parents, there's a big swimming pool, as well as amphitheater, putt-putt golf and grocery. Yogi has a similar **Jellystone Park** (9200 Turkey Lake Road, Orlando; 407-351-4394) that's three miles from Universal Studios. Budget.

The Cadillac of RV camping, **Outdoor Resorts of Orlando** (Route 192 just east of Route 27; 800-842-9115) sprawls across 150 beautifully manicured acres. Paved lanes crisscross the park, which boasts 980 RV sites, an executive golf course, tennis courts and huge clubhouse. There's fishing and sailing on a 165-acre lake, and swimming in the olympic-size pool and children's pool. There's no tent camping, but you can rent an RV on a weekly basis. Budget.

If you prefer to camp in the buff, check out **Cypress Cove Nudist Resort** (4425 South Pleasant Hill Road, Kissimmee; 407-933-5870). Tucked inside a 260-acre forest, the purist's retreat hosts couples as well as families who have RVs and tents. You can camp in the slash pines, or along a 50-acre lake (small boats welcome). There's a swimming pool, full-service restaurant and motel villas for those more tuned to life's luxuries. Budget.

Among the fun things you'll find at **Fort Summit Camping Resort** (2525 Frontage Road, Davenport; 813-424-1880) are air-conditioned log cabins and bathhouses. The cabins sleep up to five people in their double and bunk beds and have cable television hookups. There are also 300 RV and tent campsites, sprinkled across the flat pastureland, as well as a heated swimming pool and children's wading pool, fenced playground and video gameroom. One drawback: Fort Summit is ten miles from Disney World, though free shuttles are provided. Budget.

Hook-and-line fanatics should consider staying at a fish camp. **Harbor Oaks Marina and Campsite** (3605 Marsh Road, Kissimmee; 407-846-1321) has ten RV and tent sites that sit just off the marina. You can rent canoes, or bring your own fishing boat. Disney World is 13 miles away. Budget.

Red's Fish Camp (4715 Kissimmee Park Road, St. Cloud; 407-892-8795) is farther from Disney World—about 25 miles—but it features idyllic camping along beautiful Lake Tohopekaliga. The 68 RV sites have water, sewer and electric hookups, and an open tent camping area borders the water. There's a snack and bait shop, and boat and motor rentals. Budget.

Restaurants

The several hundred restaurants inside Disney World tend to fall into three categories: (1) Lousy, overpriced fast food (2) Decent, overpriced fast food (3) Quality, upscale dining.

Unfortunately, many fall into the first group, particularly in the Magic Kingdom where families spend a lot of time. For the convenience of eating on Mickey's turf, you often have long lines and crowded dining. Even at Epcot's four-star restaurants, tables are squeezed together, and diners are sometimes hurried through their meals.

But Disney dining isn't all bad. Indeed, where else do you find elegant restaurants that welcome you, dressed in shorts and sneakers, with your kids and stroller? Even better, most restaurants have good children's menus (though not always kid-size prices) and special touches such as coloring books and Disney character visits. Restaurants outside Disney World may lack some of these effects, but you can find some interesting places away from theme-park confines.

A little advance planning will help avoid long waits for any restaurant. If you're visiting in-season, avoid the Disney rush hours (11:30 a.m. to 1:30 p.m. and 5 to 8 p.m.). Or skip lunch by eating a big breakfast before you go to the theme parks, then buy a mid-afternoon snack from a vendor. The vendors, located throughout Disney's theme parks, peddle everything from pretzels and hot dogs to baked potatoes and ice cream.

Within this chapter, the restaurants are categorized by theme park, with each restaurant entry describing the establishment as budget, moderate, deluxe or ultra-deluxe in price. Dinner entrées at *budget* restaurants usually cost $8 or less; *moderately* priced restaurants range between $8 and $16; *deluxe* establishments tab their entrées above $16; and at *ultra-deluxe* dining rooms, $24 will only get you started.

If you're staying at a Disney resort, you can make lunch and dinner reservations at full-service restaurants several days in advance by calling 407-828-4000. Otherwise, make reservations at the restaurant as early as possible on the day you plan to dine.

MAGIC KINGDOM RESTAURANTS

The fast food at the Magic Kingdom needs no introduction—its reputation for poor taste precedes it. Still, everyone ends up eating it eventually out of necessity. To help you know where to eat, here are my best of the worst:

❖ On Tom Sawyer Island, **Aunt Polly's Landing** (Adventureland) has peanut butter-and-jelly sandwiches that come with an apple and a cookie.

❖ The **Turkey Leg Wagon** (Adventureland) doles out big, moist turkey legs that make a quick but filling meal.

❖ **Mile Long Bar** serves tacos, barbecue chicken sandwiches and hamburgers.

❖ The **Columbia Harbor House** (Liberty Square) makes a decent Monte Cristo sandwich (deep-fried, with turkey, ham and cheese) and has good clam chowder.

❖ **Sleepy Hollow** (Liberty Square) makes the kids happy with hot dogs, brownies, chocolate chip cookies and sweet fruit punch. For parents, there are chicken salad and reuben "handwiches" (Disney's own pita pocket-style sandwiches).

Unless you're a glutton for gastronomic abuse, stay away from these places: **Adventureland Veranda** and **Tomorrowland Terrace** (the hamburgers are horrible); Tomorrowland's **Plaza Pavilion** (the hoagies are scary); and any fast-food restaurant in Fantasyland. Besides having bad food, they're the most crowded eateries in the Magic Kingdom.

Five Magic Kingdom restaurants offer full-service dining. Two of those, Tony's Town Square Restaurant and the Crystal Palace, have good breakfasts and, best of all, open a half-hour before the rest of the park.

Remember the romantic scene in Lady and the Tramp where the two dogs smooch over a plate of spaghetti? They were in an Italian joint called Tony's, which has been re-created on Main Street as **Tony's Town Square Restaurant**. Scenes from the movie line the brick walls of the airy Victorian café with polished brass and painted,

---

HAM AND EGGS AND MICKEY

*Kids love eating breakfast with Mickey Mouse, Donald Duck and the rest of the Disney gang. These daily galas, called **Character Breakfasts**, feature colorful balloons, favorite Disney tunes and autographs by the animated personalities. Says one parent of her three-year-old who always begged to ride Dumbo the Flying Elephant: "Once she discovered character breakfasts, it was bye-bye Dumbo!"*

*Several Disney World hotel eateries host the costumed breakfast bunch, including the Contemporary Resort's **Character Café**, **Grand Floridian Café** and Buena Vista Palace's **Watercress Café**. Minnie Mouse stars at the Polynesian Resort's **Minnie's Menehune Breakfast**, and Chip and Dale do a morning jig at **Fort Wilderness Campground**. Epcot's **Stargate Restaurant** hosts the characters every morning, and Pleasure Island's **Empress Lilly** riverboat has a character "Breakfast à la Disney." Seating times vary, and most require advance reservations. Call 407-934-7639 for information.*

The waffles at Tony's Town Square Restaurant are shaped like Mickey Mouse faces.

white iron chairs. Like many Disney eateries, the setting is fancier than the food—standard Italian fare served in heaping platefuls. For breakfast, there are eggs and bacon, pancakes and cinnamon biscuits. Children get their own coloring book menus filled with pictures of Lady and the Tramp (waiters provide the crayons). Moderate.

The Magic Kingdom's prettiest restaurant, the **Crystal Palace** is wrapped in French windows and crowned by a sparkling glass dome. Located on Main Street, Crystal Palace is outlined in delicate white filigree and overlooks palms trees and sculpted flower beds. The moderately priced cafeteria offers hearty breakfast fare, salads and sandwiches for lunch, and roasted chicken, prime rib and pasta for dinner. Go for breakfast—it's the best in the Magic Kingdom.

The **Plaza Restaurant**, also on Main Street, serves only lunch and dinner. Across from the Sealtest Ice Cream Parlor, it's a breezy place with mirrors and windows and dressed-up fast-food fare. Kids like the burgers and milkshakes, and parents usually go for the chef's salads, quiche or fancy chicken pot pies. Moderate.

Little girls adore **King Stefan's Banquet Hall** because they get to meet Cinderella. The stunning blonde princess, draped in chiffon and crowned with a jeweled tiara, sweeps through several times a day. Another reason to go is that it's the only way to get into the Cinderella Castle in Fantasyland. For lunch there are prime rib sandwiches and a variety of salads; for dinner, you'll find prime rib and seafood and chicken dishes. Unfortunately, the food is only passable. But the fabulous surroundings and excitement of the kids more than makes up for it. Moderate.

With its stone hearth, plank floors and colonial wallpaper, the **Liberty Tree Tavern** feels warm and cozy. Located in the Magic Kingdom's Liberty Square, this charming place is an oasis of early Americana. There's an antique spinning wheel, ladder-back chairs and Venetian wood blinds. To match the decor, the lunch menu features such items as the Yankee Peddler (prime rib sandwich), Boston Seafood Melt (seafood combo in wine sauce) and Minuteman Club sandwich. For dinner, there are chicken, steak and seafood, including Maine lobster in season. The service is good and the food better than average but not worth the prices. Unless you plan to dine early, reservations are a must. Make them at the restaurant, anytime after 11 a.m. Deluxe.

EPCOT RESTAURANTS

People go to the Magic Kingdom to dream, but they come to Epcot to eat. (At least part of the time). What the Magic Kingdom lacks in decent dining, Epcot more than makes up for with fresh, innovative fare and lovely surroundings. Strangely, even the Epcot vendors seem better than those in the Magic Kingdom. Another big difference: You can't buy alcoholic drinks in the Magic Kingdom, but you can at most of Epcot's sit-down establishments.

Epcot's most popular restaurants (Les Chefs de France, L'Originale Alfredo di Roma Ristorante and the Coral Reef Restaurant) are difficult to get into. Same-day reservations can be made at one of Epcot's World Key Information Centers; if you are staying at a Disney resort, you can book up to three days in advance (407-824-4321).

FUTURE WORLD   Epcot's Future World has several mundane fast-food restaurants that you should skip. Go to the **Farmer's Market** at The Land pavilion. This lively food court, beneath a huge rotunda hung with miniature hot air balloons, offers a veritable smorgasbord of fresh, healthy, smell-and-taste-good fare. There are steamy spuds and soups, tossed pasta salads, stuffed pita pockets, deli sandwiches and barbecue chicken. My favorite counter is the bakery where white-hatted bakers will hand you a muffin right out of the oven. Kids gravitate toward the ice cream counter, while parents head for the beverage window that has beer and wine.

Upstairs from the market, the **Land Grille Room** is where you should go for fine dining. For some reason, the masses haven't discovered this wonderful place so it's usually easy to get in. The Grille Room is the only Epcot restaurant that offers a sit-down breakfast, and a good one at that. Lunch and dinner feature inventive, regional American dishes such as Navajo lasagna (layers of corn tortillas, goat cheese, spiced beef and guacamole) and Key West chicken. There are simpler offerings, too, such as pepperoni pizza. Diners nestle into intimate, velvet-lined booths and, as the restaurant revolves, get great views of the rain forest, prairie and other scenes from The Land's boat ride. Deluxe.

For a quick, healthy meal, stop by **Pure & Simple** in the Wonders of Life pavilion. In keeping with the attraction's "be good to your body" theme, the takeout eatery offers turkey and veggie hot dogs (most kids can't tell the difference), fruit-topped waffles, chili with lean venison and other low-fat fare that tastes good. Budget.

The best thing about the Living Seas' **Coral Reef Restaurant** is the sweeping view of a mammoth coral reef aquarium. From dimly lit, tiered rows, diners can watch sharks, dolphin and shrimp—then eat some. The shrimp is simmered with tomatoes, leeks and onions, and the mahi-mahi broiled and brushed with lemon caper butter. Lunch

---

Before queuing up at a Disney fast-food restaurant, check the line farthest from the door—it's often the shortest.

and dinner menus feature mainly seafood such as sashimi–style tuna and pan–seared swordfish. The food is more expensive and not as good as that at the Land Grille Room, and it's tougher to get a reservation. Deluxe to ultra–deluxe.

WORLD SHOWCASE   Critics have acclaimed the restaurants here for some of the finest ethnic and continental cuisine in the area. Many are striking replicas of famous restaurants in their respective countries and employ prominent visiting chefs. Waiters and waitresses are natives of their host countries and enjoy talking about their homelands, so don't be afraid to ask questions.

You might expect Epcot's most romantic restaurant to be in the France or Italy pavilions, but it's in Mexico. The **San Angel Inn & Restaurant** rests along a dark river actually flowing beneath a simulated night sky sprinkled with stars. The air is cool, and the tables are well–spaced and topped with pink tablecloths and flickering oil lamps. For lunch and dinner, there are Tex–Mex favorites such as chicken enchiladas and *chile rellenos* and also some interesting south–of–the–border fare. *Huachinango a la Veracruzana* is a red snapper filet poached in wine with onions, tomatoes and peppers, while *cochinita pibil* features pork baked in spiced marinade. The margaritas are delicious. San Angel is a good place to bring the kids because they can explore the adjacent Mexican market while waiting for the food and while you're waiting for the check. Moderate to deluxe.

Scandinavia has never been known for its culinary achievements, and perhaps that's why many visitors shy away from Norway's **Akershus**. For those willing to experiment, the eatery has a hot and cold buffet, or *koldtbord*, piled with smoked salmon and herring dishes, cold roasted chicken, rutabagas, lamb and cabbage and other native eats. For children, there are meatballs and macaroni and cheese. The food was not to my liking, but the restaurant, with its carved wood ceilings, turret rooms and gothic archways, was positively beautiful. Moderate.

EPCOT'S FIVE-STAR STREET VENDORS

Epcot's vendor fare goes way beyond traditional street food. Here are my favorites:
  ❖ *Warm waffles and cool kaki-gori (fruit icies), in front of Japan's pavilion.*
  ❖ *Foot-long hot dogs and popcorn (smell it and try to walk by), in front of the United States pavilion.*
  ❖ *Jumbo baked potatoes (with cheese, please), in front of the United Kingdom pavilion.*
  ❖ *Creamy bread custard, outside Canada's pavilion.*

Despite the grandeur of the China pavilion, its **Nine Dragons** restaurant is disappointing. The food, a rendition of American-style Chinese favorites, is mediocre and deluxe-priced. Maybe you pay for the opulent surroundings, a fusion of garnet-red carpets, rosewood dividers and wood tabletops that glimmer. If in the mood for Chinese, stop by the pavilion's **Lotus Blossom Café**, which offers takeout food in the $5 range.

Every meal at Germany's **Biergarten** is a party. Strolling accordion players, yodelers and an oom-pah-pah band make merry while diners feast banquet-style on German food. The rousing atmosphere is perfect for families, and kids like the cool, castle-like surroundings. Bratwurst, smoked pork loin, marinated beef with dumplings and other robust classics headline the lunch and dinner menus. Moderate.

Italy's **L'Originale Alfredo di Roma Ristorante** is the second most popular Epcot restaurant. Fine Italian dishes such as fettucine Alfredo, (whose creator the restaurant is named for), veal piccata and plenty of pasta are featured. Kids go for the spaghetti and meatballs and enjoy watching the strolling musicians. One drawback: The tables are way too close, and the place is always crowded. I was seated at a table in the middle of the room and got bumped several times by waiters. Either dine early or late, or go off-season. Moderate to deluxe.

How sad that the United States pavilion's signature restaurant is a fast-food joint. (Every other World Showcase country has at least one fine dining establishment, and some have two.) On the plus side, the **Liberty Inn** is a blessing for families. Children love the burgers, hot dogs and chocolate chip cookies (look for the kids wearing cookie on their faces), and the outdoor seating provides plenty of open space. Even better, prices are budget.

Ever been to a Benihana's? Then skip the Japan pavilion's **Teppanyaki Dining Rooms**, which does a great job of imitating the Japanese chain restaurants. Like China's restaurant, Japan's avoids true regional creations and instead offers Americanized versions of teppan table cooking. Japanese cooks put on a nice show as they slice and sear the meats, chicken and seafood right on your tabletop stove. It's a good place for families because everyone shares tables and the cooks are sociable. Deluxe.

Couscous and bastila are some of the delicious, exotic-sounding dishes served at the **Restaurant Marrakesh** in the Morocco pavilion. The first consists of tiny pasta grains served with a vegetable stew; the second is spicy almonds, saffron and cinnamon layered with filo. The atmosphere is properly North African, featuring beautiful belly dancers and a three-piece band. If the kids (or dad) want to be part of the show, mention it to a waitress. The dancers enjoy including children. Moderate to deluxe.

The most popular Epcot restaurant, France's **Les Chefs de France** boasts such classics as steak *au poivre*, grouper and salmon-vegetable

The Rose & Crown Pub's architecture reveals three pubs in one: a country pub with wood shingles, a city pub with turrets and etched glass, and a maritime pub.

mousse *en croûte*, and braised duck with venison sauce. Many rave about the food but after two visits I found it was good but not exceptional—and certainly not worth the lofty prices. The ambience is not French-romantic at all, but loud, garish and crowded. Ultra-deluxe. I prefer the pavilion's **Bistro de Paris**, a charming indoor spot with carved ceilings, brass sconces and tabletop bouquets and candles. Cuisine includes roasted fish, grilled lamb chops and veal tenderloin, all bathed in light cream sauces. Like Les Chefs de France, the bistro is difficult to book. Deluxe.

The French pavilion possesses yet a third very popular restaurant, **Au Petit Café**. The sidewalk eatery smells and looks so inviting that it's perennially jam-packed. Black-suited waiters tote steaming crocks of onion soup and plates of snails, and diners sip foamy cappuccino and watch the people go by. You can't make reservations, so either arrive early or step in the long line out front. Moderate to deluxe.

At the United Kingdom pavilion's **Rose and Crown Pub**, serving wenches deliver simple English pub fare such as fish and chips, Scotch eggs or steak-and-kidney pie. You can dine indoors amid brass and etched glass surroundings or on the patio at the edge of the lagoon. Moderate to deluxe.

Families who want a quick, hot meal should head for Canada's **Le Cellier**. The cafeteria features seafood stew, prime rib, chicken and meatball stew, poached salmon and (for kids) fried chicken. Set inside thick stone walls, this is a medieval-style place with dark, heavy wood, wrought-iron lamps and naugahyde booths. For dessert, try the maple syrup pie. Moderate.

DISNEY–MGM STUDIOS RESTAURANTS

As you might guess, restaurants in The Studios reflect a passion for Hollywood and movies. Unfortunately, Disney thought and imagination went into the decor but not the menus. Still, most food is at least passable, and the starry surroundings make it worthwhile for most people.

For a light breakfast, **Starring Rolls** (Hollywood Boulevard) has bagels, muffins and giant bearclaw pastries. It opens a half-hour before the rest of Disney–MGM, so you can get a bite before seeing the sights. Later in the day, stop by for one of the bakery's many decadent desserts.

Hollywood's storied Brown Derby restaurant is gone, but its copycat is alive and prospering at Disney–MGM. Like its namesake, the

Brown Derby (Hollywood Boulevard) is classy and clubby and out-fitted with teakwood, chandeliers and caricatures of film stars. In-cluded on the lunch and dinner menus are pasta, veal and seafood dishes and the colorful cobb salad. The latter, made famous at the original restaurant, features fresh greens topped with rows of chopped bacon, avocado, tomato, bleu cheese and turkey. The portions are large but the service is slow and the prices high. For families in a hurry or on a budget, the Brown Derby is not a good choice. Deluxe.

The **50s Prime Time Café** (Lakeside Circle) is marvelous for fam-ilies. The setting is a "Leave It to Beaver"-style kitchen where you pull up a vinyl chair to a formica table. A June Cleaver lookalike (please, call her mom) serves, then urges you to clean your plate. The food comes on those great school lunchroom plates with little compart-ments and features homey yummies such as meat loaf and mashed potatoes, granny's pot roast, Aunt Selma's chicken salad and alphabet soup. "Mom" brings coloring books and crayons for the kids and checks for dirty fingernails before dinner. Moderate.

Disney–MGM also has several fast-food eateries. **Studio Catering** (Backstage Studio Tour) serves sandwiches and coffee and is so hidden it's rarely crowded. **Backlot Express** (Backlot Annex) has decent burgers and dogs, and **Soundstage Restaurant** (Studio Courtyard) is a food court fashioned like a set from the Bette Midler film *Big Business*. All budget to moderate.

OTHER DISNEY WORLD RESTAURANTS

Away from the big theme parks, Disney World has even more to offer diners. These eateries play to smaller crowds, particularly during lunch when the theme parks are gorged with visitors.

At the Disney Village Marketplace, Mickey Mouse has his own res-taurant. **Chef Mickey's Village Restaurant** (407-828-3723) looks out on a pale green lagoon and offers water vistas from dining rooms peppered with plants. There's standard breakfast fare and a lunch and dinner lineup of chicken, pasta, steak and local seafood. If you're lucky, Mickey will serve you himself (the kids won't stop talking about it all night). Moderate.

The marketplace's **Gourmet Pantry** (407-828-3886) has a splen-did deli and bakery tucked in back. The croissants and flavored coffees are delicious, and the "Huey, Dewey and Louie" cornbeef sandwich is so thick it's tough to take a bite. Nearby, **Minnie Mia's Italian Eatery** (407-828-3883) has good takeout pizza and hot pasta dishes. Both budget to moderate.

Poolside snack bars provide the quickest (and often least expensive) meals at Disney World hotels.

Got the late-night munchies? Trails End has a pizza bar from 9 to 11 nightly.

The **Empress Lilly** (407-828-3900), moored at the marketplace, is a popular showboat restaurant that, unfortunately, does not feature outstanding cuisine. Three different theme rooms offer varied stages of formality: the polished but casual Fisherman's Deck, the intimate Steerman's Quarters and the plush, lace-and-velvet Empress Room. The menu demonstrates a New Orleans influence, running the gamut from bouillabaisse and crayfish gumbo to prime rib, seafood crêpes and andouille sausage. Deluxe.

Next door, Pleasure Island's **Portobello Yacht Club** (407-934-8888) is one of my favorite Disney restaurants. The charming Italian eatery sits waterside and is nautically furnished with rudder ceiling fans, ships' models, wood paneling and shiny brass. Service is impeccable, the atmosphere jovial and the food fresh, tasty and well-priced. There are thin-crusted pizzas, grilled over a wood fire, and breaded veal chops, garlic shrimp and lots of pasta dishes, all cooked in an open kitchen. Moderate.

For back-to-basics, family-style dining, head for the **Trails End** (407-824-2900) in Fort Wilderness Campground. The wood cabin restaurant has wagon wheel chandeliers and southern vittles such as fried chicken and catfish and barbecue ribs. The omelette and waffle breakfasts are stomach-stuffers. In the same building, **Crockett's Tavern** has ground buffalo burgers, a children's menu, and a serious cocktail called the Gullywhumper. Show up at 5 p.m. and you can watch a Disney flick during dinner. Budget to moderate.

Because of keen competition between hotels, many of the area's best restaurants can be found in its resorts. For elite Disney dining without the kids, **Victoria & Albert's** (in the Grand Floridian, Lake Buena Vista; 407-824-2383) does a six-course, fixed-price meal served by folks dressed as maids and butlers. Selections change daily, but usually include fish, fowl, veal, beef and lamb dinners, often followed by the restaurant's famous dessert soufflés. For a classy finale, diners are presented with long-stem roses and Godiva chocolates. Ultra-deluxe.

The **Outback** (1900 Buena Vista Drive, Lake Buena Vista; 407-827-3430) in Disney's Buena Vista Palace Hotel takes you down under. Australian-style food is prepared on grills in the middle of the dining room. Rack of lamb, lobster tail and 99 brands of beer are served by waiters in safari suits. To arrive at the restaurant, you ride a glass elevator car through a waterfall. The hotel's most elegant dining address is **Arthur's 27**, a penthouse restaurant that dazzles with primo cuisine and breathtaking views of the Magic Kingdom in lights. Caviar and warm duck salad head up imaginative specialties including snapper

187

in Key lime sauce and duck breast smothered in a honey-ginger sauce. Prices are fixed at ultra-deluxe for a four- or six-course meal.

Nearby, in the Hilton Hotel, **American Vineyards** (1751 Hotel Plaza Boulevard, Lake Buena Vista; 407-827-4000) pays homage to the grape. Decor, posters, wine labels and paraphernalia define the theme. Many of the creative dishes use wine sauces, such as the veal rib pistachio in Riesling sauce. Others use local ingredients such as the large Gulf shrimp sautéed in garlic butter. Deluxe.

Disney World hotels offer several eateries where you can grab a quick, relatively inexpensive meal. The Yacht Club's **Beaches & Cream** (407-934-7000) is a colorful, fanciful soda fountain that has Mrs. Stowecroft's Sundaes and the Fenway Park Burger. **Tubbi Checkers Buffeteria** (407-934-4000), in the Dolphin resort, features a cafeteria lineup of fried chicken, spaghetti and other hot dishes. Over at the Polynesian Village, you'll find burgers, fresh fruit platters and coconut hot dogs at **Captain Cook's Snack and Ice Cream Company**. All budget to moderate.

Families like the **Grand Floridian Café** (in the Grand Floridian, Lake Buena Vista; 407-824-4000) for its casual atmosphere and prices and good, innovative food. Decorated in peach and cream, the place is sprinkled with marble tables and filled with the clatter of dishes and children. There are chicken, pork, beef and seafood dishes, often with a tropical flavor. I like the chicken grilled in tamarind and ginger sauce and the Caribbean roast pork. For kids, there are burgers and fries and breakfasts with Mary Poppins. Moderate.

If you enjoy big breakfasts, go to the **Coral Isle Café** (in the Polynesian Village; 407-824-2000) and eat French toast. It's made with sourdough bread that's chocked with creamy bananas and quick-fried until puffy. The no-frills coffee house also serves eggs and cereal for breakfast, and stacked sandwiches and jumbo salads for lunch and dinner. One drawback: People have discovered the place (and its fabulous French toast) so it's usually crowded. Moderate.

JUST OUTSIDE DISNEY WORLD RESTAURANTS

Almost every Florida city has a restaurant named for Ernest Hemingway, and Orlando is no exception. This **Hemingway's** (Grand Cypress Resort; 407-239-1234) conforms to the Key West style preferred by most of these restaurants, with a casual atmosphere and seafood. Orlando's version also offers an elevated poolside location and woodsy ambience. The menu swims with grouper, pompano, squid, conch, shrimp and other salty creatures, plus a steak or two. Half portions are available for all menu items. Deluxe.

An old island atmosphere is created with wooden fanback chairs painted in pastels, a stuffed marlin on the wall and casual attitudes at **Key Largo Steaks & Seafood** (5770 West Route 192, Kissimmee;

407-396-6244). A moderately priced menu mixes steak with grouper, calamari and lobster entrées. Children's menu.

For low-priced meals with an exotic flair, check out the international food pavilion at **Mercado Shopping Village** (8445 South International Drive; 407-345-9337). You'll have a choice of fast foods from Greece, Latin America, Mexico, Italy and the United States. I tried the **Greek Place** (407-352-6930) and enjoyed Greek salad and lemon soup that rated well above the average mall food. The counter menu also offers moussaka, gyro sandwiches, dolmades and other authentic specialties. Budget.

Many local folks will point to **Ran-Getsu** (8400 International Drive; 407-345-0044) as your best bet for authentic Japanese food. The sushi bar whips around like a dragon's tail, and floor tables overlook a bonsai garden and pond. Besides sushi, the restaurant offers sukiyaki, *kushiyaki*, deep-fried alligator tail and other Japanese-Florida crossbreeds. Deluxe.

For a night away from the kids, the Stouffer Resort's **Atlantis** (6677 Harbor Drive; 407-351-5555) serves elegant French-Mediterranean cuisine on tables surrounded by nicely appointed furnishings and art. The menu contains such pleasures as grilled swordfish with port wine sauce, rack of lamb with mushroom and sun-dried tomato sauce and roasted baby pheasant. Atlantis is ultra-deluxe. If you are with the kids, the resort's less formal **Tradewinds** provides coloring book menus. Parents will find fancy sandwiches and salads and nouvelle preparations such as rainbow trout with pine nuts, dill and lime meunière. Moderate to deluxe.

Sunday brunch is an event at the Stouffer. It's held in the hotel's spacious atrium, where buffet tables are packed with everything from pasta and seafood to waffles and omelettes. There's a section just for children, featuring tacos, hamburgers, chocolate milk and sweet treats. Deluxe.

ALL YOU CAN EAT

One way families can save on food is to eat buffet-style. Numerous restaurants near Disney World specialize in buffets, offering all-you-can-eat smorgasbords at budget and moderate prices. Most places are concentrated along Route 192 and International Drive:

Gilligan's (4559 West Route 192, Kissimmee; 407-396-1212) is a no-frills eatery with all-you-can-eat seafood for dinner. Breakfast and lunch are also buffet-style. For breakfast, my favorite is the charming café Your Just Desserts (5770 West Route 192, in the Old Town shopping village; 407-396-1910). Also, try the following chain restaurants: Shoney's, Ponderosa Steak House, Olive Garden Italian Restaurant, International House of Pancakes and Sonny's Barbecue.

Tucked in the Old Town shopping village is a marvelous find for families: an old-fashioned soda fountain. **Chrissy's Ice Cream Parlor** (5770 West Route 192, Kissimmee; 407-396-6440) sells nickel Cokes, 99-cent hot dogs and other tasty, budget-priced eats such as hoagies and chili burgers. Heart-shaped iron chairs and a rickety screen door provide authentic "old town" ambience.

Local couples and families are the main patrons of **Donato's** (in The Marketplace, 7600 Dr. Phillips Boulevard, Orlando; 407-352-8772), located near Universal Studios. The wood-floored Italian deli and eatery, stashed away in a strip shopping center, serves huge portions of delicious veal, chicken, spaghetti and other saucy pasta dishes. There's also pizza and fresh seafood, and a good children's menu. Best of all, its boisterous, homestyle atmosphere make it an anomaly in this gimmicky theme park area. Budget to moderate.

UNIVERSAL STUDIOS RESTAURANTS

Universal Studios has outdone Disney when it comes to food. From fast food to cultured dining, Universal's eateries stand a notch above standard theme park fare. One of the best spots to get a quick, filling meal is **Louie's Italian Restaurant** (New York), a rendition of a Little Italy bistro. Pizza, lasagna and other pasta dishes are served cafeteria style. There's also barbecue chicken and, on the lighter side, minestrone soup and pasta salads. Moderate.

Few families can pass up **Mel's Drive-In** (Hollywood). Kids like the burgers, malts and cherry red booths with individual juke boxes, while parents enjoy the blast from the past. Classic '50s tunes throb through the *American Graffiti*-style joint, decorated in hot pink neon and formica and silver metal. Budget.

The place with the elegant atmosphere is **Lombard's Landing** (San Francisco/Amity). Nestled along a lagoon inside a warehouse, the restaurant is embellished with plank ceilings, shiny teak tables, archways, a bubble-shaped aquarium and copper fountains. Seafood dishes such as grilled salmon and crab cakes headline the deluxe-priced menu, though you'll also find prime rib, chicken dishes and a children's menu. Reservations required; call 407-363-8000.

There are numerous spots for budget-priced quickie meals. The **Beverly Hills Boulangerie**, located in The Front Lot, has croissants and pastries and stacked sandwiches. Over in the Expo Center, stop by **Animal Crackers** for burgers, hot dogs and chicken fingers. In New York, an **outdoor stand** stocks oranges, apples and other fresh fruit. And in San Francisco/Amity, **vendors** sell frozen chocolate covered bananas that are hits with the kids.

SEA WORLD RESTAURANTS

Sea World's restaurants are a medley of sit-down places, fast-food eateries and delis with food that's pretty tasty.

Al E. Gator's (407-351-3600) is proof that theme-park restaurants with corny pun names can be incredibly good. Much of the menu is devoted to classic Florida seafare, including fried grouper sandwiches, chunky conch chowder and shrimp scampi. There is gator tail, fried and served with lemon pepper cream sauce. You can sit inside or on the outdoor patio overlooking a pale green lagoon. There are a children's menu and family-style dinners where everyone helps themselves to platters of fried chicken and other comfort foods. Moderate.

For a quick sandwich, check out the **Waterfront Sandwich Grille**. Good foot-long hot dogs and stuffed baked potatoes are featured at **Hot Dogs 'n Spuds**. Both budget.

Sightseeing

Route 192, called "the gateway to Walt Disney World," leads you into downtown Kissimmee along a trail of flashing billboards and high-tech signs with ten-foot letters, all trying to persuade you to see an alligator, watch a medieval joust, get wet, ride an airboat, buy oranges or T-shirts and eat seafood. This is "tourist trap trail," also known as the Irlo Bronson Memorial Highway or Spacecoast Parkway. Despite overdosing on tackiness, the strip features a slew of family-style fun.

One of the first super attractions you will encounter is **Old Town** (5770 West Route 192, Kissimmee; 407-396-4888), a nostalgic extravaganza of shops and restaurants, with cobbled streets and fountains, a ferris wheel and a simulated roller coaster ride. A splendid place for families, the pedestrian mall is rarely crowded during the day and offers plenty of room for the kids to roam.

A few museums are tucked away in Old Town, including the **Wooden Train Museum** (407-396-7120; admission). A favorite of sons and dads, it features an audio-narrated tour of handcrafted wooden models of historic locomotives. Over 100 railroad pieces include Lincoln's funeral train, the Wabash Cannonball and early steam engines. Another museum pays homage to the king of rock n' roll. The **Elvis Presley Museum** (407-396-8594; admission) claims to have the world's largest collection of Elvis memorabilia outside of Graceland. It does have some prize articles, including a piano housed at Graceland for 12 years, antique pistols from Elvis' Beverly Hills home and, of course, a rhinestone-studded cape.

In this bizarre land of tacky tourism, things don't get much stranger than **Xanadu** (4800 West Route 192, Kissimmee; 407-396-1992; admission). Billed as the "home of the future," the ballooning white polyurethane building looks like an igloo with tentacles. Here, in the 21st century, computers select the menu according to your dietary needs and preferences, then prepare the meal in proper proportions, and—the best part—clean up. Each of Xanadu's fifteen rooms features futuristic funkiness, including an electronic hearth and art gallery, a room in a wine glass and a climate-controlled treehouse where kids can weave through a maze of tunnels. Kids under 10 are admitted free.

Once upon a time, before Disney ever built its Typhoon Lagoon water park, there were two places you went for a mix of water and slides: **Water Mania** (6073 West Route 192, Kissimmee; 407-396-2626; admission) and **Wet 'n Wild** (6200 International Drive, Orlando; 407-351-1800; admission). Today, Typhoon Lagoon lures the most vacationers, but Wet 'n Wild draws locals who want the steepest, fastest, scariest slides. Wet 'n Wild's premier attraction is The Black Hole, a $2 million, space-themed slide where you corkscrew through pitch blackness on a 1000-gallon-a-minute stream of water. And the 25-acre Wet 'n Wild has much more: whitewater rapids, a wave pool, a leisurely raft ride, knee-board water skiing and five vertical drops called the Mach 5. It also has a children's water playground with scaled-down versions of the big slides as well as kid-size restaurants.

Water Mania, on the other hand, is much smaller and offers only a handful of fast slides. It does feature some children's slides and a small wooded area perfect for family picnics.

Of the three water parks, Typhoon Lagoon naturally has far more landscaping and special effects. Water Mania, in fact, is almost all concrete, and Wet 'n Wild has only a minimum of trees and grass. Wet 'n Wild costs about the same as Typhoon Lagoon, but Water Mania is slightly less. Other factors to consider: The slides at Wet 'n Wild and

---

TUPPERWARE TIDINGS

Buuurrrrrrppp!

Excuse us, but we really can't help ourselves. See, we're here at the world's first and only Tupperware Museum (Route 441 just north of Route 192; 407-847-3111), located in downtown Kissimmee, Florida. And we're surrounded by oodles of plastic containers with those clever little grooved lids that scream to be, well, burped.

This very keen place is Tupperware's world headquarters, and it will give you the low-down on food storage. There are "historic" food containers, including jugs and urns used by ancient Egyptians. There's also a narrated tour about the makings of modern day vessels, and a kiddie playroom with (what else?) plastic toys. Our favorite part, though, is the Tupperware kitchen with pastel bowls and plates, cereal storers, butter keepers, and "multi-mugs" that—how groovy!—double as coasters.

Best of all, you can leave your plastic at home—seeing all this plastic is free.

Water Mania feature easier climbs and—oftentimes—shorter lines than those at Typhoon Lagoon. During spring and fall, Wet 'n Wild and Water Mania are usually less crowded on weekdays than Typhoon Lagoon. Wet 'n Wild closes from January and mid-March; Water Mania and Typhoon Lagoon are open year round.

"Is it really real?" is what kids ask when they visit **Mel Fisher's World of Treasure** (8586 Palm Parkway, Orlando; 407-239-6000; admission). They're referring, of course, to the $10 million worth of gold, silver, emeralds and other gleaming jewels piled around the museum. Fisher and his crew of divers recovered the booty from the ships *Atocha* and *Santa Margarita*, which sank in 1622 off the Florida Keys.

Fun 'n Wheels (6739 Sand Lake Road, Orlando; 407-351-5651; admission) is a good place to take the kids after dinner. There's putt putt golf, bumper cars and bumper boats, a water slide and video arcade. There's also a small ferris wheel for young children, and go carts for older ones who like a little speed.

Despite its whirlwind tourist reputation, **Kissimmee** manages to maintain the flavor of its bucolic cattle town beginnings. When you reach this town at the end of the road, you will find a transformation from the maelstrom behind you. Little has changed in the heart of the city since its founding in 1878. Many original buildings remain, including the courthouse and **Makinson's Hardware Store** (308 East Broadway; 407-847-2100), purported to be the state's first hardware store.

A weekly event recalls the town's beef and dairy industry roots: every Wednesday visitors can sit in on the town's cattle auction at the **Kissimmee Livestock Market** (805 East Donegan Avenue; 407-847-3521).

Located near the lakefront in downtown Kissimmee, the **Monument of States** (Monument Avenue, Lake Front Park; 407-847-3174) is built of stones from every state in the nation, plus 21 foreign countries. Built in 1943 by the townspeople, it stands as a 70-foot monument to tourism. Somewhat disheveled in appearance, it appeals to rock-hounds with its impressive gathering of flint, alabaster, coquina, meteors, stalagmites, marble, petrified teeth, lava and other specimens.

Lake Front Park lies at the end of Monument Avenue. This city park skirts Tohopekaliga Lake (called Lake Toho for short), where fishing, canoeing and bicycling are popular sports.

Another hint of Kissimmee's noncontrived lifestyle can be found in the 50-mile-long **Kissimmee Chain-of-Lakes** (407-847-2388) resort area. This string of lakes, of which Lake Toho is the largest, provides secluded activities for families. Houseboating, motorboating, sailing, bass fishing and birdwatching are offered. Follow Route 525 out of Kissimmee for a scenic oak-tunnel drive around the big lake.

For more information on the area, stop in at or call the **Kissimmee-St. Cloud Convention and Visitors Bureau** (1925 Route 192, Kissimmee; 407-847-5000).

Southwest of downtown Kissimmee, kids can spend a day on the farm. The **Green Meadows Children's Farm** (Ponciana Boulevard five miles south of Route 192, Kissimmee; 407-846-0770; admission) offers 40 acres of pretty countryside where children can milk a cow, ride a pony, take a hay ride and help feed up. A perfect break from theme park crowds and noise, the quiet retreat is home to over 200 animals. Arrive during October, and you can pick pumpkins.

North along Route 441, you will find a pair of giant alligator jaws beckoning you to enter **Gatorland Zoo** (Route 441, Kissimmee; 407-857-3845; admission). Here you can see over 4000 Florida alligators and crocodiles, along with exotic snakes, birds, monkeys and one tapir. Not as much a tourist trap as it sounds, this refuge maintains a natural cypress swamp setting, carpeted with ferns and brightened with orchids. Scenes from *Indiana Jones and the Temple of Doom* were filmed in this jungle atmosphere. If your kids are brave (and you don't mind forking over a few extra bucks), they can have their picture taken with a baby alligator or a snake.

Shopping

Both at Walt Disney World and outside its confines are many ways to spend your shopping dollars. Within the Magic Kingdom, Epcot and Disney–MGM Studios, fantasy stores fuse atmosphere into the illusory surroundings. Cinderella Castle, for instance, has a cache of twinkling jewels and medieval-style swords and axes. Shops also carry Disney *everything*, from Mickey sunshades and underwear to Donald Duck cookery. It's easy to spend hours (and mega-bucks) in the Disney shops, but you'll end up wasting valuable sightseeing time. Unless you're a shopaholic, save the heavy duty shopping for a mall. On the other hand, Disney's best stores include some so unusual they qualify as sightseeing.

MAGIC KINGDOM SHOPPING

On Main Street U.S.A., shops help create the ambience of a charming American town. The odorous **Main Street Market House** stocks dried herbs, teas and Mickey Mouse cookie cutters. Kids love the mystical **House of Magic**, where they can try on monstrous masks and try out magic wands. **Main Street Confectionery** is a wonderful old-time candy store with illuminated shelves of chocolate and giant candy canes.

Adventureland has two covered markets offering exotic treasures. One, **Adventureland Bazaar**, features African jewelry and prints.

Caribbean Plaza has such tropical goodies as shell jewelry and pirate swords and hats.

Next door in Frontierland, **Bearly Country** is lined with glazed ceramics, pillows and other decorative items with a Navajo flair. **Frontierland Trading Post** excels in gifts and leather goods in a western and Mexican vein.

One of my favorite Magic Kingdom shops is Liberty Square's **Yankee Trader**. Like a New England general store, it's brimming with jams and jellies, pretty country furnishings and nifty kitchen gadgets.

Stores in Fantasyland naturally appeal to children. **Tinkerbell's Toy Shop** has princess-style gowns for little girls and model cars for boys. There are stuffed animals and wooden toys at **Nemo's Niche** and Alice in Wonderland clothing at the **Madd Hatter**. Few can resist a peek inside the **King's Gallery**, at the base of Cinderella Castle. With its twinkling blown glass, miniature castles and medieval-style costumes, the place seems magical. **Mickey's Christmas Carol** smells like cinnamon and looks like a yuletide party. Pick up your Mickey tree lights and ornaments here.

Mickey's Starland and Tomorrowland have little in the way of interesting shops. If you must browse, go to Tomorrowland's **Space Port** and check out the campy "futuristic" gifts.

EPCOT SHOPPING

The Future World half of Epcot offers a few novel stores. **Broccoli & Co.** (The Land) has health food cookbooks, jewelry shaped like vegetables and other fun food things. In **CommuniCore West**, a robot will custom paint a T-shirt for you.

World Showcase shops are part of the Epcot cultural experience. Each pavilion highlights goods native to its host country and often showcases works from visiting artists and crafters. Store architecture

PACKAGE PICKUP

*If you're a sucker for Mickey Mouse T-shirts, Goofy caps and other silly souvenirs (don't try to hide it—we know you are), here's good news: You don't have to lug your packages around all day. Any time you make a purchase at a Disney World theme park or Sea World, you can have the store clerk forward your bags to **Package Pickup**. Then you collect them on your way out of the park. For Package Pickup locations inside Disney World, check with Guest Relations at each theme park. Inside Sea World, check with Visitor Information.*

often emulates the beautiful designs of each country, so take time to peruse the buildings.

Fashioned like a town square at night, **Plaza de Los Amigos** (Mexico) is a festive market scattered with baskets, gourds, colorful papier-mâché and other south-of-the-border wares.

During medieval times, Scandinavian peasants painted their old furniture to give it style and color. The painted furnishings at Norway's **Puffin's Roost** are done in a method called rosemaling, which uses floral designs and inscriptions. The shop, which also has beautifully painted ceilings and floors, carries Norwegian souvenirs made of glass, pewter and wood.

China's **Yong Feng Shangdian**, or "Bountiful Harvest," is an exquisite gallery of silk tapestries, porcelain masks, carved chests and other Oriental treasures. For children, there are plastic snakes and swords.

The Germany pavilion boasts no less than nine shops, including the engaging **Glas and Porzellan**. Like many German craft shops, the place has dozens of built-in cabinets and cubbyholes lined with figurines. **Der Teddybar** has filled-to-the-top toy chests as well as model Volvos and Mercedes Benz cars. Clocks, beer steins and wood carvings can be found next door at **Volkskunst**.

Chocoholics should head for **Delizie Italiane** (Italy), an oasis of gourmet Italian chocolates. The marble-floored **Il Bel Cristallo** specializes in crystal and porcelain but has some funky Mona Lisa prints.

Kids can get their coonskin caps and Daniel Boone rifles at **Heritage Manor Gifts** (United States). Out front, vendors sell dulcimers and American flags.

In the true spirit of capitalism, Japan's pavilion has its own department store. At **Mitsukoshi Department Store**, you'll find an assortment of elegant Japanese furniture, tableware, jewelry, kimonos and much more.

Merchants at the exotic **Moroccan** pavilion peddle such authentic goods as tasseled fez hats, finger bells, woven rugs and bellows. Horn and drum players stroll while you shop.

France is a wonderful place to shop. The **Plume et Palette** has French reproduction art, crystal and porcelain, while **Tout Pour le Gourmet** features goodies for the gourmet cook. **La Maison du vin** stocks a good selection of French wine, and **Galerie des Halles** proffers heavenly chocolates.

Each United Kingdom shop signifies a different architectural period. The **Tea Caddy**, purveyor of English teas, is fashioned like a thatched cottage from the 1500s. The tudor-style **Magic of Wales** offers Welsh crafts and mementos, while the Queen Anne-style **Queen's Table** displays figurines and crystal.

Indian and Eskimo crafts, moccasins and such are offered at **Northwest Mercantile**, in the Canada pavilion.

DISNEY–MGM STUDIOS SHOPPING

The place for Hollywood mementos is **Sid Cahuenga's One-of-a-Kind** (Hollywood Boulevard). You can pore through original playbills and autographed photos of stars such as Al Pacino and Burt Reynolds. Across the street, **Oscar's Classic Car Souvenirs** is lined with fuel pump bubble gum machines and classic car models. Head to Hollywood Boulevard's **Sweet Success** for your candy fix.

Star Wars junkies should blast off to **Endor Vendors** (Backlot Express), which sells books, masks and other souvenirs based on the movie. For Muppet maniacs, the **Muppet Store** (Backstage Studio Tour) is a treasure trove of toys, T-shirts and more Muppet merchandise. My favorite Disney–MGM store is the **Loony Bin** (Backstage Studio Tour), where the inventory centers on cartoons. Among the great gag gifts are Bugs Bunny's air freight cartons (look for the Tasmanian devil inside) and Wile E. Coyote's Acme kits for catching the Road Runner.

OTHER DISNEY WORLD SHOPPING

The Pleasure Island (407-934-7781) shops have some really out-of-the-mainstream stuff. The avant garde **Changing Attitudes** has leather and lace getups, counterculture T-shirts and mod artwork and jewelry. Nearby, Roger Rabbit's sexy cartoon girlfriend has her own shop. **Jessica's** tempts with sheer red lingerie, red ties and shirts, and other items emblazoned with the cartoon's knock-em-dead figure. **Avigator's** will outfit you in expedition wear.

The Disney Village Marketplace (407-828-3800) was created so you could buy Disney souvenirs without paying theme-park admission. The lakeside gathering of decorative shops and eateries is a good place to spend a rainy afternoon or a relaxing evening (stores stay open until 10 p.m.). One store, **Mickey's Character Shop**, boasts the most Disney paraphernalia anywhere. It's a jolly place flooded with marching band music and mouse merchandise. The mood is just as joyous at **You and Me Kid**, a child's dreamworld of giant electric trains, fairy tale gowns, Big Birds in sneakers and other fantasy toys. At **Board Stiff**, you'll find psychedelic surfboards and hip clothes to wear to the beach. On a more serious note, **Personal Message** features high-tech gifts, clocks and photo frames.

When mom is shopping at Disney Village Marketplace, dad and the kids can rent mini-speedboats at the nearby marina.

JUST OUTSIDE DISNEY WORLD SHOPPING

Old Town (5770 West Route 192, Kissimmee; 407-396-4888) is a tourist-belt shopping center offering specialty wares and trendy items in an old-fashioned ambience. Brick-lined streets re-create a nostalgic atmosphere of nickel Cokes, merry-go-rounds, ice cream parlors and city squares.

In Old Town, **Swinging Things** (407-396-7238) carries a line of imported hammocks and wind chimes. At the same location, **Mango Republic** (407-239-6012) deals in T-shirts, cotton fashions, straw hats and other items with Caribbean soul. Old Town's **The Rolls** (407-396-4888) is a car lover's mecca, carrying coffee mugs, T-shirts and even toilet paper emblazoned with car names. **The General Store** (407-396-4888) corners the market on old-fashioned funky stuff, with gifts such as hot dog-shaped telephones and Hershey's chocolate soap dispensers. The storefront at **The Great Train Store and Exhibit** (407-396-7120) sells model trains, engineer caps and other railroad nostalgia and toys. **Old Town Magic Shop** (407-396-6884) carries an enticing collection of tricks and magic books, with a free lesson for every trick purchase.

One of the largest gatherings of factory outlets is **Belz Factory Outlet Mall** (5401 West Oakridge Road; 407-352-9611). Over 80 stores sell discounted books, jewelry, electronics, clothing and dinnerware. One shop at Belz called **Everything But Water** (407-351-4069) sells swimwear and accessories.

At **Mercado** (8445 International Drive; 407-345-9337) village, shoppers are entertained while they browse the brick streets and Mediterranean-style storefronts full of ethnic shops. Here you'll find **Treasures from Nature** (407-352-1808), which deals in Native American silver jewelry, distinctive pottery and unusual wood carvings. **Exclusively East Gallery** (407-351-2626) sells very expensive Oriental vases, statues and wallhangings. The **Conch Republic** (407-363-0227) in Mercado sells Key West aloe lotions and singer Jimmy Buffet's line of tropical clothing and jewelry.

Also in the Mercado, **Coral Reef** (407-351-0100) carries unique artwork including Oriental *chokin* items as well as some remarkable pieces by a Gainesville artist working with crushed pecan shell and powder. In **Hello Dolly** (407-352-7344) collectible dolls are sold. Spiffy clothing and gifts for the car enthusiast await at **One For the Road** (407-345-0120). Pick up your MGM and Universal Studios movie paraphernalia and T-shirts at **Once Upon A Star** (407-363-4449).

If the cowboy bug bites, mosey on over to **Great West Boot Outlet** (5531 International Drive; 407-345-8103) to get outfitted in one of the 5000 pairs of boots.

UNIVERSAL STUDIOS SHOPPING

Universal Studios' imaginative shops make for some interesting browsing. The twisted plastic faces at **Hollywood Make-up and Masks** (Hollywood) would scare Boris Karloff, and that's why kids love this place. If you're in the market for a knock-em-dead swimsuit, **It's a Wrap** (Hollywood) has the latest in minuscule neon styles. Top it off at **Brown Derby Hat Shop** (Hollywood), where black and whites of the stars decorate the wall.

Young children can spend an afternoon in **Animal House** (Expo Center), where they get to wade through stuffed Pink Panthers, Woody Woodpeckers and other cartoon favorites. Over in San Francisco/Amity, **San Francisco Imports** offers pearls, jade, kimonos and other Oriental imports with fantasy pricetags. Planning a trip to the banana republic? Stop in **Safari Outfitters Ltd.** (New York) for jungle wear. Hitchcock fans should head for **The Bates Motel Gift Shop** (Production Central), which stocks plastic knives, terry cloth robes and shower curtains (without the bloodstains).

SEA WORLD SHOPPING

Sea World's handful of shops are of the souvenir variety, and offer little in the way of interesting browsing. For those who insist on a campy memento, there are stuffed Shamus, dolphins and sea lions and an assortment of ocean-themed T-shirts.

PARADES ACROSS THE WATER

*Every night, the tranquil, pitch-black Seven Seas Lagoon gets a jolt of electricity. Like someone flipping on a big light switch, the waters come alive with the **Electrical Water Pageant**. This 1000-foot caravan features thousands of tiny lights arranged to resemble sea creatures. As they weave around the lagoon, the shimmering "creatures" reflect across the water and appear to be swimming.*

You can see the beautiful pageant from the Polynesian Resort, Grand Floridian, Contemporary Resort, Fort Wilderness Resort and the Magic Kingdom when it's open until 11 p.m. The parade usually starts at 9 p.m. but travels past each site at various times. Call 407-824-4321 for specific times. If you're not staying at any of the resorts, simply ride the monorail or Disney bus to one. My favorite spot is the twinkling lakeside gazebo at the Grand Floridian.

Nightlife

The Disney area, so resplendent with sightseeing gimmickry, has debuted its own brand of entertainment. The biggest night game in town is Disney's Pleasure Island, a flashy playground of bars, restaurants and shops. Nearby, area restaurants take dinner theater a step further, to "dinner arena." The entertainment is usually more noteworthy than the food at these extravaganzas. Most require advance reservations, especially on weekends. Included here are most of the major dinner attractions, along with a sampling of more low-key gathering spots and watering holes.

If you don't want to be in the Comedy Warehouse show, avoid the last seat in the fifth row next to the telephone. (Otherwise, expect a phone call).

DISNEY WORLD NIGHTLIFE

The Magic Kingdom of nightlife, **Pleasure Island** (407-934-7781) plays to virtually every nighttime entertainment fantasy. The six-acre pleasure palace cranks with six themed nightclubs and outdoor stages where singers and dancers reel with energy. A New Year's Eve-type celebration, complete with fireworks, laser lights and party favors, happens every night around midnight. One cover charge gets you into every club. Or, get there before 7 p.m. and there's no cover (restaurants and shops are open during the day; bars open at 7). Anyone under 18 must be accompanied by an adult, and you must be at least 21 to order alcoholic drinks. Exceptions are CAGE! and Mannequins Dance Palace where you must be at least 18 to enter.

Every Pleasure Island club has its own style of show, from country and western two-steppers to psychedelic gyrators. You can come and go between all the clubs except for the Comedy Warehouse, which has several shows that fill up fast each night. Plan to see the first comedy show (usually at 7:25 p.m.) or the last one (around 12:30 a.m.); the shows in between typically have a 30-to-45-minute wait.

The reason people flock to the **Comedy Warehouse** is its hilarious improvisation that—surprise!—pokes fun at Disney World. You'll hear Disney employees plotting to swipe tourist dollars and see a cob-webbed tourist who's been waiting...and waiting...to ride Space Mountain. The employees, called "polyester robots," also sing a great little tune about how Disney "gives you a thrill then gives you the bill." The warehouse decor is appropriately loony, with Mickey Mouse drums, giant crayons, fake palm trees and other kitschy stuff strung everywhere.

Pleasure Island's **Adventurers Club** looks like a safari gone mad. Everywhere you look there's African-style weirdness: shrunken heads, propellers, a barstool with elephant legs, gargoyle sculptures, a hippopotamus head. One entire room is filled with masks that, every hour or so, come alive. Besides the talking mask shows, eccentric "travelers" tell tall tales to tourists.

The beat pounds so loud and hard at **Mannequins Dance Palace** it shakes your ribs. Billed as a "high-tech" nightclub, the steel-and-strobe palace pulsates in an atmosphere accented by cool fog. Waitresses tote trays of test tube shooters, and Madonna-style dancers strut their stuff on a revolving dancefloor.

With its dozens of video screens flickering in the night, **CAGE!** is Disney's rendition of an underground video club. Virtually everything that can be painted is done in black, and the rest is steel beams, catwalks and twisted metal. Recorded sounds range from heavy metal to progressive.

Who but Disney would combine art deco and country-western? At Pleasure Island's **Neon Armadillo Music Saloon**, surroundings appear western moderne: Mexican blankets, wagon wheels and saddles combined with chrome and neon. Like the decor, the live entertainment leans toward hip country.

XZFR Rock and Roll Beach Club has psychedelic carpets, black padded rails, fishing nets and parking meters. You can dance to everything from recorded Beach Boys to Led Zeppelin, or shoot some pool upstairs.

Disney nightlife does exist outside Pleasure Island, mainly in the form of dinner theater. At **Polynesian Revue and Mickey's Tropical Revue** (Polynesian Village Resort, Disney World, Lake Buena Vista; 407-824-8000) two different shows appeal to adults and children with an outdoor South Seas motif. During the Polynesian revue, hula dancers and fire jugglers entertain while diners enjoy barbecue fare. Disney characters dressed à la tropical perform for kids during Mickey's revue.

GATHER 'ROUND THE CAMPFIRE

Of all the Disney World activities, few get higher ratings from families than the Fort Wilderness Campfire (407-824-8000). The old-fashioned gathering, open only to those staying at a Disney resort, is held nightly at a wooden trading post enveloped in mossy slash pines. It's a people event, with marshmallow roasting and sing-a-longs where everyone joins in on camping classics like "My Bonnie Lies Over the Ocean." Kids go crazy when Chip and Dale show up and beg for chocolate chip cookies (bring a handful). For the finale, a full-length Disney movie is shown on an outdoor screen.

While parents are visiting Pleasure Island's nightclubs, teenagers can catch a movie at the island's ten-screen theater.

The show at **Top of the World** (Contemporary Resort, Walt Disney World, Lake Buena Vista; 407-824-8000) features Broadway's greatest hits performed by a troupe of dancers and singers. If you can't make the show, have a drink at the adjacent lounge and check out the spectacular view of the Magic Kingdom.

At the **Hoop-Dee-Doo-Revue** (Fort Wilderness Resort; 407-824-2900), the Pioneer Hall Players crack corn in an Old West setting with appropriate chow. By far the most popular Disney revue (it can take several months to get a seat), it is also, in my opinion, the least entertaining. The dancing and singing are average at best, and the jokes are just plain silly. Worse yet, it costs big bucks. My advice: Skip this one and see the Magic Kingdom's Diamond Horseshoe Jamboree.

Among other lively watering holes, the **Rose & Crown Pub** at Epcot's United Kingdom pavilion is a prime place to toss back a brew. On the waterfront, it's warm and clubby and beautifully designed with polished oak, leaded glass and brass. Afternoon or evening, you can count on a jolly crowd.

Over at Epcot's Germany pavilion, the **Biergarten** inspires good times with a Bavarian beer garden atmosphere. An oom-pah-pah band and yodelers entertain. Japan's relaxing **Matsu No Ma Lounge** has bonsai planters, teakwood tables and splendid views across Epcot. The sushi platters and exotic rum fruit drinks are excellent.

The beachy **Copa Banana** at the Dolphin resort has great frozen libations and tabletops that look like slices of fruit. Late at night, an early 20s crowd packs the live rock 'n roll bar.

Disney–MGM Studios' **Tune In Lounge** makes you feel like you stepped into a '50s television sitcom. Fashioned like a cozy living room, the place has cushiony couches, TV trays and waiters dressed like the Beave. You also can get a drink at the studios' **Catwalk Bar**, a spacious second-floor roost overlooking the Soundstage Restaurant.

The Empress Lilly showboat's **Baton Rouge Lounge** (Disney Village Marketplace; 407-828-3900) features comedy entertainment with music. Cover.

The Giraffe Lounge (Hotel Royal Plaza, Walt Disney World Village, Lake Buena Vista; 407-828-2828) is a splashy, crowded dance spot featuring live music.

Nearby, **Laughing Kookaburra Good Time Bar** (Buena Vista Palace, Walt Disney World Village, Lake Buena Vista; 407-827-2727) lists 99 varieties of beer and features live dance music in an Australian-theme setting.

JUST OUTSIDE DISNEY WORLD NIGHTLIFE

The **Arabian Nights** (6225 West Route 192, Kissimmee; 407-239-9223) dinner attraction features chariot races, Arabian horse dancing and white Lippizaner shows.

Little Darlin's Rock n' Roll Palace (5770 West Route 192, Kissimmee; 407-396-6499) in Old Town boasts the spectacular showmanship typical of this area's attractions. In a grandiose palace, rock 'n' roll takes a trip down memory lane. A house band performs nightly, often followed by old touring rock-and-roll bands of fame. Cover.

Fried chicken and cowboy shenanigans are served up at a dinner attraction called **Fort Liberty** (5260 East Route 192, Kissimmee; 407-351-5151).

Most out-of-towners are scared off by the shabby appearance of the **Big Bamboo** (4849 West Route 192; 407-396-2777), and that's why Disney employees made it their favorite haunt. The little cinderblock building is cluttered with Mickey Mouse paraphernalia (some marvelously cynical) and is ripe with Disney gossip. The Bamboo serves beer in mason jars on toilet paper coasters and reels with big-band music every night.

Murphy's Vine Street Emporium Dance Palace (4736 West Route 192, Kissimmee; 407-396-6500) spotlights live dance music every night. The word palace aptly describes the majestic proportions of this popular spot. Cover.

Another dining novelty, **Medieval Times Dinner Tournament** (4510 Route 192, Kissimmee; 407-396-1518), brings back the Middle Ages. Here you eat fowl with your fingers and watch jousting tableside. The **Mardi Gras** (8445 International Drive; 407-351-5151) dinner

---

THE ULTIMATE ILLUMINATION

*Epcot's **IllumiNations Laser Show** is a must-see. This grand finale could easily be the highlight of your Disney visit. Staged at 9 or 10 nightly over the World Showcase lagoon, the program is a stunning visual concert of colored fountains, stirring music and laser lights that dance across the pitch-black sky (Epcot turns its lights off). IllumiNations goes much further than most laser shows, creating powerful images across shooting streams of water, the Spaceship Earth globe and the World Showcase countries.*

The largest and most sophisticated laser show in the world, IllumiNations uses two types of lasers: argon for green and blue light and krypton for red. Some of the lasers are mounted on World Showcase pavilions, while others rest on a 50-ton barge in the lagoon. The show's pyrotechnic finale features some 650 fireworks in six minutes—nearly two fireworks per second!

attraction, as you might imagine, has a New Orleans theme. Brightly painted papier-mâché masks, clowns and balloons create a carnival atmosphere. Entertainment comes from a jazz band and cabaret performers.

Medieval dinner entertainment is offered at **King Henry's Feast** (8984 International Drive; 407-351-5151). Magicians, acrobats and King Henry himself come to the stage. The outside looks like a castle, complete with moat and notched turrets. Inside are swords, shields and heavy pewter wine and ale tankards that combine with grand chandeliers to create a Middle Age ambience.

The **Plantation Dinner Theatre** (9861 International Drive; 407-352-0008) sits in the lobby of the Heritage Inn. It features light drama in intimate Victorian surroundings.

The entertainment at **Mark Two** (3376 Edgewater Drive; 407-843-6275) is more traditional dinner theater. Local troupes perform Broadway classics.

UNIVERSAL STUDIOS NIGHTLIFE

Part of an international chain, the **Hard Rock Café** (5800 Kirkman Road, Orlando; 407-363-7655) is an uproarious rock n' roll shrine that plays to big crowds. Memorabilia covers every inch of the place There's Elton John's outrageous suit and Elvis' jeweled costume, and even some bricks from the Beatles' first Liverpool stage. A nostalgic spot for mom and dad, without the kids.

SEA WORLD NIGHTLIFE

Sea World has joined the dinner show circuit with its **Polynesian Luau** (407-363-2195). Held nightly at a lakeside restaurant, it showcases hip-swinging island women, fire-eating men and a tropical menu of sweet 'n sour pork, seafood and strawberry colada cheesecake. The food and entertainment more than satisfy, and the community seating is perfect for families who like to socialize.

The oceanarium also stages an array of evening stadium shows. Depending on the time of year, you can see pyrotechnics at the **Starlight Laser and Fireworks Spectacular** (Atlantis Water Ski Stadium) and brilliant dancing fountains at the **Water Fantasy Show** (Sea World Theatre). Shamu the killer whale presents his own evening extravaganza in **Shamu Night Magic** (Shamu Stadium). For showtimes and dates, call 407-351-3600.

NINE

Orlando

Orlando. Mention the word and most people envision Mickey Mouse, **205**
Cinderella's castle or perhaps even an imaginary town on Main Street
U.S.A. But this is no imaginary town. In fact, like the Disney World
"community," Orlando is growing at a rapid pace that makes it the
boomtown of the South.

With the stream of new residents and jobs, Orlando the city is spilling over into an ever-expanding metropolitan area. The population of
the three counties that make up Orlando and its environs has mush-
roomed in the past decade to more than one million. Eighteen million
passengers arrive at Orlando International Airport every year, three
times the number of ten years ago. New factories are booming, with
high-tech companies creating jobs at three times the national average,
Two of the stalwarts of Desert Storm—the Patriot missile and infrared
sights for night warfare—are made just a few miles from Disney's Star
Wars fantasy ride.

Nicknamed "Hollywood East" because of the influx of movie-in-
dustry theme parks, the Orlando area is attracting some real-life
"beautiful people" as well, including the likes of director Steven
Spielberg, who bought a home in the city.

Others are discovering the region, too. Tammy Faye Bakker, the
wife of jailed evangelist Jim Bakker, has moved what's left of their New
Covenant Ministries to a warehouse on Orlando's outskirts. Campus
Crusade for Christ, whose stated ambition is to bring the gospel to
billions by the next century, is moving its headquarters from San Ber-
nardino, California to the Orlando area. Social worker Jerry Schall
claims to have discovered the Fountain of Youth in a forested area 35
minutes from Disney World.

From the 19th century Orlando has captured the imagination of
entrepreneurs, dreamers and zealots alike. Together with the area's
other residents, they have moulded it into the quintessential American

More than 800 flights come and go from Orlando International Airport each day, making it the 20th-busiest facility in the world.

town. During the 1880s, a group of New England pioneers rode a one-way train to Orlando and began working their architectural charm. Around the gin-clear lakes they built crisp, white colonial estates and graceful frame homes trimmed in verandas. Among the moss-covered trees they built a Spanish-style college, the first in Florida. Then they seasoned the city with art, introducing theater, painting, sculpture and literature. In 1908, locals proclaimed Orlando "The City Beautiful." It was perhaps the earliest attempt at national promotion.

The Great Depression set Orlando back, but not for long. Through the '30s and '40s, wealthy Northerners and Midwesterners arrived and built stately winter homes. Others, too, poured on the architectural charm. Famous families such as Sears and Edison created sumptuous winter hideaways in the northern suburb of Winter Park. Spanish Mediterranean estates were the choice of home for many.

By the 1950s, Orlando began to feel real growth. The opening of Cape Canaveral, only 45 miles away on the coast, launched a wave of industry. But it did little to prepare the city for the tidal wave that rolled in 20 years later: Walt Disney World.

The 1971 opening of the Magic Kingdom gave Orlando a jolt and propelled it into one of the fastest-growing vacation centers in the world. With the "magic" of Disney came big-time highways and mega shopping malls, overnight tourist attractions and hundreds of new restaurants, and eventually more hotel rooms than any other city in the nation. It meant national attention and brought people from every walk of life—major investors and get-rich-quick entrepreneurs, religious zealots and drifters, and vacationing middle America—who transformed this New England-style sleepy town.

The rapid growth has carried a price. Typical big-city problems like traffic jams and air and water pollution are beginning to crop up in the greater metropolitan area. Long-time residents lament the invasion of neon and road signs and the loss of some city treasures. The last orange grove on Orange Avenue, for example, disappeared in 1977. From pastures where cows are grazing you now can see condos and fast-food restaurants. Interstate 4, which runs through the heart of Orlando, will need 22 lanes by the year 2000, according to a regional planning group. Right now it has only six.

But all in all Orlando has handled its newfound fame well. Away from the theme parks that bring travelers to Orlando's door still beats the heart of a real city. Downtown Orlando boasts imagination indeed: Mirrored towers that angle toward the sky. Fountains that stream a rainbow of colors. Lakeshores that flourish with museums, galleries,

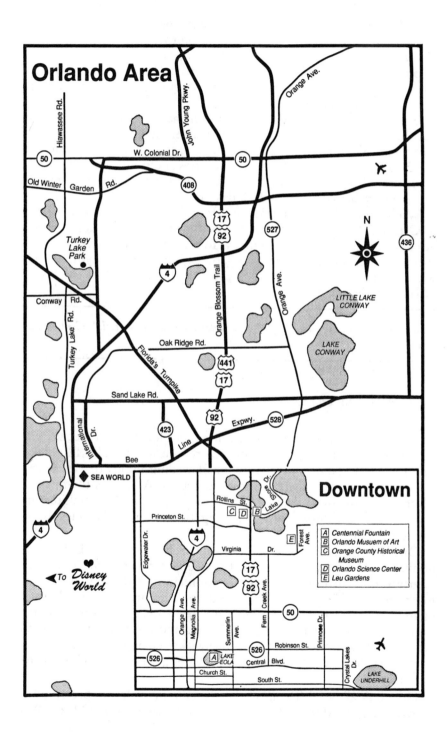

Orlando Area

Hiawasee Rd.

John Young Pkwy.

Orange Ave.

W. Colonial Dr.

50

50

Old Winter   Garden   Rd.

408

17
92

527

N

436

Turkey
Lake
Park

4

Orange Blossom Trail

Conway   Rd.

Turkey Lake Rd.

LITTLE LAKE
CONWAY

Florida's Turnpike

Orange Ave.

Oak Ridge Rd.

LAKE
CONWAY

441
17

Sand Lake Rd.

International   Dr.

92

423

Expwy.

528

Line

Bee

◆ SEA WORLD

4

♥
To *Disney
World*

Downtown

Rollins   St.

Shore Dr.

Lake

C   D   B

Princeton St.

Edgewater Dr.

4

Virginia   Dr.

E

Forest Ave.

	A	Centennial Fountain
	B	Orlando Musuem of Art
	C	Orange County Historical Museum
	D	Orlando Science Center
	E	Leu Gardens

17
92

Orange Ave.

Magnolia Ave.

Summerlin Ave.

Fern Creek Ave.

50

526

A LAKE
EOLA

526

Central   Blvd.

Robinson St.

Primrose Dr.

Crystal Lakes Dr.

LAKE
UNDERHILL

Church St.

South St.

science centers and blocks of historic buildings. Away from downtown, turn-of-the-century neighborhoods seem timelocked in a setting of ivy-wrapped pines and carpets of manicured greenery.

As it copes with the demands of a boomtown, the Orlando area is striving to retain its charm. For mass transit, the city is putting emphasis on an old-fashioned trolley line rather than an elevated rail system. Residential subdivisions, instead of the ubiquitous tract homes, try to instill a bucolic atmosphere.

But without question, the city's true character lies within its people. For this is still very much a hometown, a genuine place where people go to raise families. Maybe this is why vacationing families find so much in common with Orlando. Activities and sights, restaurants and shops are all geared toward family life. And where else do you find urban nightclubs designed with kids in mind?

While you're here, take time out from the theme parks and tune in to Orlando. Paddle a swan boat across downtown's Lake Eola. Stroll a brick street that was laid last century. Tour an old home brimming with antiques, then linger in the rose gardens outside. Once you've seen what the city truly has to offer, you can say you've had the "real" Orlando experience.

More than five millions gallons of water flow daily through Lake Eola's Centennial Fountain.

ORLANDO AREA SIGHTSEEING

Orlando may be an hour's drive from either Florida coast, yet the city possesses some of the state's most picturesque waters. The 1200 lakes that speckle Orlando range from small wading ponds to vast waters whose dark bottoms reach impossible depths. All across town, these silvery-blue mirrors reflect a mix of historic and modern architecture and perpetuate a lifestyle of waterskiing, bass fishing and careless walks along the shore.

One of the prettiest and best-known lakes is Lake Eola (pronounced YO-la), which rests in the heart of downtown. The lake's **Centennial Fountain** was built to commemorate the city's 100th anniversary in 1975 and features a modern sculpture and a rainbow of lights at night. When the fountain was dedicated, waters were added from fountains in Spain, England, France and the United States—all nations that have ruled Florida. A lovely lakeside park, with moss-covered oaks and an Oriental pagoda, provides a spectacular view of the fountain.

Orlando's early 20th-century heydays are marvelously preserved at **Church Street Station** (129 West Church Street; 407-422-2434), a two-block pedestrian mall of restored former hotels, warehouses and a railroad depot. This festive place, home to a colorful array of restaurants, nightclubs, shops and street performers, dispenses a visual feast of wrought-iron balconies, stained-glass windows, red-brick lanes, shiny turrets, and green and grape awnings. Strolling is the thing to do here, and hundreds indulge daily.

The historic Orlando neighborhood known as Loch Haven Park offers three fine museums. The **Orlando Museum of Art** (2416 North Mills Avenue; 407-896-4231; admission) spotlights 20th-century American works, pre-Columbian artifacts, African art and rotating exhibits from around the world. They also offer classes in painting and sculpture for children ages 6 to 12, so adults can spend some leisure time viewing the exhibits while the kids prepare to be artists of the future.

The **Orange County Historical Museum** (812 East Rollins Street; 407-898-8320; admission) travels back 10,000 years with the display of a Timucuan Indian canoe, then takes visitors to the Big Freeze of 1894, which devastated the area's citrus crop, and finally rolls into the early 20th-century era of boom and depression. At the museum's back door is **Fire Station No. 3**, the city's oldest firehouse. Built in 1926 on Dade Street and moved to the museum in 1978, the station houses antique toys as well as helmets, nozzles and uniforms from the days of bucket-brigade firefighting. Children really enjoy themselves here, and they get a history lesson at the same time.

Facts are flavored with fun for both kids and adults at the **Orlando Science Center** (810 East Rollins Street; 407-896-7151; admission), also in Loch Haven Park. Here you can find out your moon weight, enter a black hole, blow giant soap bubbles, learn to produce electricity with your own energy or eat ice cream made for astronauts. Daily planetarium shows run in an adjoining facility.

Orlando's botanical fantasyland is **Leu Gardens** (1730 North Forest Avenue; 407-246-2620; admission), where a 55-acre profusion of palm trees, orchids, roses, camellias and other flowering flora border a picturesque lake. Kids feel right at home in this wild setting, where

---

THE LEGEND OF ORLANDO REEVES

No one knows for sure how Orlando got its name, but many believe it comes from a brave but ill-fated soldier named Orlando Reeves. In 1835, Reeves joined a posse scouting for central Florida Indians. He was on sentinel duty one night when some Indians, disguised as pine tree logs, snuck into the soldiers' camp. Reeves spotted the intruders, fired his gun and saved his companions. Unfortunately, he was pierced by an arrow and died on the spot. Soon people started calling the town Orlando, and eventually that became the official name.

they can run free on soft grass and smell the flowers. Parents will want to join the guided tour of the handsome 1880s frame home, which showcases the lifestyle of a wealthy turn-of-the-century family.

A fantastic way to see Orlando is from the clouds. Hot air ballooning has soared in popularity in the area, particularly with families. Several ballooning enterprises offer sunrise flights with spectacular views of the city and outlying lakes and theme parks. Cinderella Castle, Space Mountain and Spaceship Earth are highlights. **Balloons by Terry, Inc.** (3529 Edgewater Drive; 407-422-3529) includes a brunch at Lili Marlene's Restaurant in its flight pattern. Or try **Rise & Float Balloon Tours** (5767 Major Boulevard; 407-352-8191). To ride, children sould be tall enough to see over the edge of the balloon's basket.

Remember the old Batman and Superman comic books? You'll find them among 70,000 vintage comic books and cartoon drawings crammed into the tiny **Cartoon Museum** (4300 South Semoran Boulevard #109; 407-273-0141). Much of the cartoon art was created by museum owner Jim Ivey, a colorful, cigar-smoking man who once drew political cartoons for the *Washington Star, San Francisco Examiner* and *Mad Magazine*. Parents and older children are guaranteed to like this zany cartoonist and his ever-changing collection of funnies. Young children, however, may be disappointed to find the museum doesn't feature Saturday-morning cartoons—which to them are the real thing.

Right outside Orlando on Route 426, the town of **Winter Park** delights families with its tree-lined avenues and lovely, oldtime **Central Park** (Park Avenue, between New England and Canton avenues) complete with benches, fountains and a stage. Folks here like to say that Winter Park is not a suburb of Orlando but the "superb" of Orlando. They're referring, of course, to the town's picture-book setting of winding brick streets, palatial turn-of-the-century homes, blue jewels of lakes, hidden courtyards and grand oak and cypress trees dripping with Spanish moss. Here, expensive foreign cars populate the streets, and art galleries are nearly as plentiful as shops.

Families can explore Winter Park's pretty scenery aboard the **Scenic Boat Tour** (312 East Morse Boulevard; 407-644-4056; admission). The peaceful, one-hour cruise weaves through canals draped in vines and across lakes where perfect lawns slope to the water's edge. Children enjoy the tame boat ride and the abundance of native water birds, and adults get to relax amid Florida scenery at its undisturbed best.

Just north of Winter Park lies the lovely bedroom community of Maitland. Here the **Maitland Art Center** (231 West Packwood Avenue, Maitland; 407-539-2181) hosts a changing array of contemporary sculpture and paintings that appeal to adults and children. Most interesting, though, are the buildings themselves: a cluster of Mayan and

Aztec designs built singlehandedly by an artist in the 1930s. Over the years, the six-acre spot has become a retreat for avant-garde artists and actors. Today, the lovely Garden Chapel on the grounds is a popular spot for weddings.

Getting a bird's eye view of big and beautiful fowl is the highlight of a visit to **Florida Audubon Society State Headquarters** (1101 Audubon Way, Maitland; 407-260-8300). Children are particularly intrigued by the bald eagles, owls, falcons, vultures and other birds of prey who live here in a huge aviary. As one docent noted, "How often does a child get to stand five feet from a bald eagle and look him dead in the eye?" The society also offers an instructional area where the whole family can brush up on their bird sense.

A little farther north in Longwood, the **Bradlee-McIntyre House** (150 West Street, Longwood; 407-332-6920) exemplifies the mansions that heralded the golden days of steamships. Built in 1855 in nearby Altamonte Springs, it was moved to its present location in the early 1970s. The architecture and appointments have been restored to their Queen Anne style.

Kids can't climb the cypress at **Big Tree Park** (General Hutchinson Parkway, north of Longwood; 407-323-2500), but they can marvel at its enormous size. With a height of 126 feet and diameter of 18 feet, the nubby giant is the largest bald cypress tree in the nation.

For more information on Orlando-area sights, visit the **Orlando/ Orange County Convention & Visitors Bureau, Inc.** (8445 International Drive, Orlando; 407-363-5871).

Who's the oldest resident in Central Florida? Most likely it's the enormous cypress tree in Big Tree Park, which is thought to be 3000 years old.

ORLANDO AREA LODGING

Unlike the array of family-style lodging in the Disney World area, Orlando's accommodations are geared more toward corporate visitors and adults traveling without children. Still, a few places really do make families feel at home while at the same time providing the welcome surroundings of a "real" city. Except for the Gold Key Inn, all of the following hotels invite children under 18 to stay free—with parents, of course.

With its sleek, curving concrete and glass tower, the **Radisson Plaza Hotel** (60 South Ivanhoe Boulevard; 407-425-4455) is one of the showcases of downtown Orlando. Like the outside, the inside is an eye-catcher. Sunshine streams through a dramatic glass atrium in the lobby, and rose-colored marble floors create a stylized look. Families will appreciate the extra space offered in the 337 guest rooms, outfitted with plush carpets and oak furnishings. Most rooms afford panoramic views of the city and adjacent Lake Ivanhoe. For parents who want some time alone, the hotel will arrange in-room babysitting. Deluxe rates, with moderate-priced specials throughout the year.

Downtown's other signature sleeping address is the **Harley Hotel** (151 East Washington Street; 407-841-3220). Built in the early 1960s and completely refurbished in 1991, the six-story hostelry enjoys a superb location along Lake Eola. The lobby decor harkens to earlier days with dark woods, brass and crushed velvet. By contrast, guestrooms feel ethereal with their pastel hues, downy comforters and dust ruffles and marble-topped dressers. Despite the Harley's standing as a corporate hotel, many families find it an inviting place to stay. Moderate.

Howard Johnson (305 West Colonial Drive; 407-843-8700) has a noisy but convenient location right next to Route 4. A 1990 refurbishment provided the 13-story building with a cozy yet modern appearance. The 276 guest rooms proffer contemporary appointments and fine city or lake views. Families will appreciate the heated outdoor pool, gameroom, laundry facilities and restaurant with children's menu. Moderate.

Not far from downtown, the **Plaza Inn** (603 Lee Road; 407-644-6100) is a good choice for families. Spread across ten acres, the inn is a cluster of low-slung buildings, two swimming pools, a toddler pool, gameroom, huge playground and extensive fitness center. Accommodations are generic motel style, though many rooms have kitchenettes and pull-out sofa beds. Ask for a quiet room near the back and away from the bustling highway. Budget.

If you need a resting place near Orlando International Airport, I recommend the **Gold Key Inn** (7100 South Orange Blossom Trail; 407-855-0050). An anomaly among the area's glitzy resorts, the two-story hostelry provides a warm, homey atmosphere with a brick fireplace in the Early American-style lobby and cushy armchairs and reproduction English prints in each of 208 guest rooms. A swimming pool, gameroom and restaurant framed with gardens round out the amenities. Children under 12 stay free. Moderate, with frequent budget specials.

In Winter Park's lovely Park Avenue area, the **Langford Resort Hotel** (300 East New England Avenue; 407-644-3400) features 226 rooms, dressed up simply and offering a hint of hotel days gone by. The lobby decor lingers between eclectic and tacky with a mix of Seminole Indian murals, velour sofas, cypress tables and terra-cotta floors. Families find solace in the outdoor swimming pool and playground surrounded by jungle gardens, meandering footpaths and a waterfall. Moderate.

To get the best Orlando lodging deal, you'll have to camp out. One place you might check into is **Orlando Holiday Travel Park** (1600

West 33rd Street; 407-648-5441), a 42-acre campground southwest of downtown. Families frequent the park during summer, taking advantage of the neighboring lake where they can fish from the shore or launch a boat. A swimming pool, children's playground, gameroom and recreation hall provide plenty of campground diversions. RVs welcome year-round; pop-up campers and tents are permitted only from May through September. Budget-priced, with super rate busters available through the campground's "family plan."

ORLANDO AREA RESTAURANTS

Orlando may as well have invented the term "surf and turf." Only an hour from the Atlantic coast and plopped in the middle of the state's beef locker, local restaurants can proudly offer the freshest of both worlds. Many hotels offer coupons for restaurant discounts, and you'll find coupons in the telephone book as well.

Your best bet for downtown dining is at **Church Street Station** (129 West Church Street; 407-422-2434), which encompasses over a dozen eateries that offer everything from gourmet pastas and blackened gator tail to plain-jane burgers and homemade fudge for the kids. **Lili Marlene's** is the most upscale, offering a deluxe-priced menu of steaks and chicken, pasta and seafood dishes. Youngsters can order from the Junior Aviators menu, where entrées come with french fries and ice cream. The place is bathed in wood, from the plank floors and glossy booths to the airplane props that dangle from the ceiling.

Church Street's **Cheyenne Saloon** is where you go for Texas-style vittles such as spare ribs, beef brisket and chili that's mild enough for the small fry. It's a high-class joint with elaborate carved railings, polished wood bars and a ceiling that soars. Moderate.

If your taste leans toward "Nawlins"-style cooking, head over to **Crackers**, also in Church Street Station. Despite its swanky surroundings, the pub caters to families and offers a lineup of seafood gumbo

---

ICE CREAM BIRTHDAY PARTIES

It's tough to throw a big birthday bash for your child when you're on vacation, but why not celebrate with a little ice cream? **Larry's Old Fashioned Ice Cream and Yogurt** *(8001 South Orange Blossom Trail, in the Florida Mall; 407-857-7271) provides the balloons and banana splits; you provide the kids. Menus are customized for each party and can include cakes with candles and ice cream or yogurt served most any way. (Larry's serves only all-natural ice cream and yogurt.) Reservations should be made at least five days in advance.*

(with the precise amount of okra), blackened gator tail, crab legs and red beans and rice. Moderate.

Nearby, **Pebbles** (17 West Church Street; 407-839-0892) is one of the few elegant, New American-style restaurants that welcomes families. Flickering oil lamps, high carved ceilings and well-spaced tables create an intimate mood perfect for such dishes as smoked duck and scallops with Asian spices and chicken vesuvio (with garlic, capers and perciatelli pasta). The nutty cheesy salad and goat cheese baked in marinara sauce make sumptuous starters. Children can go kid-style with hamburgers and pita pizza. A prime locale with, or without, the kids. Moderate to deluxe.

Plush and panoramic, **Lee's Lakeside** (431 East Central Boulevard; 407-841-1565) overlooks Lake Eola and the Centennial Fountain downtown. The menu does surf and turf superbly, with such specialties as châteaubriand bouquetière, tournedos, King crab and lobster. A crock of cheese with breadsticks and wonderful piña colada muffins accompany each entrée. If it sounds a bit too elaborate for the kids, don't worry: The children's menu features everything from burgers and hot dogs to fried chicken and grilled cheese. Deluxe, with early-bird specials during weekdays.

For fresh and reasonable seafood, try **Gary's Duck Inn** (3974 South Orange Blossom Trail; 407-843-0270). It's housed in a flat, red building with walls done in knotty pine and typical nautical trimmings. The specialty of the house is red snapper. Families can enjoy budget prices during early-bird specials on weekdays. The rest of the time, prices are moderate.

Número Uno (2499 South Orange Avenue; 407-841-3840) is held in high regard among Orlando residents for its Cuban cuisine. The family-run eatery offers simple decor and a menu of standard Cuban specialties such as rice and beans, roast pork and bean soup. Budget, with weekday lunch specials and half portions available for children.

It's called **La Cantina** (4721 East Colonial Drive; 407-894-4491), but it serves steaks, not tacos, and they come with side dishes of spaghetti, not refried beans. Despite the possible confusion, La Cantina serves some of the best steaks to be found in this beef capital. The surroundings are as comfortable as the food is good. Moderate, with early-bird specials and a children's menu.

A firm fixture in the ever-changing world of restaurants is **Chris's House of Beef** (801 John Young Parkway; 407-295-1931). Since 1957, this purveyor of perfectly aged steaks has fed meat lovers, who are allowed to choose their cuts from a glass showcase. There's also a selection of seafood and vegetarian platters, plus a catalog of over 400 wines and an ample salad bar. Moderate.

If you're hankering to quietly eat a steak away from tourist crowds, **Cattle Ranch** (6129 Old Winter Garden Road; 407-298-7334) is the place. Thick cuts are tossed onto a blazing orangewood fire for extraordinary flavor. Cowpoke elegance describes the ambience; down-home good describes the moderately priced eats. Pint-size portions are guaranteed to make the kids happy.

If authentic Mexican food in a packed *casa* is your style, try the homemade guacamole, refried beans and burritos at **Paco's** (1801 West Fairbanks Avenue, Winter Park; 407-629-0149). Kids usually go for the tacos, or the chef will fix them a special quesadilla (minus onions, peppers and other "yucky" stuff). Don't be turned off by the shabby look of this place—it's the real McCoy. Budget.

Ask children what they like best about **Angel's Diner and Bakery** (3084 Aloma Avenue, Winter Park; 407-657-1957) and they'll proba-bly say it's the free bubblegum you get with your check. Ask the par-ents, and they'll tell you it's the budget-priced food reminiscent of grandma's cooking. Pot roast, lasagna, meatloaf and spaghetti are the mainstays of this retrograde diner, fitted with cherry-red booths and outlined in chrome. Individual juke boxes are parked at every table.

Kids with short attention spans have plenty to keep them occupied at the **Bubble Room** (1351 South Orlando Avenue, Maitland; 407-628-3331). Every inch of the place is covered with oddball stuff, from matchboxes and toys to mirrors and movie-star mugs. Overhead, bub-ble lights wink and miniature trains scoot around, while servers (dressed like Boy Scouts) sport the goofiest hats imaginable. The show continues on the menu, a lengthy offering of chicken, steak, seafood and other basic eats with pun names. Naturally, children get their own punny version. Don't pass up one of the 15 decadent desserts. Deluxe.

Kids who finish their meal at the Bubble Room get a Clean Plate Club badge.

ORLANDO AREA SHOPPING

Church Street Station (129 West Church Street; 407-422-2434) is a cobblestone and wrought-iron complex of saloons, restaurants and shops.

Within this complex, the **Church Street Exchange** is filled with specialty shops, and an immense gameroom filling one floor. When the kids get bored with shopping, they'll be more than happy to join the throng of youngsters that crowd in here day and night. Before they disappear, however, they may want to check out the disappearing tricks and other wizardry at **Old Town Magic Shop** (407-872-1425).

In Church Street Station's Bumby Building, the **Buffalo Trading Co.** (407-841-8472) sells western and Indian antiques, in keeping with the shoot-'em-up theme of the mall. In the same building, the **Bumby Emporium** (407-422-2434) deals in gift items and Church Street souvenirs.

For an update on children's entertainment and events around Orlando, call 407-740-6500 and press 2118 (touchtone phones only).

A few blocks from Church Street Station, **Caribbean Records & Variety Store** (539 West Church Street; 407-423-7552) offers Jamaican music, artwork and jewelry.

Orlando has no lack of shopping malls. **Florida Mall** (8001 South Orange Blossom Trail; 407-851-6255), while conventional, stands out because of its huge size and its pastel fairy tale setting. Children naturally enjoy the imaginative surroundings, which feature lots of arches and toy stores. There's even a pavilion with kiddie rides and games. Over 150 retailers, including several department stores, make this one of the largest malls in the southeast United States.

When locals say they're going shopping on "The Avenue," they of course mean Park Avenue. This Winter Park thoroughfare, considered *the* place to shop, is lined with the savviest of stores that can coax some serious dollars from your pocket. Even if you don't have a bundle to spend, it's always as fun to look.

The Black Sheep (114-B Park Avenue South, Winter Park; 407-644-0122) specializes in handpainted needlepoint canvases, imported wools, silks, fabrics and accessories.

OK Kiddo (212 Park Avenue, Winter Park; 407-647-1662) carries such goodies as freeze dried astronaut ice cream, sidewalk chalk, and trendy, casual clothes for toddlers. Kids have their own area in the back, where they can watch TV and relax on bean-bag chairs.

In a French-country-type store off Park Avenue, **Vieille Provence** (121 East Welborne Avenue, Winter Park; 407-628-3858) sells European antiques, pine furniture, imported fabrics and miscellaneous gift items.

Three Sheets to the Wind (316 Park Avenue, Winter Park; 407-644-4488) will wrap you in luxuriant linens and bathrobes. Unusual home furnishings are also featured.

Not surprisingly, this posh town boasts an exclusive toy shop. The European collectibles at **Rune Stone** (326 North Park Avenue, Winter Park; 407-644-9671) include such pricey items Madame Alexander dolls, Norfin trolls and Mohair Steiff teddy bears.

Winter Park Stamps (340 Park Avenue North, Winter Park; 407-628-1120) claims to have the largest collection of Chinese stamps in North America. The store's United States stamps alone number several hundred thousand and date back to the 1840s.

ORLANDO AREA NIGHTLIFE

When it comes to family-style nightlife, **Church Street Station** (129 West Church Street; 407-422-2434) is an anomaly. The vibrant entertainment complex readily admits children to all but one of its six nightclubs. For the most part, the entertainment is wholesome enough for children but lively enough to entertain adults. A single admission (children under three are free) gets you into every establishment.

The most famous address is **Rosie O'Grady's**, which features rousing Dixieland entertainment: cancan dancers, Dixie bands, tap dancers and vaudeville acts. On the quieter side at Church Street Station, **Apple Annie's Courtyard** guests are entertained by live bluegrass and folk tunes. At **Cheyenne Saloon**, a lot of strummin', pickin' and foot stompin' goes on in a huge former opera house. Here you'll have a chance to see some Florida-style clogging, a dance tradition borrowed from the mountains. The one place children are *not* admitted is **Phineas Phogg's Balloon Works**, a bawdy but colorful disco dance bar.

Not far from Church Street Station, **Pebbles** (17 West Church Street; 407-839-0892) is a classy spot to drink to mellow music.

For a cozy pub atmosphere, go to **Bull & Bush** (2408 Robinson Street; 407-896-7546), have a Guinness and play some darts.

Popular with the trendy, after-work set, **Mulvaney's Irish Pub** (27 Church Street; 407-872-3296) has an acoustic lineup.

For a taste of culture, check out what's happening on stage at the **Bob Carr Performing Arts Center** (401 Livingston Street; 407-849-2577). The elegant 2500-seat theater hosts major dance, opera, symphony and touring Broadway performances throughout the year.

The **Theatre for Young People** showcases favorite fairy tales and kid-style musicals and comedies from September through May. Shows are staged at the **Civic Theatre of Central Florida** (1001 East Princeton Street; 407-896-7365), which also presents regional and community theater for adults.

The place to be seen in Orlando is **Shooter's** (4315 North Orange Blossom Trail; 407-298-2855), a sprawling lakefront complex with

---

PLAY ORLANDO'S PLAYGROUNDS

Nothing breaks up a rigorous day of sightseeing like an afternoon at the park. Orlando's many fine playgrounds feature state-of-the-art equipment, jumbo sandboxes, landscaped surroundings and shady benches for parents. Some of the best: **Delaney Park** *(Delaney Avenue and Delaney Park Drive; downtown Orlando),* **College Park Playground** *(Westmoreland Drive and New Hampshire Avenue) and* **Dover Shores Playground** *(Gaston Foster and Curry Ford roads). In Winter Park, try* **Lake Baldwin Park** *(South Lakemont Avenue and Glenridge Way).*

For more information, call Orlando's Department of Parks and Recreation at 407-246-2285.

Tiny Winter Park has over 30,000 trees—just along its streets!

occasional live bands. With multiple bars, beaches and a swimming pool, the place jams at night. During the day, however, it's a fine spot to take the kids.

Country-and-western music tops the charts at **Sweeney's Place** (11599 East Colonial Drive; 407-273-9600).

The crowd at the **Crocodile Club** (118 West Fairbanks Avenue in Bailey's Restaurant, Winter Park; 407-647-8501) is ultra-toney; the music, compliments of a deejay, is Top-40.

Rollins College's **Annie Russell Theatre** (Holt Avenue, Winter Park; 407-646-2501) hosts year-round theater performances.

The Mill (330 West Fairbanks Avenue, Winter Park; 407-664-1544) serves up just-brewed beer, relaxing jazz and acoustic guitar. Children are welcome every Sunday through Tuesday night.

Harper's Tavern (537 West Fairbanks Avenue, Winter Park; 407-647-7858) is a popular local watering hole with dependably good Top-40 bands. Cover.

You can cut a rug at **Studebaker's** (994 North Route 434, Altamonte Springs; 407-774-3335), a hoppin' neon bar with deejay-spun tunes from the '50s through the '80s. Cover.

ORLANDO AREA BEACHES AND PARKS

Charming **Eola Park** (407-246-2827) is a fine place for family picnics or simply strolling the lakeshores. Draped around downtown's Lake Eola, it's the quintessential city park, with fountains and luxuriant gardens and paddle boats shaped like swans. A tot lot makes the youngsters happy, while adults can relax in the Oriental gazebo. Located at the corner of Rosalind and Eola streets.

Turkey Lake Park (407-299-5594) centers around a lake known as the headwaters of the Everglades. Designed for family pleasure, the park features two sandy beaches, a swimming pool, nature and bike trails and flora that thrive here in the midst of the metropolis. Children will enjoy the re-created cracker farm and petting zoo. You can camp here and catch pan fish in the lake. Located at 3401 Hiawassee Road.

The 1500-acre **Moss Park** (407-273-2327) is sandwiched between two lovely lakes. Shade and a nice sand beach give this metropolitan fringe park its oasis feel. Along with the playground, tennis courts and picnic areas, much of the park's acreage remains in a natural, undeveloped state. It's not heavily advertised, but the locals know it well. Camping is permitted. Located off Route 15A on Moss Park Road, southeast of Orlando's Route 528.

The Sporting Life

SPORTFISHING

The whole family can drop hook, line and sinker in one of Orlando's many lakes. Several guides guarantee fish, including **Bass Charmer Guide Service** (2920 West Washington Street; 407-298-2974), **Bass Bustin' Guide** (5935 Swoffield Drive; 407-281-0845) and **Bass Challenger Guide Service** (8617 Trevarthon Road; 407-273-8045).

WATERSKIING, WINDSURFING AND PARASAILING

Ski Holidays (Route 535; 407-239-4444) takes you waterskiing and rents jet skis in Orlando's land of lakes. You can rent a small boat or take lessons in windsurfing, parasailing, waterskiing and jet skiing at **Splash-N-Ski** (10000 Turkey Lake Road; 407-352-1494).

GOLF

Orlando's gentle, green terrain and wide-open spaces make it a perfect place to tee off. Try one of these public courses: **Alhambra Golf Club** (4700 South Texas Avenue; 407-851-6250), **Meadow Woods Golf Club** (13001 Landstar Boulevard; 407-850-5600) and **Hunter's Creek Golf Course** (Route 441, four miles south of Florida's Turnpike; 407-240-4653). Just north of Orlando you'll find **Winter Pines Golf Club** (950 South Ranger Boulevard, Winter Park; 407-671-3172) and **Sabal Point Country Club** (2662 Sabal Club Way, Longwood; 407-869-8787).

ICE SKATING

As unlikely as it may seem, steamy Orlando possesses two rinks—**Ice Rink International at Dowdy Pavilion** (7500 Canada Avenue; 407-363-7465) and **Orlando Ice Skating Palace** (3123 West Colonial Drive; 407-299-5440).

THE "MAGIC" OF ORLANDO

*Lately, the biggest game in Orlando isn't Disney World, but basketball. Ever since the **Orlando Magic** rolled into town in 1989, they've played to a packed Orlando Arena (4600 West Amelia Street; 407-649-3200). Basketball offers a great family outing—and a great way to see Orlando's magic.*

TEN

Side Trips from Orlando

There is a saying among Floridians that the farther you go from Disney
World, the closer you get to the true wonders of their state. Truth is, however, you need not venture far from Disney's door to find the poetic scenery that the theme parks can only try to imitate: billowing green hills, lakes framed with bulrushes and tiny historic towns that seem plucked from a fairy tale.

These rural rhythms start just outside the Orlando metropolis and head in every direction, creating a circle of splendid sightseeing for the family that wants to take in the "magic kingdom" of Florida. The circle takes in both Florida coasts, from the technological Space Coast and fast-paced Daytona Beach to metropolitan Tampa and sun-washed St. Petersburg and Clearwater. Except for the West Coast cities, everything is within an easy hour's drive of Orlando. For some of these adventures, just an afternoon (or morning) of your time will be plenty. For others, you'll want to consider staying overnight to enjoy all the sights and sounds.

Let's go!

Northeast of Orlando, the towns of Sanford and DeLand recall the 19th-century steamship era with riverboat attractions and glorious mansions that rich visitors left in their wake, in styles ranging from spiffed-up cracker to Victorian gothic. Sand pine forest and spring waters still refresh travelers tired of resort hubbub. Remember the magic number 72: it's the temperature these springs maintain, as well as the average temperature of upper central Florida.

State parks and national forests in this area also offer refuge to the crowd weary—and to alligators, Florida panthers, deer, wild turkeys and migratory birds. Fishing camps take the place of towering hotels, and fried catfish pushes steak au poivre off the plate.

In the hills south of Orlando, citrus reigns. Here temperatures average in the high 70s and the climate is generally rainier than along the coast. Blossom-scented tranquility settles in between pretty, little towns named either for the many nearby lakes or for the escape from cold they offer: Winter Haven, Lakeland, Lake Alfred, Frostproof, Lake Wales.

West of Orlando, sleepy towns such as Clermont, Bushnell and Howey-in-the-Hills paint a portrait of rural quaintness. The Withlacoochee River winds toward the Gulf above a state forest bearing the same name. Like the areas north and south of Orlando, this western region boasts countless waters: crystal springs, lakes and rivers that gush and gurgle and teem with fish, aquatic realms that have given life to fertile agricultural lands. Those acres have produced still another side of central Florida—rows of citrus trees that lie like neatly plaited hair, as well as farms of winter vegetables and miles of cattle scrub.

Over on the East Coast, the beaches are launching grounds for vehicles that rocket people into outer space. Epcot may provide a glimpse into the future, but the Space Coast *is* the future. Since NASA established a space center here in the 1960s, the area has turned into a bedroom community for astronauts, scientists and their support staff. A beautiful stretch of beach offers sensational viewing points for space launches.

On the other end of the technological spectrum, this area contains some of the finest beaches and wildlife refuges in the state. For 40 miles north to Daytona Beach, the Atlantic Ocean alternately laps and crashes against a seemingly endless wide ribbon of sand. This giant sand box contains great surfing spots as well as beaches where the waves are gentle enough for small children. Virtually all of this coast is separated from the ocean by a series of lovely barrier islands. Between these islands and the mainland is the Intracoastal Waterway (called a river in some locales), where calmer inland waters provide safe passage for pleasure craft everywhere on the coast. Most of the fun, a lot of the area's history and even a glimpse into the future can be found on the islands.

No single focal point highlights this region, but it is bound by one sensibility—an overwhelming consciousness of the ocean's proximity. The salt air, casual atmosphere, emphasis on water sports and abundance of exquisite seafood provide constant reminders. And, although development has obstructed views in some areas, particularly Daytona Beach, virtually every square foot of beach is open to the public.

The geography in this region is fairly consistent: flat, sandy beaches fringed with palm trees and imported Australian pines (not true pines, by the way). The climate is, on the whole, temperate.

Oddly enough, the best sightseeing route here is not well known. It is possible—and recommended—for visitors to drive the entire coast along Route A1A. This beach-hugging road lopes through resort towns and retirement enclaves and villages not much bigger than in-

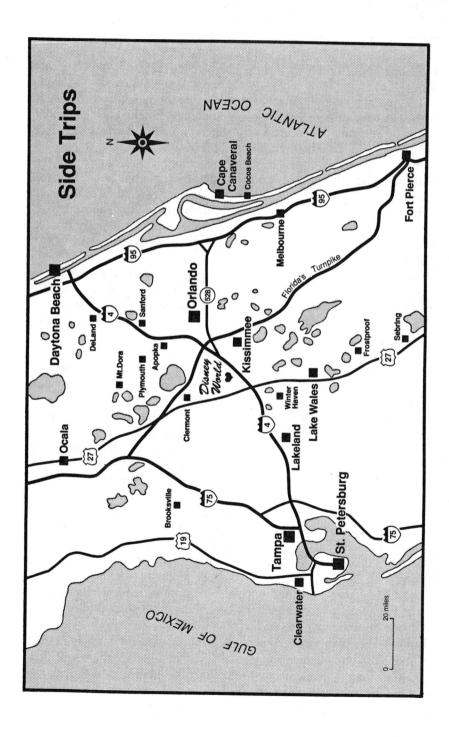

Camping out? The Florida Campground Association (1638 North Plaza Drive, Tallahassee, 32308-5364; 904-656-8878) can help you find a place.

---

tersections. Route A1A runs through the barrier islands, often within earshot of the surf.

The most developed of east Florida's resort towns is Daytona Beach. Daytona is now known as spring-break capital for the college crowd, but during summer it becomes a haven for families. Younger folks love this high-energy beach town for its boardwalk, amusement-park atmosphere and concessions and great swimming. Automobile traffic is still tolerated on the beach, but professional racing has been removed inland to the tracks at the Daytona Beach Speedway. In fact, all beach driving is hotly disputed and may end soon, as environmentalists argue that the cars interfere with Mother Nature, especially the sea turtles who come up to lay their eggs on Florida's beaches in the early summer.

Whether or not the cars disappear, plenty of pristine areas remain in the Space Coast and Daytona Beach area. And where else can you take your children from outer space to the deep ocean in a single day?

Certainly such paradoxes exist across the state on the West Coast, where visitors find a pleasing balance between the wild and the wilds. In big-city Tampa, skyscrapers seem to shoot up overnight. The town's pace is set by whizzing jai alai orbs, zooming corporate successes and neon nightlife. Yet wildlife can be found even in this soaring metropolis, on the Serengeti Plains of Busch Gardens/The Dark Continent, where thousands of exotic animals roam freely. The old ways are preserved in parks, the renovated downtown area and at shrimp docks.

Across Tampa Bay lie two gleaming jewels, St. Petersburg and Clearwater, whose spirits are stoked by the gorgeous Gulf of Mexico. Once the butt of retirement-home jokes, St. Petersburg now enjoys a livelier image, thanks to the beautiful young people who populate its shell-strewn sands. But the heart of the beach action still throbs in Clearwater, just north of St. Petersburg. A futuristic pier, restored downtown and dynamic, sun-soaked beaches make this the Gulf Coast's most popular playground. True to its name, the city's shores are lapped by see-through waters tinted a pale jade.

The Gulf Coast is blessed with the same semitropical climate and flora as Florida's burgeoning East Coast. Plus it has something the Atlantic side doesn't: seaside sunsets.

But whether your intention is to see a spectacular sun or an enthralled son, take a day trip or stay over, you can only experience these wonders if you travel away from the theme parks and into the real Florida. A side trip will help you discover the state's true character, the character that is held sacred by those who call Florida home.

Day Trips

There is so much to explore within an easy drive of Orlando that it's possible to visit a crowded theme park in the morning, then spend the afternoon in the country. No matter which direction you take out of town, getting there is half the fun as you discover bucolic byways that lead to a slower, crowdless dimension.

Traveling north of Orlando takes you through a pastoral profile of folded green hills, plantation homes, boiled-peanut shacks and lakes that dip into the horizon. Along the way here, where agriculture is still king, you can stop at a roadside vegetable stand and shoot the breeze with a farmer. You can drive a narrow road through citrus groves, or wade (gingerly) through a cactus farm.

To find all this and much more, head north on Route 1792, which leads into Sanford. Route 441 north will take you to Mount Dora.

The old steamboat town of **Sanford** is today known as the "Celery Capital of the World." Still retaining its riverside personality, Sanford also blends agricultural, historic and metropolitan characteristics.

The **Seminole County Historical Museum** (300 Bush Boulevard, Sanford; 407-321-2489) depicts the town's diversity with exhibits covering the citrus industry, cattle ranching and vegetable farming. Railroad and steamboat memorabilia and furnished rooms of a typical steamboat-era mansion are also featured.

For a narrated tour of St. Johns River wildlife and a peek at its great steamboat days, ride aboard **Captain Hoy's Riverboat Fleet** (Sanford Boat Works, Route 415, Sanford; 407-330-1612; admission). Alligators, osprey, manatees and bald eagles will greet your passage as they did a century ago.

Rivership Romance (433 North Palmetto Avenue, Sanford; 407-321-5091; admission) leaves out of Monroe Harbor Marina on a popular day or evening river sightseeing trip aboard an old-time paddlewheeler. The Friday and Saturday evening cruises include dinner and dancing.

More information on Sanford awaits at the **Greater Sanford Chamber of Commerce** (400 East First Street; 407-322-2212).

As you follow Route 17-92 out of Sanford, along glistening Lake Monroe, you will come to the **Central Florida Zoological Park** (Route 17-92, Lake Monroe; 407-323-4450; admission). This 110-acre zoo may well be the highlight of your northern day trip, as the kids gape at the ostriches, llamas and 400 other exotic animals on display. Thatched-roof shelters make ideal spots for a family picnic.

Having a shopping attack? Sanford's Flea World (433 North Palmetto Avenue; 407-321-1792) has bargain prices as well as a zoo for the kids.

A few miles west of Sanford lies one of the prettiest towns in Florida. **Mount Dora** is a storybook village of gingerbread mansions, lakeside inns and 19th-century ambience. The downtown boasts brick and wrought-iron structures, New England touches, one of the state's proudest antique store districts and a "mountainous" Florida elevation of 184 feet. Stop in at the **Mount Dora Chamber of Commerce** (341 Alexander Street; 904-383-2165), housed in a restored railroad station, for a guide to the area's antique shops and historic homes.

Among the showiest of these regally preserved mansions is the **Donnelly House** (Donnelly Street between 5th and 6th avenues), an ornate fantasy castle in Steamboat Gothic style, accented with stained glass and hand-carved trim. Built in 1893 for one of the city's founders, it is now used as a Masonic Lodge. Across the street, shady Donnelly Park provides shuffleboard and tennis courts.

Housed downtown in the old city firehouse and jailblock, **Royellou Museum** (between 5th and 4th avenues off Baker Street; 904-383-3642) features the largest collection of bayonets this side of West Point and historic photographs as well as temporary exhibits.

The **Miss Dora** (Route 441, Tavares; 904-343-0200; admission) takes tours out of Gator Inlet Marina into the Dora Canal, the channel that runs between Lake Dora and Lake Eustis. These lovely cypress-studded waters have been preserved from logging to provide refuge for various waterfowl and migratory birds.

Florida Cactus, Inc. (2542 South Peterson Road, Plymouth; 407-886-1833) will change any preconceived notions about cactus being merely green, prickly plants that grow in desert wastelands. Families can see the amazing plants growing across the United States—a 24-by-12-foot map of the country is made of cacti, a different variety representing each state. Red, yellow and pink ones, cacti that form a

---

CYPRESS GARDENS

*One of Florida's oldest and most popular destinations is **Cypress Gardens** (Route 540, Winter Haven; 813-324-2111; admission), with its lush scenery and aquatic shows that feature hoop-skirted Southern belles, human pyramids on skis and air dancing on the high wire. "Critter Encounter" lets kids play with animals, including a 500-pound tortoise. Kodak's "Island in the Sky" takes you on a ride to a world towering 16 stories above the botanical gardens. On the grounds you'll also find an old Southern town that harkens back to the antebellum era, and Lake Eloise, where a world-famous waterski revue is staged. This precursor of modern amusement parks offers at least a day's worth of entertainment; visitors can stroll through the gardens or board canal boats.*

At Bok Tower Gardens, small children love hand-feeding the squirrels, birds and fish. Peanuts and bread included in park admission.

75-foot-circumference electric clock, small cacti, gigantic cacti: Florida Cactus does more than you ever cared to imagine.

South of Orlando lies a peaceful, countrified world where grazing cattle speckle the horizon and townsfolk spend lazy afternoons on the front porch. Here in Florida's heartland, citrus scents the air with its blossoms in spring and ripe juices in winter. This gentle landscape also harbors some singular Sunshine State oddities—spooky hills, singing towers and human pyramids on skis—guaranteed to liven the family outing.

Known as the Highlands area, this section lies along Florida's central spine. From the Orlando area, take Route 4 to Route 27 and follow it south. Soon you'll come to the town of Winter Haven, home to the **Water Ski Museum and Hall of Fame** (799 Overlook Drive; 813-324-2472). The memorabilia, photos and literature trace the development of waterskiing from 1922, when the sport was born in Minnesota, to modern times. The dramatic videos of barefoot and trick skiing are favorites here with children.

The quirkiness of **Lake Wales** can be seen by the town's main attractions: an eccentric dollhouse-like country inn, a singing tower and a "spooked" hill. Start exploring the area north of town at the first of these, **Chalet Suzanne Inn Village** (Chalet Suzanne Road, Lake Wales; 813-676-6011), and have a peek at the quaint Old World restaurant, inn, gift shops and ceramic studio. Tours can be arranged through the soup cannery, where the restaurant's trademark dishes are canned. Its signature romaine soup was sent to space with Apollo 16. In the tiny ceramic studio in the midst of the meandering cobblestone village, you can watch craftspeople making dishware and personalized gifts.

A trip to **Bok Tower Gardens** (Route 17A, Lake Wales; 813-676-1408; admission) is a treat for the senses: exotic blossoms scent leaf-paved paths, and squirrels chatter atop towering oaks. Here, in 1928 Dutch immigrant Edward Bok built a 200-foot carillon tower of Georgia marble and St. Augustine coquina stone to show his appreciation for the beauty he felt America had brought into his life. He planted the 128 acres around the singing tower in magnolias, azaleas and plants from the Orient to create an atmosphere of peace. The carillon, a registered historic structure, rings out classic harmonies every half hour to add a special magic to this place.

The thing I found spookiest about **Spook Hill** (North Avenue and 5th Street, Lake Wales) was the convoluted route you must take to get there if you follow the signs. To make it simpler, take a left on North Avenue when returning to town from Bok Gardens. At the bottom of the hill, you must turn around to experience the mystery here: "spooks" power your car back up the hill. A legend accompanies the mystery, and kids are guaranteed to love it.

Lake Wales itself is a pretty, little town that lassoes a lake. For a scenic view of the water and its lakeside mansions and park, follow **Lakeshore Boulevard**. The history of the area, including the building of the railroad that settled inland Florida, can be seen at **Lake Wales Museum** (325 South Scenic Highway; 813-676-5443). The museum, housed in the city's first structure, sits next to a historic railroad car.

Sebring is best known for its **Sebring International Raceway** (813-655-1442), where the 12-Hour Endurance Race is held each March. Aside from the roar of engines, this is a pretty, lake-mottled town blending a sense of heritage, a touch of sophistication and a dash of the outdoors. For more information, stop at the **Greater Sebring Chamber of Commerce Tourist Information Center** (2001 Route 27 South; 813-385-3232).

The area west of Orlando is known as the Green Swamp and is an important underground aquifer system in Central Florida. Typical Green Swamp terrain includes cypress marshes, sandhills, pine forests and hardwood hammocks.

To explore this western section of inland Florida, head west out of Orlando on Route 50. The tour begins at the **Florida Citrus Tower** (141 North Route 27, Clermont; 904-394-8585; admission), which offers a sweeping view of miles of fruit groves. A tram tour keeps acrophobics closer to the ground to view the same area. There's also a citrus packing plant, glass workshop, candy kitchen and gift shops.

View one of Florida's younger enterprises—winemaking—at **Lakemont Winery & Vineyards** (19239 Route 27 North, Clermont; 904-394-8627). The winery opened in 1989 and uses all Florida-grown grapes. Families can view a short slide show, take a guided tour

---

THE PLACE WHERE IT'S ALWAYS CHRISTMAS

*While you're exploring central Florida, make sure you show the kids Christmas. Christmas, Florida, that is. This peaceful, rural town, located on Route 50 about 25 miles east of Orlando, is decorated with humble frame homes, moss-covered woods and a three-story Christmas tree that twinkles year-round. At the **Fort Christmas Museum** (Route 420 two miles north of Route 50; 407-568-4149), children can climb stairs and wooden walkways and peek out rifle holes. The whole family can explore artifacts and learn how 2000 soldiers built the fortress in two days, starting on December 25, 1837. The original building rotted, and the current replica opened in 1977, on Christmas Day.*

of the facilities, and sample some vintages (kids get grape juice). Most children enjoy learning about winemaking, but those who don't can watch cartoons.

History can be fun for the kids over in bucolic Bushnell. Here you can view the site where the Second Seminole War began at the **Dade Battlefield State Historic Site** (off State Road 476; 904-793-4781). The museum and nature trail commemorate December 28, 1835, when a tribe of Indians ambushed troops under Major Francis L. Dade. The Dade Massacre began seven more years of bloody and costly battles in Florida.

From there you can forge into the **Withlacoochee State Forest**, which lies between Inverness and Brooksville (see "Day Trips Beaches and Parks" section in this chapter). Stop at the **Hernando County Chamber of Commerce** (101 East Fort Dade Avenue, Brooksville; 904-796-2420) to find out more about the area.

DAY TRIPS RESTAURANTS

Several delightful restaurants reflect the pastoral flavor of the region north of Orlando:

Perched on a rising hill, **Townsend Plantation** (604 East Main Street, Apopka; 407-880-1313) enables diners to view grazing horses, white picket fences, restored Queen Anne buildings, a pond and floral gardens from the main dining room. The three-story building has several other dining areas—a room of white wicker and bentwood chairs, one dominated by a fireplace, and a third whose theme is a child's rumpus room. Southern-style food is served by the bowlful at moderate prices. A sampling of the house specialties: frogs' legs and pasta, Cajun alligator tail, country ham with redeye gravy and chicken with garden herbs (grown right outside the door). Children's menu.

"Catfish is king" proclaims the menu at the locally favored **Wekiwa Marina Restaurant** (1000 Miami Springs Road, Longwood; 407-862-9640). You can find them in the clear spring waters right outside the restaurant. Inside they're fried and all-you-can-eat. In proper cracker style, barbecue ribs, frogs' legs, hushpuppies and cheese grits can also be enjoyed in the spartan riverside setting. Moderate. Children's menu.

Old whiskey stills, washing machines and studio cameras—all copper of course—establish the theme at **Copper Cove** (201 Cassadaga Road, Lake Helen; 904-228-3400). Set against a wooded glen, the budget-priced eatery dishes up home-cooked vittles like grilled ham steak and fried chicken, biscuits and gravy, and french toast.

The homestyle cooking at **Original Holiday House** (704 North Boulevard, DeLand; 904-734-6319) has drawn crowds since the late 1950s. Guests serve themselves buffet style in this well-preserved old home. Choices include leg of lamb, fish, roast beef and salad. Budget to moderate, with special prices for children.

Rocking chairs sit on the wide, front porch of Lakeside Inn's **Beauclair Dining Room** (100 South Alexander Street, Mount Dora; 904-383-4101). Formal elegance reigns inside, where heavy valanced curtains are tied back around windows overlooking the pastoral inn grounds. The moderate-to-deluxe-priced menu offers nouvelle entrées such as raspberry duckling and filet mignon stuffed with oysters and topped with an oyster sauce. Despite such culinary formality, children are regular diners, and get royal treatment by waiters who recite daily kids' specials.

South of Orlando, four restaurants enjoy local and statewide acclaim:

Tasty seafood and prime steaks have given **Christy's Sundown** (Route 17 South, Winter Haven; 813-293-0069) its top billing with locals and critics. Antiques and works of art combine to create a Mediterranean mood. Lobster, stone crab, shish kebab, Kansas City steaks and Alaskan King crab run in the moderate price range.

For a romantic tryst without the kids, don't miss **Chalet Suzanne Restaurant** (Chalet Suzanne Road, Lake Wales; 813-676-6011). A premier Florida restaurant and inn, it is legendary for its fine cuisine served in a Swiss-style chalet. Its signature romaine soup is canned on the premises as are other soups bearing the Chalet Suzanne label. The tables, set with fine European china, offer either a stunning overlook of the lake or seclusion behind stained-glass walls. Chicken Suzanne, curried shrimp, shad roe and lobster Newburg are among the proffered entrées. Ultra-deluxe.

One of the loveliest places to eat in all of Florida is on the patio of the **Garden Café** (Route 17A, Lake Wales; 813-676-1408) at Bok Tower Gardens. Here, with a view of the chiming, pink monument and its surrounding green-and-floral al fresco decor, you feel cut off from modern tempos. The fare is nothing more than counter-service sandwiches, soup and hot dogs, but the pastoral ambience and serenades from Bok Tower can't be beat by the swankiest restaurant. Budget.

A spot of great local repute, the **Olympic Restaurant** (504 Route 27 North, Avon Park; 813-452-2700) seems to serve the entire town at lunch-time. The dining area is a couple of sprawling rooms with some Greek pictures on the wall. The food is plain good eating: budget-priced country-fried chicken, fried seafood platter, barbecue spare ribs, spaghetti and sandwiches. Some smaller portions are available for children.

West of Orlando, **El Conquistador** (Howey-in-the-Hills; 904-324-3101) matches the Spanish flavor of the Mission Inn resort where it is located. The menu is as simple as the surroundings are elegant, but the few featured dishes do show imagination—blackened breast of chicken with mushrooms and shallots served over pasta with pesto sauce, for example, plus such continental standbys as shrimp scampi, wienerschnitzel and veal Oscar. Deluxe. Smaller portions are available for children.

DAY TRIPS BEACHES AND PARKS

Just outside Orlando, dense forests and an abundance of rivers, lakes and springs create some of the state's most appealing parks. And in case you want to take more than a day trip to absorb all of this beauty, I have noted the parks that permit camping.

The 200-acre **Kelly Park** (407-889-4179) features highly productive clear-water Rock Spring, which has created a large swimming pool. The park shows off some of the area's loveliest natural attire of oaks and palm trees. Boardwalks have been built on some of the nature trails. Swimming's great, and you can camp here. Located on Kelly Park Drive, one-half mile off Route 435 near Apopka.

At **Wekiwa Springs State Park** (407-884-2009) you'll find sand pine forest and wetlands on an extensive springs system. These spring-warmed waters have created a popular swimming spot for Orlando refugees. The area around the spring swimming pool is cemented, with wooden bridges that cross the crystalline waters and lead to a sandy beach. Trails take you through wet forests along the springs and to various other plant communities. A family campground accommodates tents and RVs. Special children's programs are led by park staff. Located off Wekiwa Springs Road between Apopka and Route 4.

At the spot where the St. Johns River bulges into a lake, **Lake Monroe Park** (407-668-6522) maintains natural charm beneath tunnels of spreading oak. Used mostly for boating and fishing by locals, it is quiet and secluded. Camping is permitted. Located on Route 17-92 between Sanford and DeBary.

At **Hontoon Island State Park** (904-736-5309), you'll see Indian mounds, bald eagles and cypress trees—all viewable from an 80-foot observation tower—and a replica of a Timucuan Indian totem that was found here. But no cars or motorcycles: this 1650-acre spit of land lies in the middle of St. Johns River and requires boat transportation to reach. A ferry comes here daily.

Camping is permitted and you can fish for bass, crappie and other freshwater panfish. Rangers lead tours and point out the island's plants and animals. The ferry landing is located at 2309 Riverridge Road near DeLand.

DeLeon Springs State Recreation Area (904-985-4212) promised a fountain of youth to wintering visitors as far back as the 1890s and was named for the original seeker of anti-aging waters. A great deal of wildlife can be spotted along the nature trails here, and there's good swimming and fishing. Remains of an old Spanish sugar mill stand near the spring, a favorite local swimming hole. Located on Route 17, seven miles north of DeLand.

Lake Griffin State Recreation Area (904-787-7402) is a natural boating and fishing haven on the shores of a large lake. Much of the park is marshy and not good for swimming. Locals will tell you this is the place to see "floating islands," a phenomenon caused by chunks of shoreline breaking away into the lake. Camping is permitted. Located on Route 27 about four miles south of Fruitland Park.

A bird sanctuary and county recreational area, **Trimble Park** (904-383-1993) lies on a peninsula jutting into Lake Beauclair. The lake, known principally to locals, is huge and beautifully trimmed in mossy oaks and cypress. You'll have to watch closely for one inconspicuous sign on Route 441 that signals the turnoff for the park, which takes you down a winding, scenic road. Mainly a fishermen's mecca, this park is also a satisfying find for privacy-seeking campers. Located at 5700 Trimble Park Road off Earlwood Road near Mount Dora.

A natural recreational refuge on Lake Tohopekaliga's south shore, **Southport Park** (407-933-5822) is years away from metro mania. The secluded, difficult-to-find spot is a prime fishing area. Carpets of grass and live oak hammocks make the grounds comfortable and attractive, perfect for family picnicking. Camping is permitted. Located on Southport Road, east of Route 531 and about 20 miles south of Kissimmee.

A secluded, rustic fishing and camping haven, **Lake Arbuckle Park** (813-534-6075) features seven acres of cypress- and oak-studded grounds on Lake Arbuckle. Fishing's good here, and camping is permitted. Located eight miles off Lake Reedy Boulevard east of Frostproof.

CRUISING WITH MICKEY MOUSE

*One of the very best side trips a family can take is a cruise to the Bahamas. Three- and four-day cruises leave weekly from Port Canaveral aboard **Premier Cruise Lines** (400 Challenger Road, Cape Canaveral; 800-888-6759), which goes to Freeport, Nassau or the Abacos out-islands. Premier has teamed up with Disney World to combine family-oriented cruises with a vacation at Disney's theme parks. Mickey, Pluto, Captain Hook and Mr. Smee join the ocean voyages, leading the kids on adventures while parents do their own thing. Children get their own daily schedules, with nonstop events from early morning to late night. They also get Pluto's Playhouse, a Space Station Teen Center and their own menus for lunch and dinner (hot diggity dogs and pirate's cheese pizza are favorites). Premier also offers special family-size cabins, single parent rates and lower-priced kids' quarters for parents who want added privacy.*

During the summer, over 500 children usually sail on each Premier Cruise Line cruise. That's half the passengers!

Alligators and orchids can be seen from a "trackless train" that tours the cypress swamps and semitropical jungles in popular **Highlands Hammock State Park** (813-385-0011). Hiking trails also travel some of its 3800 acres, and a paved bicycling loop traverses the hammock. The park is named for the high, forested terrain found on Florida's central ridge. Children love spotting the white-tailed deer that reside here, as well as the otters, Florida scrub jays and occasional bald eagle and Florida panther. Camping is permitted. Located west of Sebring off Route 27 at the end of Hammock Road.

A preserved segment of Green Swamp, **Lake Louisa State Park** (904-394-2280) lies over an important underground aquifer system. The park skirts the shores of Lake Louisa and also encompasses Bear Lake. Typical Green Swamp terrain is found here: cypress marshes, sandhills, pine forests and hardwood hammocks. Good swimming and fishing in the lakes. Located off Route 561 south of Clermont on Lake Nellie Road.

The second-largest state forest in Florida, **Withlacoochee State Forest** (904-796-5650) encompasses 113,000-plus acres. Four separate tracts are designated: Forest Headquarters, Croom, Richloam and Citrus. These are subdivided into various recreation areas and forestry stations. The park focuses on the Withlacoochee and Little Withlacoochee rivers, which flow through a variety of indigenous Florida landscapes. Hiking trails penetrate the forest in several areas, allowing visitors a look at the region's diverse flora and fauna. Several campgrounds, plus good swimming and fishing. The park, which spreads through four counties, has its main entrance off Route 75 near Brooksville.

The Space Coast

Disney World may be the stuff of every kid's fantasy, but head 50 miles east to Florida's Atlantic shore, and they'll find the stuff that *real* dreams are made of—the launching pads that hurtle rockets and shuttlecraft toward other worlds. Space Mountain, after all, is just a ride. On Florida's Space Coast, a peek at real exploration awaits eager young minds and their parents alike. So strap yourself in and journey to Kennedy Space Center on Merritt Island.

Once on the East Coast, scenic Route A1A hugs the shoreline on its way north toward Cape Canaveral. Except for a few condominium

The idea for Space Mirror was conceived by an Orlando architect as he watched the space shuttle Challenger explode in the morning sky on January 28, 1986.

complexes, virtually nothing lies between the roadway and the beach as the two-lane highway cuts through small residential communities.

While you can't actually blast aboard one of the space shuttles at Kennedy Space Center (at least I wouldn't recommend it), you can recapture the history of America's space exploration—plus glimpse its future—at the center's **Spaceport USA** (Route 405, Merritt Island; 407-452-2121). This fascinating complex is an absolute must-see and one of the greatest values in Florida, especially since most of the attractions are free. You should either hook up with a guide for an introductory half-hour tour or begin on your own with a walk in the *Rocket Garden*, where you can find rockets from each stage of America's space program. Established in 1958, NASA centered many of its early, manned operations at nearby Cape Canaveral, still the site of weather and communications satellite launchings. By 1964, what had become known as the NASA Kennedy Space Center was relocated to adjacent Merritt Island.

The Rocket Garden is just the beginning of what's offered here. Opened in 1991, **Space Mirror** is an immense, poignant, stunning memorial to the 14 astronauts who died in the line of duty. Their names are etched into several gleaming black granite panels that rotate atop a mirrored steel sculpture. A computer controls the four-story granite so that, uncannily, it rises and sets with the sun. All day, sunrays strike the names and illuminate them as stars. Reminiscent of Washington D.C.'s Vietnam Memorial, the $6.4 million structure is a compelling tribute to mankind's tenuous alliance with the universe.

Inside the **Gallery of Space Flight** are full-sized models of a lunar rover and the Viking Mars Lander, along with actual spacecraft. One of the most eye-opening displays is the one-tenth scale model of the rocket that sent the Apollo 11 astronauts to the moon; it's amazing to see how small the capsule was compared with the size of the entire spacecraft.

The **Galaxy Center** houses an exhibit of space-related art and two theaters. The Galaxy Theater screens multimedia presentations on various space topics. But for sheer exhilaration, you simply cannot top the 37-minute film shown on a 70-foot-wide screen in the IMAX Theater (admission). The sound system is so extraordinary that the entire theater shudders when a shuttle is launched into space. The rest of the film consists of spectacular footage shot by astronauts in the course of various missions. You will feel almost as if you, too, are looking down on the planet earth from outer space, practicing emergency evacuations and conducting experiments in weightlessness.

You should make reservations as soon as you arrive for this show as well as for the two-hour **Bus Tour** (admission) of outlying attractions inaccessible by private vehicle. Although younger children might get bored during the long tour, the bus stops frequently so the whole family can get out and explore launch facilities and rockets. Double-decker buses depart from the visitor center every 15 minutes all day long and take visitors to the 52-story Vehicle Assembly Building, a replica of a control room that lies within good snapshot distance of one of the two launch pads near the ocean.

Also on Merritt Island are the offices of the **Cocoa Beach Tourism and Convention Council** (400 Fortenberry Road; 407-452-4390), a good place to pick up free maps and brochures.

The remainder of Merritt Island, north of the Kennedy Space Center, is largely devoted to the **Merritt Island National Wildlife Refuge** (407-867-0667) and the Canaveral National Seashore (see "Space Coast Beaches and Parks" section in this chapter).

Within Merritt Island refuge, two auto tour routes guide visitors to prime viewing sites. One road, **Black Point Wildlife Drive**, leads into habitats for such unusual species as the anhinga, a bird that swims in the canals with only its snakelike head visible above the water.

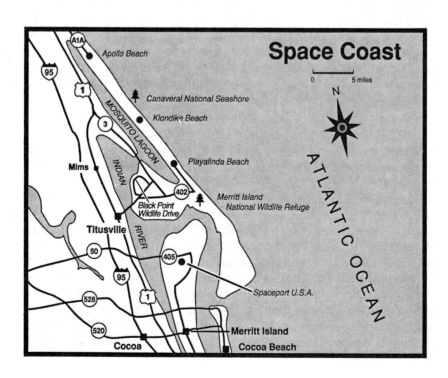

In Cocoa Village, SunRay T-shirts (105 Brevard Avenue; 407-632-6666) has good deals on Kennedy Space Center T-shirts.

On the mainland, the coast's attractions include the **Brevard Community College Planetarium** (1519 Clearlake Road, Cocoa; 407-631-7889; admission), offering several perspectives on natural history and the space age. Parents will find the comfortable theater a relaxing refuge, while kids think the skyscape shows and full-dome motion pictures are "far out!" The planetarium boasts the largest telescope available to the public in the entire state and a lobby filled with space memorabilia.

A short drive away on the same campus, the **Brevard Museum of History and Natural Science** (2201 Michigan Boulevard, Cocoa; 407-632-1830; admission) takes visitors back in time through exhibits of Victorian furniture, Indian tools and pottery and the remains of extinct animals. As for natural history, the museum maintains an extensive shell collection and 22 acres of nature trails.

The wildlife that inhabits the upper reaches of the St. Johns River (one of the few North American rivers that runs south to north) is best viewed from a boat. Half-hour airboat rides at the **Lone Cabbage Fish Camp** (Route 520, six miles west of Route 95, Cocoa; 407-632-4199) cruise the inland marshes for a close-up look at exotic flora and fauna.

Mother Nature and the trappings of the space age exist side by side in the Cape Canaveral area. Every time a space shuttle blasts off in a cloud of steam and smoke, the waterfowl and other wildlife on surrounding Merritt Island are momentarily disturbed before returning to the peaceful routine established by their kind over the centuries.

SPACE COAST LODGING

Most of the accommodations in the area are near the ocean, and the better ones can be found in Cocoa Beach. The city of Cocoa, separated from the beach by the Banana River, Merritt Island and the Intracoastal Waterway, is a few miles closer to the Kennedy Space Center.

The **Brevard Hotel** (112 Riverside Drive, Cocoa; 407-636-1411) must have been terrific in its glory days. This pale, two-story inn was built in 1923; today, it has the tone of a very quiet but totally respectable establishment. Inside the large, mustard-yellow lobby, french doors face out onto the Indian River. Upstairs, too much wood makes the rooms look dark. But you should have no trouble booking one overlooking the river, and you'll be within easy walking distance of Cocoa's shops and sophisticated restaurants. Three suites are available, with two bedrooms and adjoining bath, that will accommodate a family of four or five. Budget.

The **Inn at Cocoa Beach** (4300 Ocean Beach Boulevard, Cocoa Beach; 407-799-3460) offers the best of everything. All the rooms in this four-story, T-shaped inn are beautifully decorated with fine furniture, plush carpeting and little touches like throw pillows, stools and framed artwork. Attractive drapes cover sliding glass doors that open onto private patios. There are gorgeous views of the ocean right out front, and it's possible to witness space launches from the second-floor rooms. This place has a residential charm all too rare in an area dominated by chain hotels. Deluxe to ultra-deluxe.

One of the biggest surprises in Cocoa Beach is the **Howard Johnson Plaza-Hotel** (2080 North Atlantic Avenue; 407-783-9222). Forget the image of screaming orange and blue so familiar to highway travelers—this is a different Howard Johnson's. Take the lobby, for instance, a gleam of marble and sparkling tile with wicker settees and a high ceiling. Upstairs, luxurious rooms are sleekly furnished in pale woods and come in peaches-and-cream or aqua-and-turquoise colors. The hotel has two adult pools and a kiddie pool, and children under 18 stay free. Moderate to ultra-deluxe.

The **Days Inn Oceanfront** (5600 North Atlantic, Cocoa Beach; 407-783-7621) strikes me as a bargain only if you insist on a second-story room facing the courtyard. Otherwise, your door will open onto either a pathway to the ocean or an unattractive parking lot. Peach and seafoam green decor is contemporary in a bare-bones kind of way. Families can relax at the pool or play shuffleboard. Eight suites equipped with modest cooking facilities are tabbed in the moderate range.

If you'd rather sleep where you can smell the ocean breezes, consider camping at the **Oceanus Mobile Village and RV Park** (152 Crescent Beach Drive, Cocoa Beach; 407-783-3871). The tidy camp-

---

LUXURIOUS CAMPING

The *place to camp on the Space Coast—or perhaps anywhere in Florida—is the* **The Great Outdoors RV/Golf Resort** (*4505 West Cheney Highway, Titusville; 407-269-5004). This 3000-acre retreat combines outdoor living with resort luxury. Carpeted with soft grass and sprinkled with palms and pines, it boasts an 18-hole championship golf course, 14 freshwater fishing lakes, a department store-size recreation center, tennis and croquet courts, and a state-of-the-art health club. Children delight in the nature trails lined with animal feeders. Deer, wild turkey and even bobcats reside here. You can bring your own RV (no tent or pop-up campers permitted), or rent one of the modern cottages equipped with carpeting, full kitchens and bedrooms. RV sites are budget-priced; cottages are moderate-priced—and a real family deal.*

ground enjoys a superb location along the Banana River, a stone's throw from the Atlantic Ocean. After you park your RV or pitch a tent, you can fish off a 245-foot pier or take a dip in the heated pool. Of course, the glistening white beach, waiting across the river, is sure to be the highlight of your stay. Budget.

A little hoola with your meal, perhaps? Test your luck (or coordination) with the plastic hoola hoops at Herbie K's Diner.

SPACE COAST RESTAURANTS

Most towns have one restaurant revered as a local institution. On the Space Coast, that place is **Bernard's Surf** (2 South Atlantic Avenue, Cocoa Beach; 407-783-2401). It's been on the same corner since the 1940s, boasting the freshest crab, lobster and fish in the county. Bernard's is divided into three parts: a raw bar, a formal, dimly lit dining room and a lounge rimmed by red leatherette booths. An oversized menu is required to list the steak, rib and chicken offerings as well as dozens of seafood dishes, all in a variety of combinations. There's also a generous menu for the small fry in the family, as well as early-bird specials with prices guaranteed to make the big fry happy. Moderate to deluxe.

Families will feel right at home in **Alma's Italian Restaurant** (306 North Orlando Avenue, Cocoa Beach; 407-783-1981). This old-fashioned Italian eatery feels warm and inviting with its maze of small rooms. The moderately priced menu lists classics such as spaghetti and veal and kid-pleasing pizza, while the wine cellar boasts 200 vintages. Arrive early for dinner and enjoy budget specials.

Blue-plate specials, tabletop juke boxes and gum-popping waitresses make **Herbie K's Diner** (2080 North Atlantic Boulevard, Cocoa Beach; 407-783-6740) an ideal spot for families. This is the place to fill up on meatloaf and mountainous mashed potatoes (the real spuds), chicken parmesan and spaghetti. There's also classic '50s fare such as burgers, onion rings, fries, shakes and malts. Budget. Open 24 hours on weekends.

It's a good idea to tuck a meal under your belt before setting out for the Kennedy Space Center. Cheap and convenient is the **Kountry Kitchen** (1115 North Courtenay Parkway, Merritt Island; 407-459-3457). In this big, friendly joint, an honest country breakfast of bacon, eggs, grits and biscuits is laid out as early as 5 a.m. Or on the way back, stop in for home-style dinners: spareribs, salmon patties, chicken and dumplings, chicken-fried steaks and other hearty meals. Budget, with child's plate available.

On the main thoroughfare leading to the Kennedy Space Center is **Victoria's Family Restaurant** (320 North Courteney Parkway, Merritt Island; 407-459-1656). The exterior won't remind you much of Greece, but within the brick-and-wood interior you will find *moussaka* and its country cousins, as well as seafood and chops. Victoria's fun, simple fare is sure to please younger palates. Budget to moderate.

When the kids start screaming for ice cream, head for **Village Ice Cream and Sandwich Shop** (120-B Harrison Street, Cocoa; 407-632-2311). The hole-in-the-wall town fixture, located near posh boutiques, serves a variety of the creamy stuff (homemade, of course) as well as light sandwiches. Budget.

Between Cocoa and the Merritt Island Wildlife Refuge, a delightful mainland stop near Route 1 is **Dixie Crossroads** (1475 Garden Street, Titusville; 407-268-5000). Despite its size (350 seats), this family-style favorite made me feel right at home, with waitresses refilling my glass of iced tea every time they passed by my windowside table. And everything edible that swims in nearby waters can be found here, in plentiful helpings. Don't miss the rock shrimp, succulent and tasty thumb-sized delicacies that go well with a little red rice. Moderate, with budget lunch specials.

Nannie Lee's Strawberry Mansion (1218 East New Haven Avenue, Melbourne; 407-724-8078) is just about impossible to miss. Inside this pink Victorian confection, tables are set in practically every room, upstairs and down, within a homey setting of stained glass and floral wallpaper. The menu lists elaborate dishes such as fish Oscar along with veal, pasta dishes, chicken dinners and steaks considered the best in town. The children's menu, which features sundaes for dessert, doesn't disappoint. Dinner only. Moderate, with early-bird specials.

SPACE COAST BEACHES AND PARKS

Thick with palmettos and pines and flowering vines and bordered by a meandering creek, **Turkey Creek Sanctuary Park** (407-952-3443) is truly a purist's sanctuary. Families can roam the boardwalks through hardwood hammocks and along the bluffs overlooking the creek, using the park's signs to identify plants. The all-time favorite kid activity, though, is climbing the trail that leads up into a live oak tree. The second favorite is spotting the fish, turtles and occasional manatees that thrive in the warm creek. You can picnic creekside or in a lovely gazebo. To find the park, go to the Palm Bay Recreation Hall at 1502 Port Malabar Boulevard in Melbourne. Then follow the signs to Turkey Creek Sanctuary.

It took an act of Congress to set aside the last 25-mile stretch of undeveloped beach in eastern Florida for **Canaveral National Seashore** (407-867-2805) on Merritt Island. In 1975, the government acted to preserve some 68,000 acres of water and wilderness stretching north from the Kennedy Space Center. In this pristine setting, kids delight at the sight of alligators, turtles and even manatees that live in some of the shallow lagoons. Some 300 species of birds have been observed at the seashore, including endangered ones such as the brown pelican and the bald eagle. The barrier island, consisting mostly of pure quartz sand, was formed more than a million years ago. Evidence of ancient residents has been found stacked into a number of mounds, most notably Turtle Mound, a 35-foot-tall pile of oyster shells assembled by the Surreque Indians sometime between 600 and 1200 A.D. Vegetation has covered the mound, but it's still possible to climb up for a view of the surrounding terrain.

Klondike Beach is the central of three distinct beaches at Canaveral National Seashore. Klondike is a totally undeveloped area at the end of a hike through saw palmettos and Spanish bayonets. Angel wings, sand dollars and smooth rounded moon snails are among the shells found on all three beaches.

Though primitive, **Playalinda Beach** (407-267-1110) is Cape Canaveral's most developed beach and its most accesible. Five miles of pristine, white sand form a narrow ribbon between the high-water line and the delicate sand dunes. In June and July, kids can hide behind sand dunes to watch a nightly ritual: Turtles come ashore here to lay their eggs in the sand (reservations are required to view the laying). The swimming here is excellent, and surfing is good, but currents can be strong. Within sight of NASA's launch pads, Playalinda is usually closed for weeks prior to a launch. Located east of Titusville off Route 402.

Situated at the north end of Cape Canaveral Seashore, **Apollo Beach** (407-267-1110) is accessible by dune walkovers. Like Playalinda, it is a long strip of white quartz sand, and the swimming and surfing are great. Take Route A1A south from New Smyrna Beach.

Egrets, herons, gulls and terns form a welcoming committee on the 140,000-acre **Merritt Island National Wildlife Refuge** (407-867-0667) north of the Kennedy Space Center. A diverse habitat includes

---

FLORIDA'S BEST SURFIN' SHOP

Ron Jon Surf Shop (4151 North Route A1A, Cocoa Beach; 407-799-8888) qualifies as a tourist destination. Calling itself the world's largest surf shop, this kaleidoscopic, warehouse-size store feels like a neon beach party. Outside, a patio bar jams to live music; inside, rock fountains gush beside a glass elevator that glides between two floors. It's a haven for local teenage "dudes," though all kids love sifting through the thousands of T-shirts, swimsuits, water toys and other get-me-to-the-beach stuff that paint this store with electric color.

salty estuaries, dense marshes, pine flatwoods and hammocks of hardwood where armadillos are as common as gray squirrels. The portions of the refuge that are not marsh consist of dense vegetation that helps protect such exotic species as air plants and indigo snakes. The best times to visit are spring, fall and winter. Several species of migratory waterfowl retreat here during the coldest months of the year, making this one of Florida's prime birdwatching areas. Located on Merritt Island along Route 402, east of Titusville.

Daytona Beach

The best-known resort town on the central East Coast, Daytona Beach is famous for its 23-mile-long beach, a marvel of sparkling sand packed so hard you can easily drive a car on it. And that's what people started doing in the early 1900s, gradually developing the beach into a natural race track where speed records were set as early as 1903.

Today, automobile racing and sunshine are still the paramount attractions up and down the strip of sand that stretches from Ponce Inlet north to Flagler Beach. There is history here, too, in archaeological remains and the ruins of old plantations, and in the gracefully aged lighthouses.

Poised near the inlet separating New Smyrna Beach from Daytona Beach, the second-tallest lighthouse on the East Coast, the 175-foot-tall **Ponce de León Inlet Lighthouse** (South Peninsula Drive, Ponce Inlet; 904-761-1821; admission) affords a breathtaking view of the inlet as well as the surrounding communities. Built in 1887, the so-called "Light Station at Mosquito Inlet" is no longer in service, but the entire facility, including the keeper's cottages, is open to the public.

The centrally located **Destination Daytona** (126 East Orange Avenue, Daytona Beach; 904-255-0415) offers tips and guidance for area visitors.

Another way to get your bearings in Daytona Beach is by leaving the driving to someone else, such as a riverboat captain. The **Dixie Queen II Riverboat** (841 Ballough Road, Daytona Beach; 904-255-1997; admission) runs sightseeing cruises up and down the Halifax River. Older kids find room to roam the three balconied decks, while parents can camp out and enjoy the passing sights: huge homes along Riverside Drive, waterfront parks, fast-moving windsurfers and the occasional surfacing manatee.

Housed in a former bank that is Daytona Beach's finest example of Beaux-Arts design, the **Halifax Historical Museum** (252 South Beach Street; 904-255-6976) is best known for the six murals depicting local attractions such as the Ponce de León Inlet Lighthouse. But more fascinating is a highly detailed wood-carved model of the Boardwalk area circa 1938, with hundreds of thumb-sized people filling the

The beautiful Lucille Leigh Collection (142 East Granada Boulevard; Ormond Beach; 904-673-2042) sells exquisite home accessories.

bandshell. This elegant museum's historical displays range from artifacts retrieved from nearby plantation ruins to a smattering of memorabilia from the early days of car racing.

A single stretch of Volusia Avenue near the Daytona Beach Municipal Airport constitutes a sporting paradise in itself. The famous **Daytona International Speedway** (1801 Volusia Avenue; 904-253-7223; admission) replaced the beach as the prime racing locale in 1959. Today, families can travel the banked, two-and-a-half-mile, tri-oval race track that drivers like Cale Yarborough and Richard Petty helped put on the map. Unless you're a qualified racer, however, you won't be driving, but riding in a tour bus. The most renowned of many events hosted here is the Daytona 500, which attracts hundreds of thousands of visitors each February.

Things in Daytona Beach didn't always move so fast, as you can see at one of the city's most interesting museums where a giant sloth is displayed next to contemporary Florida artworks. Far from the beaten track, in a forested setting in Tuscawilla Park, the **Museum of Arts and Science** (1040 Museum Boulevard, Daytona Beach; 904-255-0285; admission) boasts an eclectic collection including 19th-century drawings and one of the largest displays of Cuban artwork in the United States. What children enjoy most, though, are the museum's planetarium and a natural science exhibit.

You can show the kids the days of southern plantations at **Bulow Plantation Ruins State Historic Site** (off King's Road north of the Old Dixie Highway, Bunnell; 904-439-2219). A mile-long unpaved road leads through dense undergrowth to a picnic area; the ruins lie another quarter-mile away to the left. Looming out of the jungle like a movie prop from *Raiders of the Lost Ark* is a series of crumbling coquina shell ruins, all that remains of an 18th-century sugar mill. An interpretive center nearby tells the story of the plantation's development by slave labor, its prosperous production of sugar cane, cotton, rice and indigo, and its ultimate destruction by the Seminole Indians who burned plantations in anger over being displaced by settlers.

DAYTONA BEACH AREA LODGING

Route A1A is one long canyon of hotels and motels that try to differentiate themselves with decorative themes ranging from Polynesian to Mayan. In fact, many of them are very much alike on the inside, and almost all are equidistant from the beach.

A few stoplights south of the frantic midtown action, the beach has the same sun, the same clean sand, but fewer people. In front of the **Day Star Motel** (3811 South Route A1A, Daytona Beach; 904-767-3780), you can at least find a square of sand to call your own. For budget prices, you get two double beds and a pool open 24 hours a day, so the place attracts a lot of families and seniors. For a little more, you get a large oceanfront efficiency. These accommodations aren't beautiful, but they are clean and well maintained. Children under 12 stay free.

The aroma of potpourri greets visitors at **Captain's Quarters Inn** (3711 South Route A1A, Daytona Beach; 904-767-3119). The five-story inn is well suited to families, since every room is a spacious suite. Plus, the atmosphere feels a lot like home: country provincial patterns, oak dressers and plump pillows piled up on the sofa. The homey style extends to private balconies furnished with rocking chairs. Deluxe to ultra-deluxe.

One of the most unusual hotel configurations I've ever seen belongs to **Perry's Ocean-Edge** (2209 South Atlantic Avenue, Daytona Beach; 904-255-0581), a complex of 204 units. You can rent an oceanfront motel room or enclosed garden room, but families will find the most

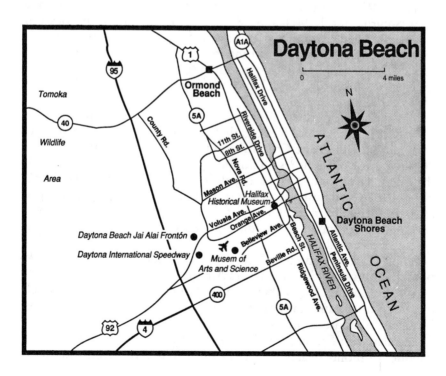

space in an apartment suite or garden efficiency. Three swimming pools—including a huge solar-heated one with a retractable roof—a toddler pool, whirlpool, shuffleboard courts and small putting green are among the many amenities. Moderate-priced rooms; deluxe-priced efficiencies. Children under 18 stay free.

Families who don't mind a 15-minute drive to the beach should consider staying at **Indigo Lakes Resort** (2620 Volusia Avenue, Daytona Beach; 904-258-6333). A lush oasis of velvet green fairways, sharp blue lakes, ponds and trees, it boasts all-weather tennis courts and an Olympic-size pool. This self-contained resort also harbors a fitness trail, shuffleboard and volleyball courts and gamerooms. The focus here is on the outdoors; the rooms are spacious, very comfortable and equipped with a private patio or balcony. Priced moderate to deluxe.

A wooded oasis amid city surroundings, the **Nova Family Campground** (1190 Herbert Street, Port Orange; 904-767-0095) features 200 sites for RVs, pop-up campers and tents. True to its name, the facility attracts vacationing families to its shady environs. There are a swimming pool and kiddie pool, gameroom, recreation hall and convenience store. The beach lies ten minutes away. Budget.

DAYTONA BEACH AREA RESTAURANTS

A brick courtyard embellished with wrought iron makes a lovely entrance to **Riverview Charlie's** (Riverview Inn, 101 Flagler Avenue, New Smyrna Beach; 904-428-1865). True to its waterfront location, this glass-walled restaurant does best with its seafood, including local shellfish as well as Boston scrod and mahimahi. Chicken and sirloin are also available at moderate prices. Children particularly like it here because they can watch the dolphins playing in the water outside. Plus, they get their own menu.

The question at one spot is not so much *if* you want catfish, but *how* you want it: blackened, fried, garlicky, Cajun-style, baked or broiled with lemon. But **Aunt Catfish's** (4009 Halifax Drive, Port Orange; 904-767-4768) also dishes up flounder and plenty of other seafood. In this rustic riverfront restaurant, entrées come with "country fixin's" like cole slaw and hushpuppies, just the kind of full meal you'd expect in such a friendly place. Great for families, Aunt Catfish's features a good children's menu and budget-priced early-bird specials. Otherwise, prices are moderate.

Ships' lanterns and etched glass create a nautical theme at **Blackbeard's Inn** (4200 South Atlantic Avenue, Daytona Beach; 904-788-9640). Located closer to Ponce Inlet than to central Daytona Beach, this cozy restaurant features steak and prime rib as well as seafood. Moderate. Children's menu and early-bird specials.

Popular with families, the **Delta Restaurant** (790 South Atlantic Avenue, Ormond Beach; 904-672-3140) rests across from the ocean and supplies fine views from its glass-enclosed atrium. Prime rib, seafood, gyros and *souvlaki* are a few of the American and Greek-style offerings at this family-run establishment. For children, there are spaghetti, burgers and mini pizzas. Moderate.

DAYTONA AREA BEACHES AND PARKS

When the locals tire of the crowds in central Daytona Beach, they head south to the less well-known beach at **Lighthouse Point Park**. Bypassed by Route A1A, this Ponce Inlet facility is often overlooked except by travelers in search of the Ponce de León Inlet Lighthouse. The southern portion of the park is a tree-shaded greensward with a children's playground. You can picnic while watching the fishing boats in the marina. To the east is a particularly beautiful stretch of pale sandy beach where it's possible to take long walks in relative peace and quiet. The swimming is good here, especially for young beginners, and there are plenty of stores nearby. Located at the end of Atlantic Avenue south of Daytona Beach.

The promotional brochures proclaim **Daytona Beach** to be 23 miles of hard sand beach, but technically only four miles of that lie within the city limits of Daytona Beach. To the south is Daytona Beach Shores, to the north, Ormond Beach, both virtually indistinguishable from Daytona Beach.

Aside from the expanse of clean beige sand (500 feet wide at low tide), the most striking aspect of the beach is the presence of automobiles. Motorists are required to park perpendicular to the ocean, in single file, and to restrict their beach driving to poorly marked "lanes." A speed limit of 10 mph is enforced, but it is still distracting to have to look both ways before proceeding into the surf, and parents, of course, should keep careful watch over their children.

The swimming, however, is excellent here, with shallow, sandy shelves perfect for the short stuff. You can surf at the north end of the

---

MARINELAND

About 40 miles north of Daytona Beach, Route A1A runs right by **Marineland** *(904-471-1111; Marineland; admission), a roadside attraction that was built in 1938 to facilitate underwater filming. Though nowhere near the scope of Sea World or Disney World's Living Seas, this faded seaside complex does offer a fine porpoise show that's popular with small children. Performed several times a day in an ocean-view amphitheater, it stars a cast of endearing and well-trained sea mammals. Between the shows, you're apt to catch a special effects film or a trainer feeding a shark.*

On your way to Tampa, consider stopping at Lakeland's Florida Southern College: It boasts the largest number of Frank Lloyd Wright buildings in the world.

beach. Located between Ocean Dunes Road and Plaza Boulevard off Route A1A.

The approach to the 949-acre preserve at **Tomoka State Park** (904-677-3931) travels along a driveway worthy of an antebellum plantation (which it once was), with magnolia trees and moss-draped oaks threatening to overtake the road. Flanked by the Halifax and Tomoka rivers, Tomoka State Park has lush, coastal hammocks dense with shrubs and trees. Raised boardwalks allow visitors to explore the moist, low-lying swamps and marshes. You can camp here, and there's plenty for a family to do—picnic, join a riverboat tour, go saltwater angling, rent canoes or visit the interpretive center. Located at 2099 North Beach Street in Ormond Beach.

With frontage on the ocean as well as on the Intracoastal Waterway, the windswept **Flagler Beach State Recreation Area** (904-439-2474) offers close encounters with a variety of wildlife. A short nature trail winds through taller sand dunes, where scrub oaks and shrubs make an excellent habitat for the Florida scrub jay. On the inland side of the park, fiddler crabs and wading birds wander through the marsh grasses and shallow waters near the boat basin. On the ocean side, sea turtles lay their eggs (in early summer) in the rough coquina-shell sand above the high water mark on this narrow, undeveloped beach.

You can camp here, and the swimming and fishing are excellent. Located at 3100 South Route A1A, Flagler Beach.

Tampa

To many, Tampa means Busch Gardens and Buccaneer football. But to those who take the time to explore, and to the accelerating numbers who are making this West Coast hub home, Tampa is seen as a sophisticated network of growth stemming from carefully nurtured agricultural and fishing roots. Located about 75 miles from Orlando, this thriving city boasts dazzling corporate towers that rub elbows with spruced-up historic buildings and re-created street markets. The result is sophistication with a homey feel.

One of the biggest renovation projects undertaken was **Harbour Island**. Once weed infested, today its cobblestone streets lead to a world-class hotel, luxury condominiums and the **Harbour Island Market** (813-223-9898), an indoor fantasy mall. The PeopleMover monorail carries passengers to and from the island and around the downtown area.

The neighborhood across the water from the island is also looking up. The **Franklin Street Mall** allows pedestrian outdoor shopping among restored boutiques that sit in contrast with Tampa's skyscraping and skyrocketing downtown commercial image.

"Hands-on" displays at the **Museum of Science and Industry** (4801 East Fowler Avenue; 813-985-5531; admission) mean experiencing a hurricane and touching a shark's tooth. This, Tampa's largest museum, is an open-air facility that has fun with scientific phenomena.

The 300-ton **José Gasparilla** (813-223-8130), the world's only full-rigged pirate ship, is docked on Bayshore Boulevard near downtown, for viewing. The kids won't be able to roam the decks, but they always enjoy looking.

Another pastime is watching the shrimp boats come in to unload their catches at the **shrimp docks** (22nd Street Causeway). If you don't catch any activity from the shrimpers, it's still a good place to watch waterfront activity and see gargantuan sea craft passing by.

Visitors to Ybor City, the well-known cigar making center, can still see expert craftsmen roll cigars by hand and view factories as they

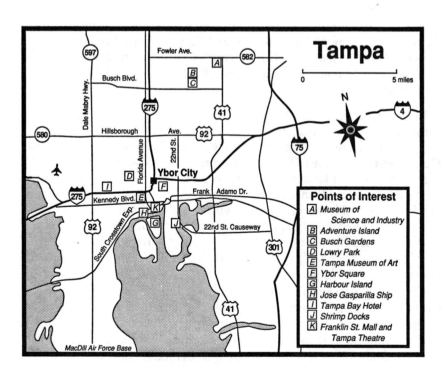

Points of Interest
A Museum of Science and Industry
B Adventure Island
C Busch Gardens
D Lowry Park
E Tampa Museum of Art
F Ybor Square
G Harbour Island
H Jose Gasparilla Ship
I Tampa Bay Hotel
J Shrimp Docks
K Franklin St. Mall and Tampa Theatre

Can you spare a dollar? Everything's $1.00 (813-223-6847), on Tampa's Harbour Island, has shelves of goodies priced at a buck.

---

operated in their heyday. Cobblestone streets, Spanish-tiled storefronts and wrought-iron detailing take you back to the days when Cuban, Jewish, German and Italian immigrants lived here.

Villazon and Company (3104 Armenia Avenue; 813-879-2291) offers guided tours around its mechanized cigar factory. Amid the fragrance of cut tobacco, modern-day methods of twisting and rolling are demonstrated.

The **Ybor City State Museum** (1818 East 9th Avenue; 813-247-6323; admission), once a Cuban bread bakery, depicts the history of the area near Preservation Park, a turn-of-the-century street of cobblestone and wrought iron. Three renovated structures demonstrate typical cigar workers' homes. In one, the **Ybor City Chamber of Commerce** (1800 East 9th Avenue; 813-248-3712) is housed. Stop here for a self-guided walking tour map of Ybor City.

At **Ybor Square** (8th Avenue and 13th Street; 813-247-4497) arts and crafts, antique marts, specialty shops and a nostalgia market are located where cigars were once manufactured. In the square at **Tampa Rico Cigars** (813-247-6738), visitors can still watch a craftsman roll cigars by hand.

For information on Tampa and its environs, stop in at the **Greater Tampa Chamber of Commerce** (801 East Kennedy Boulevard; 813-228-7777) or the **Tampa/Hillsborough Convention & Visitors Association** (111 Madison Street, Suite 1010; 813-223-1111). Both are located downtown.

BUSCH GARDENS AREA   The number one attraction in the Tampa metropolitan area, number two in the state (after Disney World), and one of the country's foremost zoos is **Busch Gardens/The Dark Continent** (3000 East Busch Boulevard; 813-987-5082; admission). The 300-acre beer factory-cum-theme park takes visitors to 19th-century Africa via the 20th-century technology of a monorail system and skyride. The wilds are juxtaposed with the wild; jungle animals placidly roam the Serengeti Plains as thrill seekers get dunked, spun and set on their heads by different amusement rides. Tropical bird gardens, belly dancers, beer sampling and food and gift stands are all presented in exotic surroundings.

One thing you won't find too much at Busch Gardens is Disney-style lines. During summer and popular holidays, *a few* rides (roller coasters, river rapids, etc.) sometimes feature a wait of 30 to 45 minutes. During the rest of the year, you can usually walk right on. What you will find in Busch Gardens are eight themed sections:

Timbuktu, fashioned as an ancient desert marketplace, is home to the tortuous looping roller coaster called the Scorpion. Riders know it as the snake with a 62-foot plummet and curves banked from 0 to 60 degrees. For children or the weak of stomach, several midway-style rides offer tamer encounters. In **Morocco**, elaborate tiles and keyhole architecture re-create an exotic walled city. Snake charmers and roving sheiks perform in the streets, while indoors at the Moroccan Palace, you can watch a superb ice skating show. A monorail snakes above the 80-acre **Serengeti Plain**, offering visitors up-close views of African herds. Giraffes, zebras, hippos, antelope, elephants, Nile crocodiles, ostriches and other exotic animals roam free on this veldt-like prairie. You can also see the animals from a locomotive, skyride or promenade around the plain.

Children are enchanted by **Nairobi**, where an animal nursery cares for fledgling birds and delicate gazelle. There's also a petting zoo with goats, ponies and deer, and Nocturnal Mountain, where families can view animals in their own nighttime setting. Over in the bustling African town of **Stanleyville**, a log flume ride excites the whole family. Bigger thrills, however, await at **The Congo**. Here, the Python roller coaster rockets visitors along 1200 feet of track that corkscrews into two 360-degree spirals. There's also the Congo River Rapids, a family-style raft ride through caves and under waterfalls. Some 2000 exotic fowl hoot, caw, flit and fly around the area aptly named **Bird Gardens**. Several koalas also hang out here in eucalyptus trees, drawing big crowds all day. Nearby, **Crown Colony** is meant to imitate a British-African village. The area's highlight is a Victorian restaurant, though the beautiful, renowned Clydesdale horses also make their home here.

Next door to and owned by Busch Gardens, **Adventure Island** (4545 Bougainvillea Avenue; 813-971-7978; admission) is a 19-acre water theme park featuring an endless surf pool, innertubing chutes and waterslides with names like Calypso Coaster and Caribbean Corkscrew. The latter offers a high-speed journey through transluscent braided slides. Parents will enjoy the leisurely "Rambling Bayou" float ride, while toddlers feel right at home in the kiddie pool. When they're not on the speed slides, teens hang out at the video arcade. Like its African neighbor, Adventure Island seems set in a tropical jungle, with palm trees, vines and ferns.

At **Lowry Park** (7530 North Boulevard; 813-935-5503) storybook characters entertain the young and young at heart. This attraction is set up as a city park, replete with bubbling fountains, shade trees and picnic areas. From there, childlike fancy takes over. Foot bridges look

If you survive Busch Gardens' Scorpion, you can say you've pulled over three Gs (gravitational forces).

like rainbows and ferris wheels spin. Safety Village is set up to look like a miniature town, complete with homes, a fire station and various shops. Here children learn the rules of the road in a universe their size. To top it off, there's even a zoo (admission).

Busch Gardens' Dwarf Village playground, located in the Bird Gardens, is a favorite place for toddlers—and parents who need a rest.

TAMPA LODGING

Most of the accommodations in the city are chain hotels catering to the business traveler or overnight guest. Those looking for a fun-in-the-sun resort should head across the bay to St. Petersburg and the necklace of islands that adorn it. If you plan on staying awhile in the bay area, I recommend rooming there. For those seeking a few days of metropolitan stimulation and culture, I have found a few Tampa hotels that excel.

Overlooking intracoastal waterways, the **Radisson Bay Harbor Inn** (770 Courtney Campbell Causeway; 813-281-8900) is about the only place in Tampa you'll find a beach with your lodging. Private balconies in the 257 modern rooms overlook the bay or the city. Deluxe and ultra-deluxe tabs buy you lots of extras: restaurant, lounge, sailing and windsurfing, tennis courts and pool. They can recommend a babysitting service, and children under 18 stay free.

On the outside, the **Guest Quarters Suite Hotel at Tampa Bay** (3050 North Rocky Point Drive West; 813-888-8800) looks like a Mayan temple dedicated to the god of bay waters. Inside the look is decidedly 20th century, with subtle shades, dark woods and modern family conveniences. All 203 units are suites, renting in the deluxe and ultra-deluxe range. The facility provides swimming and hot tub facilities.

Holiday Inn Downtown–Ashley Plaza (111 West Fortune Street; 813-223-1351) sits downtown on the riverfront near the Tampa Bay Performing Arts Center. Its 312 units include plushly carpeted rooms and suites decorated in modern mauves and teals. Moderate to deluxe. They recommend local babysitting services; children under 16 stay free.

On Harbour Island in the downtown hub, the **Harbour Island Hotel** (725 South Harbour Island Boulevard; 813-229-5000) spells luxury in the form of 300 posh rooms with bay vistas, along with sophisticated clubs and restaurants. Dark woods panel the lobby areas, and moving sidewalks will carry you around the hotel. Ultra-deluxe.

More homey and less glitzy is the family-operated **Tahitian Inn** (601 South Dale Mabry Highway; 813-877-6721). You will find comfortable, clean rooms and a swimming pool at this budget-priced motel.

The **Safari Resort Inn** (4139 East Busch Boulevard; 813-988-9191) theme comes from its proximity to Busch Gardens. The lobby fits in with its luxurious rattan chairs and the bamboolike trim around the check-in area. The 99 rooms are decorated in jungle tones. There are also a pool, restaurant and lounge. Budget.

Tampa offers little in the way of campgrounds. However, heading west toward Clearwater you will find **Bay Bayou Traveler** (12622 Memorial Highway, Tampa; 813-855-1000), a tidy place with large grassy lots for parking an RV or pitching a tent. Amenities include a heated swimming pool and Jacuzzi. Families are the main summer customers; during winter, seniors frequent the park. Some sites are located along a creek. Budget.

Another good bet for camping is the **Hillsborough River State Park** (See "Tampa Beaches and Parks" section in this chapter).

TAMPA RESTAURANTS

Local seafood—pompano, grouper, shrimp and stone crab—makes a culinary splash at most Tampa restaurants, washed with the new wave of American cuisine. Standing at the crossroads of Cuban, Spanish, Greek and Scottish subcultures, and influenced by its international port role, Tampa offers fare that tends to be continental while maintaining the homespun flavor of its surrounding agricultural communities.

Crawdaddy's Restaurant & Lounge (2500 Rocky Point Road; 813-281-0407) is a theme eating spot done in poor white trash chic. Outside, you feel you've stumbled into the backyard of a Carolina mountain man. A tin smokehouse, long johns on the clothesline and a junked truck, together with the broken-down shacks that house the restaurant, are some of the props. Inside, things are considerably more comfortable and pleasant. Parlor lamps, curtained booths and carved, highback chairs are designed to look timeworn and to provide a unique eating experience with picture-window views of the bay. The menu concentrates on seafood. Moderate, with a good children's menu.

INDIANS, SNAKES AND ALLIGATOR WRESTLING

While you're in the Tampa Bay area, you might consider a side trip to the nearby **Seminole Culture Center** *(5221 North Orient Road; 813-623-3549; admission). It contains a Seminole Indian village of chickee (thatched-roof) structures and a museum demonstrating the way of life of these long-time Florida residents. Alligator wrestling and snake shows are the sensational aspects of the center—and big hits with the kids.*

The phone book-size wine list at Bern's Steak House boasts 6500 labels from 19 different countries!

Saltwater aquariums, exotic music and articles that have washed ashore give **The Castaway** (7720 Courtney Campbell Causeway; 813-281-0770) its South Seas ambience. However, the food is mainly steak and seafood with some pasta and chicken dishes. Families can enjoy budget prices with early-bird specials. Otherwise, prices are moderate.

Mirabella's Seafood (327 North Dale Mabry; 813-876-2844), with its big neon fish sign and shanty look, has endured as a roadside eatery since the early days of Florida. The fish is guaranteed fresh and provided by the restaurant's own waterfront seafood house. Moderate. Children's menu and early-bird special.

Bern's Steak House (1208 South Howard Avenue; 812-251-2421) is the place you go *without* the kids. This is Tampa's top shelf, and the restaurant often pointed to as Florida's best steak house. The heavy, rococo decor gives it a slightly garish feeling, but be assured, things don't get any fresher than Bern's homegrown herbs and vegetables. It has outstanding steaks and the largest wine selection in the area. Desserts are enjoyed upstairs in glass booths equipped with televisions and radios for after-dinner relaxation. Deluxe.

Dishes at **Selena's** (1623 Snow Avenue; 813-251-2116) epitomize the Florida melting-pot effect. Creole and Sicilian are married together here to produce garlicked seafood with sides of sausage, red beans and rice. Furnishings are classic: refinished oak antiques and flowered wall-coverings. Moderate to deluxe. Children's menu.

In the historic cigar-factory district of Ybor City, restaurants principally feature Cuban food. The Cuban sandwich, Ybor City's gastronomic mainstay, creates a sense of friendly rivalry among restaurateurs, who all claim theirs is the best. Basically, this is little more than a sub sandwich. The difference is the Cuban bread, baked in yard-long loaves using a time-honored method that produces something totally unrelated to a sub bun. Most importantly, they're made with stuff kids tend to like—ham, pork and swiss cheese. Other area specialties include Spanish soup, black beans and rice, paella, flan and Cuban coffee.

Silver Ring Café (1831 East 7th Avenue; 813-248-2549) holds the reputation as maker of the best Cuban sandwich. These are produced in a showcase window for your entertainment. The decor of this long-established luncheonette is so old and out-of-date, it's "in." Seating is at a long formica counter, at tables or on stools facing little shelves along the wall. Antiques clutter the window, and an old-fashioned juke box still spits out tunes.

New Orleans ambience and food take Ybor City diners on a cultural departure at **El Pasaje Café Creole** (1330 9th Avenue; 813-247-

6283). Once a popular Spanish club, the restored building swings with jazzy background music, lively atmosphere, architectural drama and spicy Creole concoctions. The prices are budget to moderate for blackened fish, crawfish, jambalaya and crab cakes..

The **Columbia Restaurant** (2117 East 7th Avenue; 813-248-4961) is both landmark and restaurant extraordinaire. The block-long building demonstrates a Spanish influence in its ornate tiling, archways, balconies and grand chandeliers. Although the waiters wear dinner jackets and musicians serenade tableside, the Columbia is casual, reasonable and especially suited to families. Its menu is priced in the moderate to deluxe range for traditional and inventive Spanish dishes: paella, pork *salteado, boliche* and *pompano en papillot,* for example. For children, there are chicken fingers, spaghetti and Cuban sandwiches.

Latam Restaurant (2511 West Columbus Drive; 813-877-7338) has incredibly inexpensive châteaubriand. But if you desire elegant atmosphere with your fine food, you will be disappointed. The eatery is housed in an unassuming facility with naugahyde decor. It also serves Cuban specialties, spaghetti and chicken. Budget, with slight discount for children.

TAMPA BEACHES AND PARKS

Hillsborough River State Park (813-986-1020) includes 3000 forested acres and a suspension bridge that spans the placid river. Within the park sits Fort Foster, a reconstructed Seminole War fort garrisoned by soldiers of the United States Second Artillery. Actually park service guides, they are dressed and equipped in replica outfits. The park includes canoe rental and camping facilities, and you can swim in a man-made lake. Located on Route 301, six miles southwest of Zephyrhills.

A stretch of sand lying along the Courtney Campbell Causeway, the nine-mile **Ben T. Davis Municipal Beach** bridging Tampa and Clearwater has pretty landscaping, and the sand is soft and white. This is the Tampa area's only saltwater beach, and the locals swarm here. True beach lovers go the distance to the other side of the Pinellas County peninsula across the causeway to the beaches of Holiday Isles.

A REAL BREW-HA-HA

If you've ever wondered how beer is made, take the self-guided **brewery tour** *at Busch Gardens. Plenty of families enjoy the aromatic, informative trek through the distilling, aging, canning and bottling stages. There are even a "Brew Hall" of memorabilia and free beer samples for grownups at the end. The tour is included in park admission.*

St. Petersburg Area

Resting on a peninsula across the bay from Tampa, St. Petersburg is about two hours from Orlando. What brings travelers here from all over Florida, and the world, are a dazzling thread of islands woven to the mainland by five bridges. This thread, often known as the Holiday Isles, has developed into highrise heaven thanks to its gorgeous beaches and lucid waters. Pleasure seekers of all ages are attracted to this paradise playground where the most strenuous activity is building sandcastles.

Activity in downtown St. Petersburg centers around **The Pier** (800 2nd Avenue Northeast; 813-821-6164), an inverted pyramid-shaped structure that houses shops, restaurants and an observation deck. The view from here overlooks the seaside city in all its splendor and is especially scenic at night. One office of the **St. Petersburg Chamber of Commerce** is located in the lobby of The Pier; another is nearby at 100 2nd Avenue North (813-821-4069).

Sunken Gardens (1825 4th Street North; 813-896-3186; admission), with its jungle-like ambience, is a must for families. The grounds were created in a sinkhole from which the water was drained. The fertile pit was then landscaped with exotic plants and stocked with tropical birds. Children delight in the monkeys, crowned cranes, muntjac deer and hornbills wandering among bougainvillea, hibiscus and giant ferns.

From downtown, head west to the Gulf and comb the strand of sandy islands. To make the island tour, take Pinellas Bayway across the peninsula that comprises Pinellas County, to Fort de Soto Park. North of the five islands that form the park, the town of Tierra Verde eases into the holiday carnival scene that its neighbor, St. Petersburg Beach, begins. The sun and watersports action continues along this sandy rim all the way to Clearwater Beach—a splendid finale to the family's Gulf-front tour.

The **London Wax Museum** (5505 Gulf Boulevard, St. Petersburg Beach, 813-360-6985; admission) imitates Madame Tussaud's of London with over 100 carved figures, including some of Disney's characters, the pirate Gasparilla and Elvis Presley.

From St. Petersburg Beach, the **island chain** along Gulf Boulevard includes Treasure Island, Madeira Beach, Indian Rocks Beach, Belleair Beach and Clearwater Beach. These Gulf-front islands are separated from the mainland by a narrow trickle of water that broadens at both ends.

Between Treasure Island and Madeira, a boardwalk with salty shops, restaurants and charter boats has cropped up at **Johns Pass Village and Boardwalk** (12925 East Gulf Boulevard, Madeira Beach; 813-

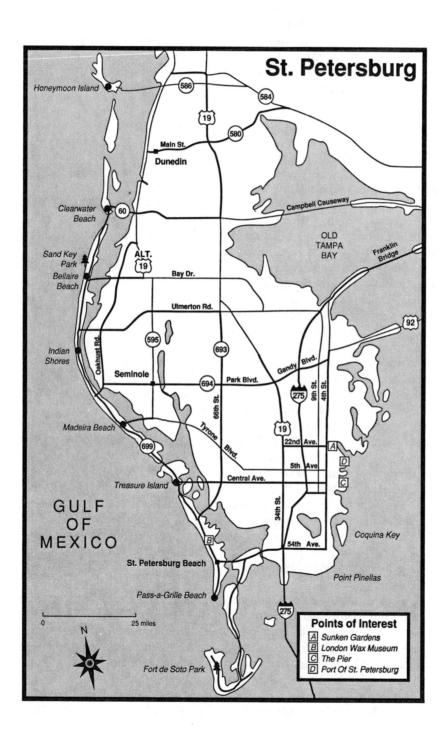

St. Petersburg

Honeymoon Island

586

584

19

580

Main St.

Dunedin

Campbell Causeway

Clearwater Beach

60

OLD TAMPA BAY

Franklin Bridge

Sand Key Park

ALT. 19

Bellaire Beach

Bay Dr.

Ulmerton Rd.

92

Indian Shores

Oakhurst Rd.

595

693

Gandy Blvd.

Seminole

694

Park Blvd.

275

9th St.

4th St.

66th St.

Madeira Beach

Tyrone Blvd.

19

699

22nd Ave.

A

5th Ave.

D

Treasure Island

Central Ave.

C

GULF OF MEXICO

34th St.

Coquina Key

B

54th Ave.

St. Petersburg Beach

Point Pinellas

Pass-a-Grille Beach

0   25 miles

N

275

Points of Interest

A Sunken Gardens
B London Wax Museum
C The Pier
D Port Of St. Petersburg

Fort de Soto Park

397-7242). Patterned after a fishing community of yore, it pays tribute to the community's commercial fishing industry.

The **Suncoast Seabird Sanctuary** (18328 Gulf Boulevard, Indian Shores; 813-391-6211) works to restore injured and crippled sky-dwellers. You may catch close-up views of many species here, including the native cormorant, white heron, brown pelican and snowy egret. You can even adopt one of the feathered creatures.

ST. PETERSBURG AREA LODGING

On Pass-a-Grille Beach, low-key motels and beach houses line one side of Gulf Way, dusty sand beach the other. One colorful lodging option is the **Sunset View Guest House** (1107 Gulf Way; 813-360-1333). For budget rates, you can sleep under a homemade quilt with sea breezes wafting through jalousie windows. Refrigerators come with each cozy room in this circa-1940 building that makes you feel right at home. Guests are allowed full use of kitchen facilities.

A historic masterpiece in cotton-candy pink, the **Don CeSar Beach Resort** (3400 Gulf Boulevard, St. Petersburg Beach; 813-360-1881) greets visitors to this beach town. It stands stately and fancifully to woo guests with complete resort services in the ultra-deluxe price range. Classic Florida resort style is embodied here. Built in the 1920s, when F. Scott and Zelda Fitzgerald supposedly visited, it was converted into an army hospital during World War II. An ongoing restoration now keeps the 277 rooms, plus restaurants, lounges, conference facilities and banquet halls, in prime condition. The Don's personality combines equal doses of Mediterranean, fairy castle and beach resort. Children ages 4 to 12 can take part in the "kids limited" program, with supervised arts and crafts and a host of other activities led by retired schoolteachers. There's also a swimming pool, and the resort is right on the beach. Children under 18 stay free.

Cadillac Motel (3828 Gulf Boulevard, St. Petersburg Beach; 813-360-1748) provides some architectural interest with its 43 beachfront rooms, efficiencies and apartments. Peaked roofs, a wooden observation sundeck and a rounded bay window front upgrade the court hotel look. The rooms are pleasant, the efficiencies not without character. Two pools, a poolside lounge and 180 feet of expansive beach are other amenities. Moderate.

Guests can tour the grounds via gondolas at the exotic **Tradewinds** (5500 Gulf Boulevard, St. Petersburg Beach; 813-367-6461). Housing 422 rooms, Tradewinds takes complete care of guests with four pools, a sauna, whirlpool, tennis and croquet courts, restaurants, wide beach and children's activities. Each room includes a wet bar, refrigerator and exclusive furnishings. Ultra-deluxe.

The rooms are furnished in a modern style at the **Breckenridge Resort Hotel** (5700 Gulf Boulevard, St. Petersburg Beach; 813-360-

1833), with built-in desk and bookshelves in some rooms. Kitchenettes and balconies are provided in each of the 200 units. Lighted tennis courts, seaside eating and sipping, swimming pool and a fluffy beach complete the package. Deluxe, with no extra charge for children.

Fresh little gingerbread cottages rent for budget rates at **Villa St. Tropez Motel** (1713 North Gulf Boulevard, Indian Rocks Beach; 813-596-7133). The eight units sit across the street from the beach and are ideally suited for families. Full kitchens and a grassy sunning area with shuffleboard courts are included.

Holiday House Motel Apartments (470 North Gulfview Boulevard, Clearwater Beach; 813-447-4533) lie low along blindingly white sands. Typically beach oriented, the 31 apartments won't win awards for interior decoration but are clean and roomy and provide full kitchen facilities. At moderate rates you get a full apartment for what you would pay for a room at other hotels in the area.

Fine resort style at **Adam's Mark** (430 South Gulfview Boulevard, Clearwater Beach; 813-443-5714) is defined with accommodations and location that create a Caribbean atmosphere. The 206 modern rooms corner a wide stretch of beach and are custom designed with elegant tropical touches. Deluxe to ultra-deluxe.

The St. Petersburg area also offers numerous family-oriented campgrounds. One of the finest is **St. Petersburg Resort KOA** (5400 95th Street North, St. Petersburg; 813-392-2233), where 96 acres border a saltwater inlet dotted with islands. You can rent canoes and paddle across the inlet, or rent a bike and peddle around the palmy campgrounds. The 500 sites accommodate RVs or tents, but the real family deal is the 30 one-and two-room cabins. Best of all, there's plenty to keep you busy: a huge swimming pool, three hot tubs, miniature golf, gameroom and volleyball. Of course, the Gulf beach is only two miles away. Budget.

Fort de Soto Park (see "St. Petersburg Area Beaches and Parks" section in this chapter), is also an excellent place to camp.

ST. PETERSBURG AREA RESTAURANTS

At the pier in downtown St. Pete, **Alessi Café At the Pier** (800 2nd Avenue Northeast; 813-894-4659) impresses with blond woods, a brass espresso machine and a showcase of sinful pastries. The moderate menu features international specialties and grilled seafood, with children's selections.

Continental cuisine with a difference comes in moderate price ranges at **Good Times Continental Restaurant** (1130 Pinellas Bayway, Tierra Verde; 813-867-0774). The Old World influence takes a refreshing departure from France and Italy, to offer tastebud tantalization in the form of Hungarian chicken paprikash, beef stroganoff, filet mignon topped with glazed peaches and béarnaise, black forest cake and Czechoslovakian beer. All is served in a plain-looking facility with vinyl chairs and pool-hall paneling. Half portions available for children.

On Pass-a-Grille Beach, **Hurricane Seafood Restaurant** (807 Gulf Way; 813-360-9558) seats you outdoors with a beach view, or inside its wood-accented, casual dining room. Seafood comes in every form imaginable at moderate prices.

Pelican Diner (7501 Gulf Boulevard, St. Petersburg Beach; 813-363-9873) serves budget homestyle meals in an authentic dining car atmosphere—authentic meaning this is a survivor of a bygone era, not a replica. Corroded chrome and vinyl counter stools, blue-and-white tiled walls and individual booth juke boxes are the setting; pork chops, liver and corned beef and cabbage are the fare.

Crabby Bill's (409 Gulf Boulevard, Indian Rocks Beach; 813-595-4825) is your basic beach seafood eatery where the food is terrific and the prices even better. The oyster stew is made to order, and the frogs' legs, catfish, shrimp, crab and fish have earned the place a reputation that means long waits. Budget.

For more than a decade, folks across Tampa Bay have made faithful sojourns to the **Lobster Pot** (17814 Gulf Boulevard, Reddington Shores; 813-391-8592), a place that can feed any lobster fetish. Danish, Maine, African and Florida lobsters, served unadorned or in creamy garlic or curry sauces, headline the menu. There are fish and prime steaks as well. Fresh flowers, candles and linens assure subtle formality amid fishing nets, mounted lobsters and other seaside decor. Deluxe. Children's menu and early-bird special.

In Clearwater Beach, **Heilman's Beachcomber** (447 Mandalay Avenue; 813-442-4144) is known for its bargain Southern-style dinners of fried chicken, gravy and mashed potatoes. Locals will also tell you that this is the best place in the bay area to get good stone crab. The ambience is simple, the menu diversified, the quality consistent. Moderate. Arrive early for budget-priced dinner specials.

OYSTERS, EVERY WHICH WAY

To get the true flavor of Florida's Gulf Coast, dine at P.J.'s Oyster Bar (500 1st Street North, Indian Rocks Beach; 813-596-5898). Rolls of paper towels hang on coat hangers above the tables at this ultracasual beach nook, which doles out oysters, clams, crab and shrimp in their unadulterated state (raw and/or steamed, hold the sauce). The budget to moderate menu also offers fried, broiled, baked or steamed seafood, sandwiches and blackened specialties. Grilled cheese and chicken fingers are available for young, picky eaters.

The ship-shaped Showboat Dinner Theater (3405 Ulmerton Road, Clearwater; 813-573-3777) hosts musicals, comedies and children's theater.

ST. PETERSBURG AREA BEACHES AND PARKS

Twenty-eight miles of sugar sand sweetens Pinellas County's Gulf front. Its public beaches spread wider than anywhere else along the coast.

A precious natural respite from the beach crowds lies at **Fort de Soto Park** (813-866-2662) on five road-connected islands at the southern tip of Tierra Verde. Hiking trails take you to cannons marking an uncompleted Spanish-American War fort and around quiet paths shaded by Australian pines and live oaks dripping with Spanish moss. Secluded areas are available at both East Beach and North Beach. The sand is coarse, shelly and booby-trapped with sand spurs. Natural vegetation along the beaches grows low to the ground: cactus, sea grape shrubs and sea oats. You get a true deserted feeling with none of the development on the northern islands to clutter the view. Camping is permitted; reservations must be made at the camp office in person or at the St. Petersburg County Building (150 5th Street North, Room 63, St. Petersburg). Fishing is excellent, and a three-mile area of the seven-mile-long beach is approved for swimming. At the north end, currents are dangerous. Located off Pinellas Bayway, south of Tierra Verde.

A popular gathering place for young sunbathers, **Pass-a-Grille Beach** is a strand of fluffy sand that loops around the southern point of the island of St. Petersburg Beach. The long, wide beach is flanked by Gulf Way and its quaint homes and low-rises. The swimming is good, and facilities include showers, dressing rooms, a snack bar and picnic area.

Like most of the parks in Pinellas County, **Sand Key Park** is beautifully landscaped. The facility looks more like a resort than a city park, with lush greenery and beautiful, blond sands. A rock barrier tumbles from the beach out into the Gulf at the southern end of the park. The swimming is good, ditto the fishing. Located at the northern end of Belleair Beach on Gulf Boulevard.

Clearwater Beach is the reason thousands cross the big bridge from Tampa every weekend. The most popular West Coast beach, Clearwater combines fast-paced action and gentle surf with ribbons of shells, wavy dunes and fine sun-bleached sands. Even the name sounds rejuvenating. The beach rambles for three miles, from the wall-to-wall hotels and crowds in the south to remote spots in the north. Families usually prefer the northern end, though swimming and fishing are excellent everywhere. Located at the west end of Route 60.

Index

About the Author

Stacy Ritz, a lifelong resident of Florida, is a co-author of Ulysses Press' *Hidden Florida* (winner of the Lowell Thomas Award for Best Guidebook), *Florida's Gold Coast: The Ultimate Guidebook* and *Hidden New England*. She has written for the *Washington Post, Miami Herald, Orlando Sentinel, Palm Beach Post, Carribean Travel & Life, Detroit News, Cleveland Plain Dealer* and *San Antonio Express-News*. Formerly a staff writer for *The Tampa Tribune*, she is now an adjunct professor of journalism at Florida International University in Miami.

About the Illustrator

Glenn Kim is a freelance illustrator residing in Oakland, California. A graduate of the Acadamy of Art College in San Francisco, he specializes in editorial and animal illustrations. He is currently employed as a storyboard artist.

HIDDEN MEXICO
Covers the entire 6000-mile Mexican coastline in the most comprehensive fashion ever. 432 pages. $13.95

CALIFORNIA
The Ultimate Guidebook
Definitive. From the Pacific to the desert to the Sierra Nevada, it captures the best of the Golden State. 504 pages. $13.95

HIDDEN COAST OF CALIFORNIA
Explores the fabled California coast from Mexico to Oregon, describing over 1000 miles of spectacular beaches. 468 pages. $13.95

HIDDEN SOUTHERN CALIFORNIA
The most complete guidebook to Los Angeles and Southern California in print. 516 pages. $12.95

HIDDEN SAN FRANCISCO
AND NORTHERN CALIFORNIA
A major resource for travelers exploring the Bay Area and beyond. 444 pages. $13.95

TO ORDER DIRECT   For each book send an additional $2 postage and handling (California residents include 7¼% sales tax) to Ulysses Press, P.O. Box 3440, Berkeley, CA 94703-3440